D1744600

The US Secretaries of State and Transatlantic Relations

Transatlantic relations have been among the most crucially important areas for US foreign policy since 1945. For reasons of self-interest and with regard to common transatlantic values and political, economic and security interests, every American Secretary of State to date has dedicated a considerable period of time to America's relations with Europe. This book assesses the transatlantic policy which America's most important post-Second World War Secretaries of State have pursued. Brief profiles of each Secretary's political philosophy and his/her policy towards Europe provide insights into the continuities and changes US foreign policy towards Europe has displayed from 1945 to the present.

The book provides a synopsis of America's relations with Europe during the last six decades. It establishes an overview of the crucial problems in American–European relations and indeed in America's global role. Each chapter embeds an assessment of the respective Secretaries of State within a general survey of American foreign policy during both the Cold War and the post-Cold War world.

This book was published as a special issue of the *Journal of Transatlantic Studies*.

Klaus Larres is professor of History and International Affairs at the University of Ulster, Northern Ireland. He is the former holder of the Henry A. Kissinger Chair in Foreign Policy and International Relations at the Library of Congress in Washington, DC. He is a visiting professor in European Studies at The Paul H. Nitze School of Advanced International Studies (SAIS) at Johns Hopkins University in Washington, DC (personal website: www.klauslarres.com).

The US Secretaries of State and Transatlantic Relations

Edited by Klaus Larres

LONDON AND NEW YORK

First published 2010 by Routledge
2 Park Square, Milton Park, Abingdon, Oxon, OX14 4RN

Simultaneously published in the USA and Canada
by Routledge
270 Madison Avenue, New York, NY 10016

Routledge is an imprint of the Taylor & Francis Group, an informa business

© 2010 Board of Transatlantic Studies

Typeset in Times New Roman by Value Chain, India
Printed and bound in Great Britain by TJI Digital, Padstow, Cornwall

All rights reserved. No part of this book may be reprinted or reproduced or utilised in any form or by any electronic, mechanical, or other means, now known or hereafter invented, including photocopying and recording, or in any information storage or retrieval system, without permission in writing from the publishers.

British Library Cataloguing in Publication Data
A catalogue record for this book is available from the British Library

ISBN10: 0-415-55323-7
ISBN13: 978-0-415-55323-0

Contents

Notes on Contributors

Dieter Dettke is a former US Representative and Executive Director of the Washington Office of the Friedrich Ebert Foundation. He is Adjunct Professor at Georgetown University and Senior non resident Fellow of the American Institute for Contemporary German Studies.

John Dumbrell is professor of Government and International Affairs at the University of Durham in England.

Michael Hopkins is lecturer in American Studies at the University of Liverpool in England.

Dianne Kirby is senior lecturer in American Studies at the University of Ulster in Northern Ireland.

Klaus Larres is professor of History and International Affairs at the University of Ulster in Northern Ireland and a visiting professor in European Studies at The Paul H. Nitze School of Advanced International Studies (SAIS) at Johns Hopkins University in Washington, DC.

Christian Nuenlist is a senior researcher with the Zurich Technical University (ETH) and a full-time journalist with the *Aargauer Zeitung*, Switzerland.

Hillary Clinton

Condoleezza Rice

Colin Powell

Madeleine Albright

Warren Christopher

James Baker

George Shultz

Alexander Haig

Henry Kissinger

Dean Rusk

John Foster Dulles

Dean Acheson

George Marshall

James Byrnes

Edward Stettinius

Introduction

Klaus Larres

School of History and International Affairs, University of Ulster, Belfast, Northern Ireland, UK & SAIS, Johns Hopkins University, Washington, DC.

In the recent past, US foreign policy in general and transatlantic relations in particular have enjoyed much attention. The events of 9/11, the subsequent 'war on terror,' and not least the invasion of Iraq and its disastrous aftermath, as well as the battle for Afghanistan and many other geopolitical challenges have greatly increased general and scholarly interest in American foreign policy. Severe European–American disagreements about the Iraq war, international concerns such as Iran's nuclear ambitions, and a good degree of discord over how to overcome the worst global economic slump since the Great Depression once again have turned transatlantic relations into a fertile field of research.

Yet most attention by scholars, as well as the general public, has been levied on the president. The president's power and its limits, as well as the president's domestic and international policymaking role, have captured public imagination. This has been particularly true since the end of the Cold War, when the US president became the only true global leader.[1] Since the events of 9/11, this tendency has become even more pronounced; both George W. Bush and his successor, Barack Obama, have been at the centre of unprecedented global attention.

Yet this meant, in turn, that the secretary of state has almost been relegated to playing a mere supporting role. For instance, George W. Bush's two secretaries of state, Colin Powell and Condoleezza Rice, frequently have not been considered in their own right but merely as instruments of Bush and his administration. To some extent, most other secretaries of state since the end of the Second World War have suffered a similar fate. And even a high-profile politician such as Hillary Clinton, former first lady, former senator and presidential candidate, has hardly been able to put her own imprint on America's foreign relations as Obama's first secretary of state.

It is the purpose of the eight essays in this volume to consider the role of the various secretaries of state in formulating and executing America's foreign policy since 1945. Underlying the analysis presented here are questions about the importance of the secretaries of state under consideration and the possibility that America would have followed an alternative foreign policy if the president had chosen a different secretary of state. Last not least, the European and transatlantic policies pursued by the respective secretaries of state are considered. However, in order to evaluate the transatlantic performance of any given secretary of state, his or her transatlantic policy must be set within the wider parameters of American foreign policy and considered against the many domestic and international constraints any secretary has to contend with when dealing with America's oldest allies.

The secretary of state normally is regarded as the most senior cabinet officer and tends to sit on the president's left in cabinet meetings, while the vice president sits on his right. The secretary of state is number four in the hierarchy of succession if the president should be incapacitated or die in office, so this is indeed an important position. Still, the secretary of state is an appointed not an elected office holder and thus serves entirely at the pleasure of the president who appoints and dismisses him or her as he deems fit. It is therefore not surprising that the relationship between president and secretary of state is of utmost importance for the successful pursuit of foreign policy under any administration, whether Republican or Democratic. In addition the secretary's relationships with the other two cabinet officers who deal with foreign affairs – the national security adviser and the secretary of defence – are also of crucial importance. Naturally there are also other cabinet positions that deal at least partially with foreign affairs but the 'golden triangle' that shapes US foreign policy clearly consists of the heads of the State Department, the Pentagon and the NSC.[2]

This book focuses on an analysis of those secretaries of state who generally have been regarded as the most influential secretaries during both the Cold War and the years that followed. In particular, the policies of secretaries who dedicated a lot of time and energy to America's relations with Europe, such as Marshall, Acheson, Dulles, Kissinger, Shultz, Baker and Powell, are analysed here. Yet clearly Dean Rusk, Condoleezza Rice and Hillary Clinton are also crucially important secretaries of state whose policies deserve our attention.

In the following essays, the performances of the four-star general Colin Powell and the comparatively inexperienced Condoleezza Rice, George W. Bush's two secretaries of state, are analysed by Klaus Larres. The policies of President Clinton's two secretaries of state, the scholarly and somewhat dry Warren Christopher and the flamboyant and exuberant Madeleine Albright, are considered by John Dumbrell. Michael Hopkins then investigates the performance of George H. W. Bush's astute secretary James Baker, as well as the foreign policy of Ronald Reagan's highly influential secretary George Shultz; he also considers the performance of Alexander Haig, Reagan's first secretary of state. One of the most well-known, highly influential, and at the same time most controversial secretaries of state is the German-born Henry Kissinger, whose policies are analysed by Dieter Dettke. Subsequently, Christian Nuenlist looks at the performance of Dean Rusk, the secretary of state who was in charge of the State Department under both John F. Kennedy and Lyndon B. Johnson and thus had to deal with the Vietnam War and its transatlantic repercussions. The foreign policy and moralistic anti-communism of the somewhat dour John Foster Dulles, President Eisenhower's influential secretary of state, is considered by Dianne Kirby. Michael Hopkins focuses on General Marshall and Dean Acheson but also briefly considers Truman's first two secretaries of state, Edward Stettinius and James Byrnes. Last not least, by way of opening this volume, Klaus Larres investigates the performance of Hillary Clinton during the first few months of the Obama administration. Naturally, one can offer merely a provisional and temporary assessment of her achievements at this early stage.

All of the secretaries of state who feature in these pages have one commonality: they shaped American foreign policy, including transatlantic relations, to a considerable extent. Most of them were skilful politicians in their own right; yet ultimately their success depended on their ability to build a close and trusting relationship with their president. Moreover, the ability of these secretaries to design and execute US foreign policy in a constructive way depended to a large extent on the degree of esteem in which the world generally held the president and the authority with which he could exercise America's global power in the post-1945 world.

This book is based on a special issue of the *Journal of Transatlantic Relations* (Vol. 6/3, December 2008), enlarged by a revised introduction and a new essay on Hillary Clinton. Special thanks are due to Alan Dobson, the experienced editor of the *Journal of Transatlantic Relations*, and to the generous support extended by Stephen Thompson at Routledge.

Klaus Larres
Washington, DC, August 2009

Notes

1. See Zbigniew Brzezinski. *The Choice: Global domination or global leadership?* (New York: Basic Books, 2004).
2. Surprisingly few newer books deal with the position of secretary of state as such rather than with certain office holders. See Alexander DeConde. *The American Secretary of State: an interpretation.* (Westport, CT: Greenwood Press, 1975); Donald P. Warwick with Marvin Meade and Theodore Reed. *A Theory of Public Bureaucracy: politics, personality and organization in the State Department.* (Cambridge, MA: Harvard University Press, 1975); Barry Rubin, *Secrets of State.* (New York: Oxford University Press, 1985). The standard work, though now somewhat dated, on individual American secretaries of state is Robert Ferrell and Samuel Bemis (eds). *The American Secretaries of State and their Diplomacy.* (New York: Cooper Square Publishers, 1963ff., 18 vols); see also Edward S. Milhalkanin. *American Statesmen: secretaries of state from John Jay to Colin Powell.* (Westport, CT: Greenwood Press, 2004), and Richie Jason, *Secretaries of State: making foreign policy* (Minneapolis, MN: Oliver Press, 2002); Lawrence S. Falkowski, *Presidents, Secretaries of State, and crises in U.S. foreign relations: a model and prescriptive analysis* (Boulder, Colo.: Westview Press, 1978), and the still valuable book by Norman A. Graebner (ed.), *An uncertain tradition: American Secretaries of State in the twentieth century* (New York: McGraw-Hill, 1961).

Hillary Rodham Clinton as Secretary of State: A New Engagement with the World

Klaus Larres

School of History and International Affairs, University of Ulster, Belfast, Northern Ireland, UK & SAIS, Johns Hopkins University, Washington, DC.

Hillary Clinton was the Democratic front-runner in the presidential election campaign of 2008 until her campaign strategy veered off the tracks. Much infighting and a lack of coherent direction doomed her initially very promising bid for the Democratic nomination.[1] She narrowly lost the race to Barack Obama, who achieved an impressive victory against his Republican opponent, John McCain, in November 2008 and became the first-ever African American to be elected president. Although not unexpected, Obama's victory was a profound shock to Clinton. At the age of 60, she could have little hope of running again in eight years time, after Obama quite possibly would have completed a two-term presidency. But Hillary had abilities and willpower, not unlike those that are the hallmark of her husband, former President Bill Clinton, and she, too, proved to be a comeback kid. Rather than retreat and find solace in resuming her position as New York's respected two-term junior senator, she accepted Obama's offer to become secretary of state, the third female secretary of state after Condoleezza Rice and Madeleine Albright.

There were convincing reports that before conceding the Democratic nomination to Obama in early June 2008, negotiations between the two fierce rivals had taken place. Presumably, Clinton had intended to extract the highest possible price for withdrawing from the Democratic race and asking her supporters to give their votes to Obama. Her accrued campaign debt of over $25 million remained, however, a serious problem.[2] There were also rumours at the time that Obama agreed to give her the choice between becoming vice president or secretary of state.[3] Yet, in late August 2008 Senator Joseph (Joe) Biden was chosen to be Obama's running mate.[4]

Once Obama had won the election and become President-elect he announced in December 2008 that Clinton had been nominated to head the State Department. Hillary Clinton seems to have concluded that this position would offer her much greater possibilities for pursuing her interest in America's global role and making use of the undoubted political talent that she had shown as a member of the influential Senate Armed Forces Committee for the previous six years. It is a little-known fact that Clinton was also a long-serving commissioner of the Commission on Security and Cooperation in Europe. As secretary of state, she may have reasoned, she might be able to come across as a more independent player and thinker in the administration than would have been possible in the role of vice president. Clinton must also have realised that Obama was hardly likely to give as much influence and power to his vice president as George W. Bush had extended to Dick Cheney.[5]

When Clinton's appointment became known she was widely acclaimed as a wise choice. Even former Republican Secretary of State Henry Kissinger told reporters: 'I believe it would be an outstanding appointment. If it is true, it shows a number of things, including great courage on the part of the president elect. To appoint a very strong personality to a prominent cabinet position requires a great deal of courage.'[6] Yet this was also a clever strategic move on the part of Obama. He effectively neutralised Clinton as a political rival and competitor. It was unlikely that Clinton would be able to run against him for the Democratic nomination in 2012 if she served as one of his most prominent cabinet colleagues. As a member of his administration, she would also be unable to criticise his policy from the outside. Instead, she would have to be loyal and accept his predominant position.

When Clinton was sworn in as the 67th secretary of state on 21 January 2009, this capped a highly unusual and rather unexpected political career.[7] While still a student at Wellesley College, the then Hillary Rodham had been an active member of the Republican Party and worked on Nelson Rockefeller's campaign to obtain the Republican nomination of 1968. Attending the Republican National Convention in Miami was a turning point in her political outlook. She felt greatly antagonised by what she perceived as the convention's racist undertones and Nixon's negative portrayal of Rockefeller, so she turned towards the Democratic Party. Soon, at Yale Law School, she met Bill Clinton and eventually accepted his repeated proposal of marriage. Subsequently, she left Washington, DC, to live with Bill in Arkansas, where she began a very successful career as a lawyer and partner of Rose Law Firm in Little Rock. They got married in October 1976, and in November 1980 their only child, a daughter Chelsea, was born.

From 1979 to 1982 and from 1984 to 1992, Clinton was first lady of Arkansas, where Bill served a total of 12 years as the state's governor. Afterwards, she was the nation's very activist first lady during the eight years of her husband's presidency from 1993 to 2001. In the course of this time, her strenuous (and ultimately failed) efforts to introduce universal health care in the United States earned her much credit in Democratic circles and much enmity in Republican circles but also among Liberals who criticised her somewhat chaotic approach.[8] Subsequently, she made a mark as the first-ever former first lady to embark on her own political career, becoming a respected US senator and secretary of state in January 2009.

At the time of writing, less than three – quarters of a year have passed since her appointment; this is a narrow basis for judging anyone's political performance. It is therefore difficult to arrive at a fair assessment of her achievements as secretary of state. Yet a number of characteristic features can already be discerned.

Popularity within the State Department.

Hillary Clinton is a highly popular secretary of state within the ranks of the State Department. From her first day in office, she frequently noted the great expertise and experience of her new staff. She emphasised that the Obama administration was 'a team' and that employees of the State Department were 'members of that team.'[9] She also made it be known that she preferred career diplomats to political appointees and has vigorously campaigned to obtain more and better funding for the State Department, further endearing herself to the department's employees.

Relationship with Obama

Clinton drew a lesson from the fate of Colin Powell on the importance of having a close, trusting relationship with the president. This has led her to go out of her way to overcome the deep political and personal rift that had developed between her and Obama during their hard-fought campaign for the Democratic nomination in the spring and summer of 2008.[10] She soon succeeded in coming across as an absolutely loyal member of Obama's team and has made a great effort to praise Obama's leadership when giving public speeches and interviews.

In the summer of 2009, rumours surfaced regarding tensions between her and the president. In the course of a news conference Clinton let it be known that she was less than happy that positions at the US Agency for International Development and several ambassadorships had not been filled. Moreover, she frequently was unable to appoint candidates of her choice to important ambassadorial posts. For instance, she intended to fill the ambassadorship to Japan with Harvard academic Joseph Nye; instead the post went to John Roos, a little-known lawyer but a very wealthy fundraiser for Obama's presidential campaign.[11] Obama's decision to appoint a new US ambassador to Syria reportedly took the State Department by surprise. But Clinton could hardly object to Obama's wish to use Syria as a test-case for engaging one of the world's rogue regimes without pre-condition.[12] The move of Dennis Ross, the administration's foremost expert on Iran, from the State Department to the White House may also have displeased Clinton. Yet she did not attempt to resist Obama's request, which was meant to give the National Security Council greater depth.[13] Shortly after being sworn into office, Clinton was unable to push Richard Holbrooke as her deputy secretary of state. Instead, James Steinberg, an Obama loyalist and initial candidate for National Security Adviser, was appointed her deputy.[14]

Still, it is difficult to detect a clear rift with the White House. On the contrary, Clinton goes out of her way to praise the president. She refers to herself as Obama's chief adviser and chief diplomat, but 'at the end of the day, it is the president who has to set and articulate policy,' as she explained on 'Meet the Press' in July 2009. She added, with enthusiasm, 'I am here to say, as somebody who's spent an enormous amount of time and effort running against him, I think his performance in office has been incredible.'[15] Fred Kaplan may well have been right when he wrote in *Slate* magazine that 'relations between the White House and Foggy Bottom ... are more harmonious than at any time anyone can remember ... That's an accomplishment in itself.'[16]

There is not an inkling left of Clinton's accusations during the campaign that Obama was inexperienced and naive in international affairs, had too idealistic an outlook on foreign affairs, and wasn't tough and realistic enough when considering America's role in the world.[17] Clinton, however, cannot be regarded as a member of Obama's inner circle, which is based in the White House and largely made up of confidants and advisers from his Chicago days. Still, it is probably correct to say that Hillary Clinton is 'morphing from superstar to loyal soldier,' as exemplified by her speech at the Council on Foreign Relations in Washington on 15 July 2009 which largely elaborated on Obama's main foreign policy objectives.[18] Clinton is 'on message' with regard to the substance of Obama's foreign policy. The secretary of state has fully adopted the grand theme that has dominated the administration's approach to external affairs – a new constructive engagement with the world, or as Clinton said in her Council on Foreign Relations speech, 'a more flexible and pragmatic posture'.[19]

Neglect of Europe

Hillary Clinton has deliberately set out to become an activist secretary of state. Already during the first seven months of her new position she hit the ground running by embarking on multi-country tours of Asia in February 2009, which included trips to Japan, Indonesia, Korea, China and an eleven-day and seven-nation tour of Africa in August 2009. In previous months, she attended the ASEAN summit in Thailand, visited India, travelled to the Middle East as well as to Turkey, attended a NATO summit in Brussels, and met with her Russian counterpart in Geneva. She also visited a number of South American countries, travelled to Canada and Egypt, and participated in an international conference on Afghanistan in The Hague.[20]

It was noticeable, though, that Clinton's travels included no major trip to visit the most important European capitals during her first months in office. Vice President Biden, rather than the secretary of state, attended the important Munich Security Conference in February 2009.[21] While Clinton visited Brussels and The Hague to attend international meetings and has met most of her European counterparts when they visited Washington, she has been too busy dealing with the world's trouble spots to dedicate a special trip to see America's European allies. Moreover, she was unable to remember the correct names of some European dignitaries she met while visiting the European parliament during her journey to a NATO meeting in Brussels during early March 2009. On one occasion, she also proclaimed somewhat naively that American democracy was much older than any European democracy. Yet, on the whole, her visit was a success and greatly welcomed in Europe.[22] Clinton's relative neglect of the European continent is perfectly understandable, given time constraints and the urgency of other burning global matters. At the same time, it is also indicative of the declining importance of Europe to the Obama administration.

The president himself visited Europe three times during his first few months in office and was almost treated like a rock star by both the European public and the media alike.[23] Obama's visits created a much improved transatlantic atmosphere and led to a new reengagement with the European continent. Yet it has not led to a 'new centrality' for Europe in American foreign policy. As Justin Vaisse has argued, 'Europe is forced to take a back seat, watching from the sidelines – not without anxiety sometimes'.[24] Still, Clinton's pronouncement in March 2009 that the Obama administration would 're-energize the transatlantic relationship, strained during the Bush era'[25] has largely been realised.

Most of the administration's foreign policy decisions have met European expectations, not least the anticipated closure of Guantanamo prison and US attempts at engagement with Moscow, Tehran, North Korea and the Palestinians. Washington even kept its engagement offer open and was prepared to deal with fraudulently re-elected Iranian president Ahmadinejad despite the violently suppressed mass demonstrations in Tehran in the aftermath of the manipulated election in the summer of 2009.[26] Also, a new priority for fighting climate change, observing human rights and introducing new strategies for Afghanistan and Iraq were all greatly applauded in Europe. So was abolition of the use of the term 'war against terror' and the administration's avowed intention to return to a general policy of global cooperation and multilateralism.[27]

America's foreign policy priorities, however, are elsewhere. The European allies are still useful, and Washington greatly appreciates their supporting role in the war in Afghanistan and elsewhere. But they are no longer central to the achievements of America's global strategy, which consists of maintaining Washington's predominant position in the world and fighting international terrorism. Even when battling the world economic crisis that began in August 2007, and despite an initial coordinated burst of activity to prevent a global banking meltdown, European–American coordination proved on the whole to be less close than many analysts regarded as desirable. In fact there were some major disagreements, not least with the German Finance Minister, about the wisdom of American pressure in favour of huge global stimulus bills to inject trillions of dollars to save banks and businesses from collapsing.[28] It is clear that Washington has begun to regard world leadership as a task to be coordinated and perhaps shared with China, Russia and possibly India. As yet the European Union (EU) or any individual European countries do not feature to any great extent within this strategic framework.

While the US has largely given up viewing the EU as an economic and strategic rival for global leadership as was the case on occasion in the late 1980s and during the 1990s, Washington is still in favour of European integration. In an interview with the *Irish Times* in late March 2009, Clinton emphasised that the US still supported the principle of an ever more closely integrated European continent. She explained that 'deeper European political integration, including the enhanced EU foreign policy role envisaged in the Lisbon Treaty, is in the United States' national interest'. Clinton continued by outlining her belief that political integration was 'in Europe's interest and I believe that it is in the United States' interest because we want a strong Europe'.[29]

Hillary Clinton's visibility problem

Clinton does not appear to be the undisputed person in charge of American foreign policy, which initially she no doubt assumed she would be. The Obama administration clearly is 'a top-down administration; the president controls policy and imposes discipline'.[30] Still, Clinton, as well as everyone else, was surprised how quickly Obama developed a great interest and indeed expertise in US foreign policy. This was contrary to what he had implied during his presidential campaign and also did not reflect his previously expressed interests, which were almost all focused on domestic social and economic issues. Instead, the first six months of the Obama administration were characterised by 'a very Obama-centric policy', not only in the domestic but also in the international realm.[31]

Moreover, the Obama administration has resurrected the idea of making foreign policy with the help of special envoys, a common practice under Bill Clinton's presidency, but one which largely fell out of favour under his successor George W. Bush. At the time of writing, there are special envoys for every area in which America has a burning stake. Richard Holbrooke deals with Afghanistan and Pakistan, George Mitchell with Israel/Palestine, Stephen Bosworth with North Korea, and Dennis Ross (effectively) with Iran. In addition, there also is Vice President Joe Biden, former long-term head of the Senate Foreign Affairs Committee, whose advice Obama often requests and who frequently travels the world almost as the president's personal special envoy. There are also special envoys and representatives for climate change (Todd Stern), for Eurasian Energy (Richard Morningstar), as well as for Sudan (J. Scott Gration) and the Great Lakes Region in East Africa (Howard Wolpe).[32]

All the envoys nominally work under the general supervision of the secretary of state, but the sheer experience and heavyweight stature of the selected politicians ensured that Clinton was perhaps *primus inter pares* but certainly not undisputed boss. Although all the envoys emphasised Clinton's importance and were always ready to acknowledge their subservience to her authority,[33] the creation of an 'empire of envoys' actually caused the secretary of state to lose a substantial degree of influence over shaping a huge and important chunk of American foreign policy. Whether this has enabled Clinton's State Department to 'take on a bigger role in tackling the problems of the future – in particular, how America will lead the world in the century ahead', as claimed in a *Washington Post* article, is doubtful however.[34] Still, Clinton naturally has remained in general charge of US foreign policy over important geographical entities, such as China, India, Europe and not least Iraq, though the latter is also handled by the vice president. In particular Clinton takes the new US policy towards Russia (optimistically called 'the reset') very seriously, not least in order to achieve resolutions of the non-proliferation problem with Iran and the explosive situation in the Caucasus.[35]

In mid-June 2009, Clinton had a fall in the State Department basement and fractured her right elbow. It proved to be a complicated and very painful fracture, and as a consequence she needed to undergo lengthy medical treatment and physical therapy. She had to withdraw from a number of engagements and could not travel much. Not least, she was unable to accompany Obama on his state visit to Russia or go to the G8 summit in Italy during early July 2009. Thus, in the summer of 2009, it became ever clearer that the person who was running the administration's foreign policy was the president himself.[36]

Clinton's aides maintained, though, that the secretary of state continued to play a critical role in formulating Washington's foreign policy despite her illness. Some journalists, in particular foreign ones, were convinced that she was merely dedicating herself to 'learning the ropes before asserting herself'.[37] The American press was less kind. US journalists increasingly spoke of Clinton's invisibility and suggested that she had been 'elbowed out'. This line of argument was well captured in a critical online article in which the author sniped that it was really time 'for Barack Obama to let Hillary Clinton take off her burqa'.[38]

These and similar articles were clearly exaggerated. Yet it became obvious that Clinton did have a visibility problem in light of a president who was highly active in almost all important political areas, including foreign affairs, and the appointment of so many eminent special envoys. Yet, it must have been comforting to her that the only one who overshadowed her was the President himself. Neither her colleague in the Pentagon, Secretary of Defense Robert Gates, nor National Security Adviser Jim Jones could rival her celebrity status and not least her firm and loyal constituency within the Democratic Party. This was very different to the situation Colin Powell had been faced with.[39] Still, in the course of July and August 2009, Clinton attempted to counter the dissatisfying image of her role as secretary of state with a number of television appearances and a well-publicised visit to seven African nations. Yet Clinton had bad luck. At the beginning, her African tour was overshadowed by her husband's dramatic and highly visible journey to North Korea, where he met with the country's dictator, Kim Jong-il, and obtained the freedom of two imprisoned American journalists.[40]

A few days later, the secretary of state snapped when the question of a Congolese student was mistranslated from the French and he appeared to have asked about Bill Clinton's, rather than Obama's or her own views, on the global economic crisis. She angrily told the student in no uncertain terms that this was of no interest since she and not her husband was the secretary of state. Granted, fatigue and exhaustion may have partly explained Clinton's reaction. Still, it became obvious that Clinton's much-discussed visibility problem had not left her untouched. In fact, she herself seems to believe that she has been unable to put her imprint on American foreign policy since becoming secretary of state and that her ability to shape her country's foreign policy has turned out to be much more constrained than she and almost everyone else expected.[41]

Conclusion

During the first seven to eight months of the Obama administration, there was very little indication that Hillary Clinton may yet prove to be an exceptional secretary of state. While she came across in this role as talented, well-organised, and energetic, it quickly became obvious that the president alone set the administration's main foreign policy directions. In fact, many analysts and possibly Clinton herself believed she had too low a profile. She did not seem to be in the driving seat with regard to America's foreign policy. And this was a dangerous development, as Colin Powell's precedent had shown: once the international community realises that the secretary of state is a lightweight within the administration, most foreign ministers and heads of state will wish to deal with the president directly rather than with a weak secretary of state. Clinton is aware of this and she intended to do her best to overcome this hurdle and develop an image as a strong secretary of state who enjoys the president's confidence and is thus fully in command of the country's foreign policy.

Fortunately for Clinton, there appear to be very few points of contention between her and Obama regarding the substance of America's foreign policy. Clinton seems to agree with Obama's process-driven way of organising his administration and with most of the major foreign policy decisions taken by the administration.[42] As for the day's burning issues – the wars in Iraq and Afghanistan, policy towards Iran and North Korea, how to deal with China's and Russia's imperial ambitions, climate change and human rights – she and Obama again seem to be largely in agreement. For instance, Clinton, contrary to much press speculation, fully supported Obama's decision to increase the strength of American troops in Afghanistan as wise and necessary. It wasn't Clinton but Vice President Biden who viewed this development with scepticism.[43] Clinton and Obama also agree about the necessity to pay much greater attention to the less traditional issues of American foreign policy such as energy and environmental matters and not least international women's issues. Her introduction of a Pentagon-style new 'Quadrennial Diplomacy and Development Review' to rethink America's Foreign Aid policy is an innovative and forward-looking initiative.[44]

So far, though, neither Obama nor Clinton has developed a truly new vision for America's foreign policy in the twenty-first century. While the administration's well-meant new 'engagement' with the rest of the world is prudent and long overdue, it can hardly count as a visionary policy. Although there are some visionary elements in the administration's foreign policy, such as Obama's declaration that he was in favour of the elimination of all nuclear weapons,[45] as yet no clear comprehensive foreign policy strategy has evolved. It remains to be seen whether the president or his secretary of state, perhaps even in cooperation with their transatlantic allies, will be able to develop such a vision.

This is a formidable challenge. After all, none of the post-Cold War administrations led by George H.W. Bush, Bill Clinton and George W. Bush was capable of doing so before. Already during the first few months of the new administration one thing became clear however: the Obama administration had no intention to abdicate global leadership though it wished to exercise US leadership and hegemony in a cooperative and multilateral way if at all possible. As Secretary of State Clinton expressed it in a major speech in mid–2009: 'With more states facing common challenges, we have the chance and a profound responsibility to exercise American leadership to solve problems in concert with others.'[46]

NOTES

1. See Michael Cottle, 'What went wrong', *The New Republic*, 16 May 2008: http://www.tnr.com/politics/story.html?id=f7a4a380-c4a4-4f84-b653-f252e8569915
2. She was eventually able to clear her debt by April 2009. See http://www.cnn.com/2009/POLITICS/04/16/clinton.debt/index.html.
3. See for example http://www.nydailynews.com/opinions/2008/06/28/2008-06-28_hillary_clintons_vice_president_stock_is.html, 28 June 2008.
4. See http://www.cnn.com/2008/POLITICS/08/23/biden.democrat.vp.candidate/index.html, 23 August 2008.
5. See Barton Gellman, *Angler: The Cheney Vice Presidency* (New York: Penguin, 2008).
6. See ABC News, 16 November 2008, http://blogs.abcnews.com/politicalpunch/2008/11/kissinger-backs.html.
7. For recent accounts of Clinton's life and political career, see Carl Bernstein, *A Woman in Charge: The Life of Hillary Rodham Clinton* (New York: Knopf, 2007); Jeff Gerth and Don Van Natta, Jr., *Her Way: The Hopes and Ambitions of Hillary Rodham Clinton* (New York: Little Brown, 2007); Gil Troy, *Hillary Rodham Clinton: Polarizing First Lady* (Lawrence, KS: University Press of Kansas, 2006). See also her bestselling autobiography *Living History* (New York: Simon and Schuster, 2003).
8. See http://healthpolicyandmarket.blogspot.com/2007/10/analysis-of-senator-hillary-clintons.html, 15 January 2008.
9. 'Arrival at the Department of State,' http://www.state.gov/secretary/rm/2009a/01/115262.htm, 11 January 2009.
10. See for example *The New York Times*, 26 June 2008: http://www.nytimes.com/2008/06/26/world/americas/26iht-dems.1.14012672.html
11. http://search.japantimes.co.jp/cgi-bin/nn20090529a4.html, 29 May 2009.

12. http://www.cnn.com/2009/POLITICS/06/24/us.syria/index.html, 24 June 2009. Also http://www.wnd.com/index.php?pageId=104430, 19 July 2009; Matthew Kaminski, 'The Hillary Doctrine', interview with Hillary Clinton, *The Wall Street Journal*, 14 August 2009: http://online.wsj.com/article/SB20001424052970203863204574348843585706178.html.

13. See http://thecable.foreignpolicy.com/posts/2009/06/25/dennis_ross_move_to_nsc_announced, 25 June 2009; http://www.nytimes.com/2009/06/16/world/16diplo.html, 15 June 2009; http://www.politico.com/news/stories/0609/24221.html, 26 June 2009.

14. See http://washingtonindependent.com/20615/sargent-steinberg-will-be-clintons-deputy-at-state-holbrooke-on-the-outs, 2 December 2008; http://www.npr.org/templates/story/story. php?storyId=97775518, 4 December 2008.

15. See 'Clinton insists ties with Obama are strong', 26 July 2009, http://news.yahoo.com/s/afp/20090726/ts_alt_afp/uspoliticsdiplomacyclintonobama.

16. See Fred Kaplan, 'So happy together', *Slate* magazine, 17 July 2009, http://www.slate.com/id/2223025/.

17. See for example, http://www.msnbc.msn.com/id/19933710/, 24 July 2007.

18. Mark Landler in the *International Herald Tribune*, 17 July 2009, p. 2. The text of her speech before the CFR can be found online at: http://www.state.gov/secretary/rm/2009a/july/126071.htm.

19. Speech before the Council on Foreign Relations, 15 July 2009: http://www.state.gov/secretary/rm/2009a/july/126071.htm.

20. For an overview, see http://www.state.gov/secretary/trvl/2009/index.htm.

21. See http://www.spiegel.de/international/world/0,1518,605949,00.html, 6 February 2009.

22. See http://www.reuters.com/article/politicsNews/idUSTRE52540720090306, 6 March 2009.

23. See Joseph Joffe, 'Obama's Popularity doesn't mean much abroad', *Wall Street Journal*, 18 April 2009: http://online.wsj.com/article/SB124000916299330597.html.

24. See http://www.brookings.edu/opinions/2009/0604_obama_europe_vaisse.aspx, 4 June 2009.

25. See http://news.xinhuanet.com/english/2009-03/06/content_10959626.htm, 6 March 2009.

26. See Matthew Kaminski, 'The Hillary Doctrine', interview with Hillary Clinton, *The Wall Street Journal*, 14 August 2009: http://online.wsj.com/article/SB2000142405297020386320457434888 43585706178.html.

27. BBC Monitoring Service Europe, Portuguese paper *Publico*, 'Obama to find Europe "reluctant to cooperate"', 1 April 2009.

28. Joseph P. Quinlan, 'The transatlantic economy really is too big too fail', Europe's World, summer 2009: http://www.europesworld.org/NewEnglish/Home/Article/tabid/191/ArticleType/ArticleView/ArticleID/21380/language/en-US/Thetransatlanticeconomyreallyistoobigtofail.aspx; also http://www.gmfus.org/event/detail.cfm?id=583&parent_type=E, 11 May 2009. See also http://www.neurope.eu/articles/94029.php, 20 April 2009.

29. See http://www.irishtimes.com/newspaper/world/2009/0321/1224243196950.html, 21 March 2009.

30. See Fred Kaplan, 'So happy together', *Slate* magazine, 17 July 2009: http://www.slate.com/id/2223025/.

31. David J. Rothkopf quoted in *LA Times*, 16 July 2009, http://www.latimes.com/news/nationworld/world/la-fgw-clinton16-2009jul16,0,1210881.story.

32. For an interesting account, see David Gauvey Herbert's article in the *National Journal*, 29 July 2009, http://www.nationaljournal.com/njonline/print_friendly.php?ID=no_20090715_7067.

33. See, for example, Richard Holbrooke's comments at the Center for American Progress, 12 August 2009, http://thehill.com/leading-the-news/holbrooke-on-af-pak-know-success-when-we-see-it-2009-08-12.html; also http://www.politico.com/news/stories/0809/26047.html.

34. David Rothkopf, 'It's 3a.m. Do you know where Hillary Clinton is?' *Washington Post*, 23 August 2009, p. B5.

35. See Matthew Kaminski, 'The Hillary Doctrine', interview with Hillary Clinton, *The Wall Street Journal*, 14 August 2009: http://online.wsj.com/article/SB2000142405297020386320457434888 43585706178.html.

36. See http://www.latimes.com/news/opinion/la-oe-mcmanus26-2009jul26,0,381778.column, 26 July 2009.

37. See http://www.independent.co.uk/opinion/commentators/rupert-cornwell/rupert-cornwell-the-curious-case-of-hillary-clinton-the-missing-secretary-of-state-1752207.html, 19 July 2009.

38. See Tina Brown, 'Obama's Other Wife', The Daily Beast: http://www.greatertalent.com/GTNnews.php?articleId=427, 16 July 2009.
39. See the first chapter in this volume.
40. See for example http://www.washingtonpost.com/wp-dyn/content/article/2009/08/04/AR2009080400684.html, 5 August 2009; also http://www.nytimes.com/2009/08/16/weekinreview/16gettleman.html?_r=1, 15 August 2009.
41. For the video of Clinton's outburst, see http://celebrifi.com/gossip/Hillary-Clinton-Snaps-At-Reporter-VIDEO-617519.html; see also for example http://www.foxnews.com/politics/2009/08/10/hillary-clinton-im-secretary-state/, 10 August 2009.
42. Michael Crowley, 'The Decider', *The New Republic*, 12 August 2009: http://www.tnr.com/politics/story.html?id=3cec0b39-4950-4a27-9e03-ad8d3a07f52f.
43. See Tina Brown, 'Obama's Other Wife', The Daily Beast: http://www.greatertalent.com/GTNnews.php?articleId=427, 16 July 2009.
44. See http://www.state.gov/secretary/rm/2009a/july/125949.htm, 10 July 2009.
45. He made such a declaration in a speech in Prague in April 2009. See http://articles.latimes.com/2009/apr/06/world/fg-obama-arms-control6; already in 2007 Senator Obama expressed similar sentiments, see: http://www.nytimes.com/2007/10/02/us/politics/02obama.html
46. Speech before the *Council on Foreign Relations*, Washington, DC, 15 July 2009. The text can be found online at http://www.state.gov/secretary/rm/2009a/july/126071.htm.

George W. Bush's Secretaries of State and Europe: Colin Powell and Condoleezza Rice

Klaus Larres

School of History and International Affairs, University of Ulster, Belfast, Northern Ireland, UK & SAIS, Johns Hopkins University, Washington, DC.

By the time George W. Bush became President in January 2001 he had assembled one of the most experienced cabinets in recent US history. In particular his foreign policy team had an almost unprecedented level of experience. Due to the dispute about the outcome of the presidential election results in Florida, however, the new President did not have the customary two and a half months but just a few weeks to focus on the transition. It was not until early December 2000 that the controversial decision of the US Supreme Court not to allow the re-count of the ballot in Florida handed a narrow electoral victory to Bush over his Democratic rival, President Clinton's sitting Vice-President Al Gore.[1] Still, by the end of the year most of the main players of Bush's foreign policy team had largely been selected.

Ever since the two-term governor of Texas with little knowledge and expertise about the world outside the United States had made up his mind in the course of 1999 to run seriously for the Republication presidential nomination, a number of experienced foreign policy experts had begun to coach him. Most of them had held mid-level positions under the Republican administrations of Nixon/Ford, Reagan and George H.W. Bush and soon called themselves the 'Vulcans', after the Roman god of fire whose statue was overlooking the town of Birmingham, Alabama, the home town of Condoleezza Rice, one of Bush's most trusted advisers.[2] Important other members of the group included Richard Armitage, Stephen Hadley, Robert Blackwill, Robert Zoellick, Paul Wolfowitz, Richard Perle, Dov Zakheim, I. Lewis (Scooter) Libby, and some others.[3]

It was from this group of people as well as from an associated group of eminent and much more senior Republican foreign policy experts that Bush chose the people for the crucial foreign policy posts of his administration. Among the associated group were illustrious politicians such as George Shultz, Reagan's Secretary of State, Donald Rumsfeld, Secretary of Defence under President Ford, Richard (Dick) Cheney, George H.W. Bush's Secretary of Defence, and Brent Scowcroft, National Security Adviser under Ford and Bush senior. The 'Vulcans' and the more established politicians knew each other well as most had worked together closely in their previous government posts. All of the 'Vulcans' came to hold high-level positions in the new Bush administration. Many of them had a somewhat military outlook on foreign affairs as they had worked at the Pentagon, at least briefly, for a crucial time in their careers.

Among the most prominent of Bush's foreign policy appointments were Richard (Dick) Cheney, who became the new Vice-President with an important and unprecedented role in US national security policy; Donald Rumsfeld was again appointed to head the Pentagon; Paul Wolfowitz, who had been an Assistant Secretary of State under President Reagan, became his deputy. Richard Armitage, an Assistant Secretary of Defence under Reagan, was appointed Deputy Secretary of State.

The informal meetings of the 'Vulcans' were chaired by Condoleezza Rice, a Russian expert and mid-echelon member of the elder Bush's foreign affairs team who returned to her academic post at Stanford University in early 1993 and secured a controversial appointment as Provost. In late 2000 President-designate Bush appointed her to be his National Security Adviser and despite what was regarded by most scholars and journalists as a generally disappointing performance in this role, she was elevated to Secretary of State when Bush began his second term of office in early 2006.[4]

Colin Powell, four-star general, Ronald Reagan's National Security Adviser from 1987 to 1989 and a highly influential chairman of the Joint Chief of Staff during the entire administration of Bush senior and the early months of Bill Clinton's first term in office, was named George W. Bush's first Secretary of State. He thus became the first African American appointed to this position.[5] Although Powell had also advised Bush on foreign affairs in 1999/2000, as one of the most celebrated and prominent US politicians at the time who was often touted as being interested in running for President himself,[6] he had not been in the inner circle of Bush's advisers and never developed a very close personal relationship with him. This would come to haunt him. Powell, despite his immense foreign policy experience and impressive personality, would always remain the 'odd one out', as *Time* magazine described him in early September 2001.[7] In contrast, his much less experienced cabinet colleague and successor Condoleezza Rice developed what probably amounted to the closest relationship with a sitting President any National Security Adviser or Secretary of State has ever had.

Yet, the foreign policy which both of them pursued on behalf of the Bush Administration can hardly be regarded as a success. The Iraq war and its fallout, the unsuccessful fight against Al Qaeda in Afghanistan and elsewhere, lack of progress in the Middle East and with regard to Iran's and, to a lesser extent, North Korea's atomic diplomacy, the failure to improve tense relations with Russia, China and many other countries as well as the scant attention paid to international climate change, energy and human rights issues amounted to a less than impressive balance sheet. Not least the inability of either of them to re-create the close transatlantic partnership with Europe which had existed before George W. Bush's presidency was indicative of the general mistrust felt towards the Bush Administration in the world at large.[8]

Essentially it seems that not only the closeness of the relationship the Secretary of State enjoys with the President is crucial for the success of American foreign policy as is often and with justification claimed in the literature and by experienced politicians such as Henry Kissinger.[9] Even more important appears to be the general regard and respect for the President himself in the outside world. Thus, both Powell and Rice were perhaps fighting a losing battle once the international community, including America's closest allies, had concluded that American foreign policy under Bush essentially consisted of unilateralism writ large. The administration's foreign policy seemed to be largely ideologically driven and, as a result of the infighting in the administration between the neo-conservative ideologues and pragmatists such as Colin Powell, displayed a considerable degree of confusion, contradiction and sheer incompetence.

In the following the performance of both Colin Powell and Condoleezza Rice will be assessed; particular attention is paid to transatlantic relations.

Colin Powell

During the election campaign of 2000 Republican candidate George W. Bush went out of his way to emphasise his relatively mild conservative sentiments as well as his multilateral approach to international relations, a fact which went down very well with Colin Powell. Domestically Bush spoke of his 'compassionate conservatism' and of reaching out to all sorts of domestic audiences and groups. On foreign affairs Bush said very little during the election campaign. In November 1999, however, he had spoken of 'the modesty of true strength' and 'humility of greatness' when referring to America's foreign relations.[10] Bush would continue this line of reasoning throughout the next year. In the televised debate on foreign affairs with Al Gore in the late summer of 2000 Bush spoke of the importance of reaching out to America's allies. He explained that it really depended 'upon how our nation conducts itself in foreign policy. If we're an arrogant nation, they'll resent us. If we're a humble nation, but strong, they'll welcome us.' Bush criticised Clinton's use of the military for international nation-building. He said 'Our military is meant to fight and win war ... and when it gets overextended, morale drops'. The Republican presidential nominee declared that if elected he would be 'judicious as to how to use the military. It needs to be in our vital interest, the mission needs to be clear, and the exit strategy obvious.'[11]

A multilateral approach to international relations and the wise use of the US military sounded like music to Powell's ears. In an article written for *Foreign Affairs* in January 2000 Bush's confidante Condoleezza Rice had explained with reference to America's European allies and international institutions like the UN that a Republican administration would 'proceed from the firm ground of national interest and not from the interest of an illusory international community'. She also dismissed America's responsibility for contributing to the rebuilding of failed nation-states.[12] This caused much concern in Europe before Bush had even been elected. Colin Powell was also puzzled. However, later on he was confident that as Bush's Secretary of State and senior cabinet officer, he would effectively design the new administration's foreign policy and thus be able to steer US foreign policy within the tested multilateral framework pursued by George W. Bush's father with whom Powell had enjoyed excellent working relations.[13]

Soon, however, Powell had to recognise that many of the policies of the new Bush Administration diverged from his own political preferences. He managed to have a number of foreign policy successes by convincing Bush to support some of his proposed initiatives, in particular with regard to the Middle East, and by adopting a more diplomatic approach to resolving international issues such as the gentle persuasion of Russia to go along with Bush's intention to abrogate the ABM disarmament treaty of 1972. On the whole, however, Powell faced an up-hill struggle in his attempt to insist on the role of the Secretary of State as the President's foremost foreign policy adviser. Both Vice-President Cheney and Secretary of Defence Rumsfeld deeply distrusted Powell's more liberal and multilateral instincts. Cheney and Rumsfeld were much more conservative than Powell, distrusted international institutions and believed that only the British could be regarded as reliable allies.[14]

National Security Adviser Condoleezza Rice, whose task it would have been to mediate between the conflicting voices from State, the Pentagon and the VP's office and to present Bush with a number of divergent policy options, was careful not to become involved in the ideological conflicts soon being waged between Powell, Cheney and Rumsfeld and their respective and frequently even more hostile underlings. Rice certainly did not wish to endanger her carefully nourished role as Bush's confidante and her very personal relationship with the President and his entire family by proposing unpalatable options to him.[15] For instinctively Bush almost always sided with the conservative voices in his administration. Although the President did not wish to antagonise his popular and globally respected Secretary of State and was careful not to have Powell humiliated too often by overriding his proposals and political preferences, on the whole Bush tended to be drawn to Cheney's and Rumsfeld's much more ideological standpoints. Neither Cheney nor Rumsfeld nor indeed the President shared the crusading zeal of some of their neo-conservative advisers such as Libby, Douglas Faith, Perle, and not least Wolfowitz.[16] However, Bush was attracted by the neo-conservatives' belief in a new American exceptionalism and their conviction that, as journalist Krauthammer expressed it, America's 'unipolar moment' of world hegemony had to be exploited to remake the world on the model of American democracy. In particular the President was attracted by the idea of democratising the entire Middle East by embarking on regime change in Iraq and subsequently perhaps in some other countries in the region. Krauthammer had explained in his widely read article: 'The new unilateralism seeks to strengthen American power and unashamedly deploy it on behalf of self-defined global ends'.[17]

In stark contrast to the Vice-President and the Secretary of Defence, Powell had a much more pragmatic approach to American foreign policy-making which was close to what America's European allies had expected of the new administration. Essentially most of America's NATO allies had been convinced that Bush would follow the multilateral footsteps of his father and be greatly interested in nourishing the transatlantic relationship. It was thus little wonder that Powell's relations with most European governments and foreign ministers as well as with the chiefs of the EU, the UN and NATO were very good and, on a personal level, would largely remain so, even after the invasion of Iraq. 'Powell managed to maintain good relations around the world while supporting Bush's Iraq policy. He was seen as a moderate in a hawkish regime.' Thus, in Europe Powell was soon regarded as 'one of us'; yet this did much harm to his reputation in Washington and it strengthened the mistrust with which he was regarded by many in the Bush Administration outside the State Department.[18]

For instance, similar to the way many European leaders urged Bush to focus much more on the increasing violence in the Middle East, Powell also attempted to impress upon the new President that America was simply too important and influential to take a back-seat in the Israel–Palestine conflict though that was precisely what Cheney and Rumsfeld were advising. They were above all focused on Iraq and how to unseat Saddam Hussein rather than on overcoming the wider Middle East conflict.[19] The obvious link between resolving the Israel–Palestine question and undermining widespread anti-Americanism and support for terrorism in the region was largely ignored by the administration.

It took Powell considerable persuasion to make Bush refer to the Middle East in his speech to the UN General Assembly in November 2001. However, when Bush turned his attention to the region in his UN speech he even proposed a two-state solution to resolve the Israel–Palestine conflict; this was the first time that a US President had indicated America's interest in seeing a Palestinian state established.[20] Powell had to be even more persuasive and use much of his personal capital with Bush to convince the President to appoint retired Marine Corps General Anthony Zinni as a special envoy (called 'special adviser') to the Middle East. Zinni was meant to negotiate a ceasefire by helping to implement the Mitchell and Tenent plans to contain the escalating violence in the Gaza strip, the West Bank and elsewhere.[21]

Although Bush's Middle East initiative was greatly welcomed by almost all European governments, by this time transatlantic relations had already suffered. They had been damaged by the Bush Administration's early decision in March 2001 that it would not send the ratification of the Kyoto agreement to Congress and that the United States would not become a signature state to the founding of the International Criminal Court (ICC) as Washington feared the arrest and subsequent prosecution of US soldiers, and even American politicians when travelling outside the US, by foreign courts.[22] Also Bush's intention to develop a so-called Missile Defense Shield in continuation of Ronald Reagan's SDI/'star wars' initiative and the imposition of protective tariffs on American steel and then also on agricultural goods as well as several other contentious issues caused great European disenchantment with the new administration and its apparent lack of interest in cooperating with its European allies. The widespread suspicion that Bush had embarked on a course of unilateralism became ever stronger.[23]

In addition, the new administration's hard-line policy towards North Korea and its initial refusal to participate in the six-nation negotiations with the dictators in Pyongyang frustrated the Europeans and ran counter to Powell's preferred course of action. In fact, when he indicated to a reporter that Bush would continue Clinton's policy of engaging with the North Korean regime, the White House, and in particular Cheney, who detested Clinton, was appalled. The President insisted on Powell formally telling journalists during a visit by the South Korean leader to Washington that the administration was reviewing its policy towards North Korea and would soon adopt a new course unique to the administration. It was humiliating for Powell when he had to correct his previous statement by declaring that suggestions of 'imminent negotiations' were mistaken.[24] Powell's reputation as the 'odd man out' in the administration had been confirmed once again.

For a brief moment this changed in the aftermath of 9/11. With the catastrophe of the terrorist attacks on the World Trade Center and the Pentagon, the administration found a new unity. So did the coherence of the Western world. Since the disappearance of the Soviet Union the absence of a much needed common enemy had confused NATO for the last 10 years. Now a common enemy had appeared again. NATO made use of clause 5 of the North Atlantic treaty and offered its help in the pursuit of Osama Bin Laden. All European governments came out with ringing support for the Bush Administration and the traumatised American people. *Le Monde* declared 'We are all Americans now' and Buckingham Palace even arranged for the Household Cavalry to play the American national anthem to express its sympathy for the American nation.[25] There was widespread Western support for the war in Afghanistan against the ruling Taliban regime which was believed, correctly as it turned out, to be harbouring Osama Bin Laden, the brain behind the 9/11 attacks. Colin Powell's excellent relations with his fellow foreign ministers in Europe and elsewhere and his multilateral approach to US foreign policy was immensely helpful in those days.

Yet, as soon as the Taliban had been toppled in Afghanistan by mid-November 2001, the attention of the administration quickly shifted to regime change in Iraq and the removal of Saddam Hussein. In fact, shortly after 9/11 some in the administration such as Paul Wolfowitz and Donald Rumsfeld had wondered if the attacks on the World Trade Center could be laid at the door of the Iraqi dictator.[26] Soon the brief unity in the Western world began to dissipate. Already in his first State of the Union speech in January 2002 Bush had referred to an 'axis of evil' (Iran, North Korea, and not least Iraq) which had to be destroyed. It was not overlooked in Europe that he did not even once mention cooperation with the EU or NATO in this connection.[27] In the Bush Administration's first National Security Strategy paper of September 2002 Europe hardly featured either. Instead, this paper caused much attention with its reference to the necessity of pre-emptive warfare under certain conditions.[28]

Despite Washington's belated resort to the UN Security Council in October/November 2002 as a means of resolving the question of how to deal with Saddam Hussein's weapons of mass destruction, in continental Europe, and in particular in Germany, the general view continued to prevail that Bush and his closest advisers, such as Rumsfeld, Wolfowitz and not least Vice-President Cheney had already made up their minds and were merely looking for an excuse to invade Iraq – whatever America's European allies might say. This led to the firm conviction in Germany, France and elsewhere in continental Europe that the Bush Administration displayed a 'condescending indifference to outside opinion' with Secretary of State Colin Powell representing 'the lone voice of multilateral moderation in Bush's administration'.[29] Respected author Salman Rushdie summarised the European point of view neatly when he wrote that 'Unilateralist action by the world's only hyperpower looks like bullying because, well, it is bullying'.[30]

Yet, it was Colin Powell's performance at the UN on 5 February 2003, during which he presented the Bush Administration's many pieces of alleged 'evidence' to prove that Saddam Hussein was indeed secretly and illegally hiding a plethora of weapons of mass destruction in his country that convinced many in Europe that perhaps the Bush Administration's allegations were at least partially correct after all. Nevertheless, the French and German governments in particular were firmly resolved not to go along with Bush's intention to attack Iraq. Despite Colin Powell's best efforts to bridge the growing gulf between the United States and many European states, in particular France, Germany and the Benelux countries, it proved impossible to close the 'Atlantic gap' (Tony Judt) during the remainder of Bush's first term in office. The gap remained 'wide and almost unbridgeable'.[31]

With hindsight, when no weapons of mass destruction were found in Iraq after the entire country had been carefully examined by US and UN weapons inspectors, one of Powell's aides said that the Secretary of State's UN speech was 'the lowest point in my life'.[32] Colin Powell himself also realised after the invasion of Iraq that his reputation would never recover when many of the assertions in his UN speech were shown to be baseless. It is a matter of speculation whether or not the Bush Administration, and in particular the CIA and its chief George Tenent, deliberately misled the Secretary of State and thus the US, or whether the entire administration, including Tenent and Cheney, were simply too gullible when talking to high-level refugees from Iraq or when assessing aerial photos and other alleged pieces of evidence which appeared to indicate the existence of a vast areal of WMD in Iraq.[33]

It is also a matter of speculation why Powell did not resign from his post when it became obvious that the Bush Administration's WMD allegations were unfounded or after one of the many public humiliations he had to endure when Bush overruled him in favour of a course of action put forward by Cheney or Rumsfeld. After all, these occurrences made it perfectly clear that it was not the Secretary of State and the State Department but the Pentagon or the VP's office which was running US foreign policy. Most authors assume that despite his many disagreements with Bush and the clear lack of trust between them, as a former soldier Powell felt it his duty to be loyal to his commander in chief and Powell himself said on several occasions that he never considered resigning.[34]

In any case in the late summer and fall of 2002 and in the spring of 2003 the populations of almost all EU countries were either opposed to or strongly sceptical about going to war against Iraq on a flimsy pretext and without UN authorisation. With regard to the governments in power in most European countries, the situation was more complex. Essentially they were divided between those that felt the need to display loyalty to the Bush Administration and proclaim their adherence to an all-embracing 'war against terror', including an invasion of Iraq, and those who believed that their personal political convictions combined with strong domestic pressure would not allow them to agree to Washington's envisaged invasion of Iraq.

German Chancellor Schröder and French President Chirac were among the latter. Not least the importance of their countries' political and economic weight combined with their particularly vociferous attacks on Bush for electoral reasons in the case of the German chancellor[35] and for reasons of long-standing global rivalry and the desire to build up a European counterweight to the US in the case of the French, turned Chirac and Schröder into George Bush's most outspoken political opponents.[36] This even led Defence Secretary Donald Rumsfeld to speak of the division of the European continent into 'old' and 'new' Europe, the latter allegedly comprising not only new EU countries such as Poland and the Czech Republic but also any long-standing EU countries which supported the US position, such as Tony Blair's Britain, Berlusconi's Italy and Aznar's Spain.[37]

However, recent information has come to light about two German spies which the German government sent to Baghdad shortly after the September 2002 election, narrowly won by Schröder. The two spies were still in the Iraqi capital at the time of the American–British invasion and provided the US military with important target information. The German magazine *Stern* even writes about a 'secret deal with the US to provide on-the-spot intelligence to facilitate the bombardment of Iraq and clear the way for the US-led invasion'. According to the magazine, the German intelligence service, the BND (Bundesnachrichtendienst),

> co-ordinated plans with the American Central Intelligence Agency and the Defence Intelligence Agency. According to a leaked security service memo, dated November 28, 2002 – some four months before the beginning of the war – it was agreed that the German agents would report to a German liaison officer attached to the US command in Qatar. Intelligence requests from the Americans would be channelled to the German spies on the ground. The US, it seemed, had almost no trained intelligence officers in place to give context to the satellite photography. The two Germans became the eyes and ears of the war machine of the American superpower.[38]

Yet, this was known to only very few people within German and American governmental and intelligence circles; the public perception consisted instead of the adamant opposition and outright refusal of the Schröder government to collaborate with Washington in the Iraq war.[39]

The wider public and most commentators assumed that it took George W. Bush almost 18 months to once again exchange friendly smiles with the most adamant European critics of the Iraq war, Gerhard Schröder, the German chancellor, and French president Jacques Chirac. The German-American crisis over the war in Iraq appeared to be finally overcome when the German Chancellor paid a long overdue visit to the White House in late February 2004. To make up for the tension and long delayed political and personal reconciliation both politicians did not merely limit themselves to expressing their mutual friendship and admiration. They also announced an all-encompassing 'common agenda of action' and grandly reaffirmed a 'German–American alliance for the 21st century'.[40]

This was clearly meant to reflect the joint statement Bush and Schröder issued in late March 2001 on the occasion of the Chancellor's first and very successful visit to the White House shortly after Bush's inauguration when they spoke of German-American friendship constituting a 'pillar of transatlantic relations'. At the time the two politicians emphasised that they wished to 'open a new chapter' in both country's 'close relationship' with each other and based on their common belief in values such as 'freedom, democracy and human rights'.[41] In February 2004, during their first meeting since the Iraq war had begun, when they continued to disagree about Iraq and also disagreed about the Kyoto protocol on global warming and many others matters Bush and Schröder were able to emphasise that 'there's nothing wrong with friends having differences. And we have both committed to put the differences behind us and move forward.'[42] The President gladly accepted Schröder's offer to train Iraqi soldiers, albeit outside Iraq in the United Arab Emirates.

The beginnings of a Franco-American rapprochement were eventually laid in the course of the summer of 2004 when Bush visited France for the sixtieth anniversary of the Normandy landings. Following the 'worst moment between the two men' during Bush's and Chirac's personal meeting at the United Nations in New York in September 2003,[43] it took them nine month before they were ready to dine together at the Elysée palace on 5 June 2004. 'The atmosphere was all for understanding and, for once, each of the two used some tact', a French journalist reported.[44] Although during the G-8 meeting in Evian a few days later and the subsequent NATO meeting in Istanbul in late June 2004 relations worsened again, eventually, in the fall of 2004, a more lasting rapprochement was achieved. The crisis over the assassination of former Lebanese Prime Minister Hariri and Franco-American co-operation in putting pressure on Syria to bring about an end to the country's long occupation of Lebanon led to renewed Franco-American reconciliation.

Colin Powell contributed decisively to the rapprochement between the Bush Administration and 'old' Europe. Powell had excellent relations with the German and French foreign ministers and in general he was still regarded as the only 'moderate' in the Bush Administration. The first half of the year 2005 thus saw further improvement in both Franco-American and German-American relations. The decisive events were Bush's re-election in November 2004 and the elections in Iraq in late January 2005 which resulted in the formation of a sovereign Iraqi government, a long-standing French demand, and the departure of Paul Bremer, America's unpopular and controversial pro-consul in Baghdad. During her successful trip to Europe in February 2005 Colin Powell's successor as Secretary of State, Condoleezza Rice, convinced herself that that there was 'almost no dwelling on the past' and that 'everybody was in a very constructive mood and very much ready to move on'.[45] Eventually, under Chirac's successor Nicolas Sarkozy, who entered the Elysée Palace in mid-May 2007, Paris even embarked upon a distinctly pro-American foreign policy, at least when judged by France's traditional geopolitical rivalry with the US.

Yet, what really defused the crisis in transatlantic relations was not only Chancellor Schröder's election defeat in September 2005 and his replacement by the conservative politician Angela Merkel, who was much more pro-American though not an uncritical admirer of the US President, or Chirac's retirement in 2007 but above all the intention of the Bush Administration to open a new chapter and embark on a more multilateral course in its second term in office. After all, it was becoming increasingly clear that the difficulties of defeating terrorism in both Afghanistan and Iraq, as well as for instance the problems with North Korea and Iran, climate change and energy issues required multilateralism rather than a unilateral course of action. In early 2005, during Bush's state visit to several European capitals, including Brussels, Berlin and Paris, he indicated that his administration wished to open a much more conciliatory and co-operative chapter in transatlantic relations.[46]

This would have found the approval of Colin Powell but President Bush had decided to 'make a change'. Throughout most of Bush's first term in office Powell had remained 'the odd man out' and the President had never felt comfortable with him. While Bush kept Rumsfeld on as Secretary of Defence – as his departure would have looked like an admission of failure in Iraq – Powell, a much more respected international statesman, had to go. Bush did not even give Powell the bad news himself in December 2004 but had Andrew Card, his Chief of Staff, inform Powell by telephone. When Powell came for the customary farewell visit to the President a month later, Bush was puzzled when Powell stayed behind after a meeting with several participants and did not know why he was supposed to see the outgoing Secretary alone. Powell was angry and felt humiliated though pretended otherwise.[47] Bush, however, was relieved to replace the difficult Powell with the much more agreeable Condoleezza Rice, his trusted National Security Adviser and close confidante, who seldom questioned the President's judgement and his decisions.

Condoleezza Rice

Condoleezza Rice's appointment as Secretary of State in January 2005 was the culmination of a highly successful career. The first African American woman appointed to this position, Rice was born and spent her early childhood years in Birmingham, Alabama; however, at the age of 15 her family moved to the racially less difficult city of Denver, Colorado. Intending to become a concert pianist she dropped her career plan when she realised that she would not be able to compete with America's top pianists of her generation. Instead she studied International Relations at the Universities of Denver and Notre Dame and after competing her PhD at Denver in 1981 she became an Assistant Professor at Stanford University. With hindsight, this was the decisive move in her life which laid the basis for her subsequent rapid and unprecedented career progression.[48]

Only a year after arriving at Stanford she switched from being a registered Democrat to being a Republican although she still worked on Gary Hart's presidential campaign in 1984. In 1985 Brent Scowcroft, who had been President Ford's National Security Adviser, recognised Rice's foreign policy talent during a seminar at Stanford. He later claimed that he 'discovered' Rice for when Scowcroft became National Security Adviser again in 1989, this time under President Bush, he asked her to join him as a Soviet and Eastern Europe expert on the National Security Council.[49] With this step her career in national politics commenced. For during the turbulent years 1989–1991 Rice was right at the centre of events and managed to build up excellent relations with both Gorbachev and Yeltsin. She also played an important behind-the-scenes role in the process of German unification. In cooperation with a colleague on the NSC she later published an insightful book on her experience that is still one of the standard works on American foreign policy during the final period of the Cold War.[50]

When Bush lost the election of 1992 to Bill Clinton, Rice moved back to Stanford University. Once again she found the support of influential men. This time it was the eminent George Shultz, Ronald Reagan's former Secretary of State, who resided at Stanford's Hoover Institution.[51] Due to his influence she became a well-enumerated board member of illustrious companies such as Chevron and Hewlett Packard. Moreover, she managed to be on the committee who appointed Stanford's new President, the German-born lawyer Gerhard Casper who came from the University of Chicago. Casper was so impressed by her that he appointed her Provost and thus Stanford's chief financial officer; this was a controversial appointment as Rice had no experience whatsoever in management and budgetary matters but this did not seem to matter. After all, through the appointment of a female African American Provost Stanford conveniently managed to update its stuffy and conservative image. In an interview with the *New Yorker* magazine in 2002 Casper explained that it 'would be disingenuous for me to say that the fact that she was a woman, the fact that she was black ... weren't in my mind'.[52]

However, Rice fulfilled expectations; she introduced substantial cuts and thus managed to reduce Stanford's deficit by several million dollars. Even at this early stage it became clear that Rice did not have any ideological objectives. Her ideology consisted of succeeding professionally as Elizabeth Bumiller recognised. When in 1998 Rice met Texas Governor Bush when he visited Stanford for a policy seminar, the future President was immediately impressed. Condoleezza Rice not only possessed a charming and outgoing personality and a considerable foreign affairs expertise, she also was able to talk about basketball and soccer in a competent and most amusing and entertaining way. As a student Rice once dated a college football hero and from this time she apparently possessed 'an encyclopedia of knowledge about pro football'.[53]

Bush and Rice hit it off; an intense personal friendship began to develop which was based on a great degree of mutual trust. And, after all, she also knew former President Bush well who strongly recommended her to his son. Soon Rice was invited to follow-up briefings at Bush's ranch in Crawford, Texas, and in August 1998 she was asked to come to Kennebunkport, the Bush family resort. All this resulted in Rice becoming one of the most important foreign policy advisers and chairperson of the 'Vulcans' when Bush was campaigning for President in 1999/2000 and it led to her appointment as National Security Adviser once Bush was declared the winner of the presidential elections. The *Los Angeles Times* commented that 'Rice's ability to become an almost clone-like extension of the president – to understand what he wants, to make her only agenda his agenda and to carry out his wishes with unfailing loyalty – has made her invaluable'.[54]

As mentioned above, most scholars and journalists were not impressed by Condoleezza Rice's performance as National Security Adviser. While she failed to mediate successfully between Cheney, Rumsfeld and Powell, her most obvious mistakes came in the months before the terrorist attacks of 11 September 2001. She ignored the advice from the outgoing Clinton administration to focus on Osama Bin Laden's hostile intentions. Subsequently, in the months before September 2001, she also neglected the numerous warnings of the US intelligence agencies who pointed out to her advisers and herself that a terrorist attack on mainland America could not be ruled out.[55] As late as 4 September 2001 a frustrated Richard Clarke, the administration's counterterrorism chief, who felt that the administration paid insufficient attention to the dangers of international terrorism, told Rice in a memorandum "to imagine a day after a terrorist attack, with hundreds of Americans dead at home and abroad, and ask themselves what they could have done better'.[56] In his testimony to the 9/11 Commission Richard Armitage, admitted that the administration was moving too slowly in developing plans for fighting Al Qaeda. He said: 'I think it is the case – it is certainly in hindsight – that we weren't going fast enough … You can make your own judgments about whether we were going faster or slower than other administrations.'[57]

Moreover, in the spring of 2003, shortly after the invasion of Iraq, impressed by America's highly effective military onslaught against Saddam Hussein's regime, Rice did not respond constructively to attempts by the Iranian government to cooperate with the Bush Administration in the fight against international terrorism. Washington may thus well have missed the chance to work together with Tehran against the common enemy: the widely dispersed Taliban groups in Afghanistan and Pakistan.[58] Rice was unable or unwilling to design a coherent strategy for the 'war against terror' which would have included some rather unusual partners. To persuade Bush and Cheney to embark on such a course of action might not have been easy. Rice, like the other members of the Bush Administration, initially was strongly opposed to nation-building as a remedy for undermining the effectiveness of international terrorism. Instead in her *Foreign Affairs* essay in 2000 Rice 'decried' the Clinton's Administration's use of American assets for promoting human rights and democracy abroad as naïve, wasteful and superfluous.[59]

Similarly, after Rice was appointed Secretary of State in January 2005, she once again failed to design a forward-looking global strategy for American foreign policy in the post-9/11 world. Rice was a very effective organiser and administrator, who largely could rely on the loyalty of her Department and tended to get on well with her foreign counterparts. Yet, like her immediate predecessor Colin Powell, and the Secretaries of State during the Clinton Administration, she adopted a piecemeal approach to US foreign policy, though she was unlikely ever to admit this. Like her role model Dean Acheson, Secretary of State during President Truman's second term in office (1949–1953), Condoleezza Rice was convinced that she was 'present at the creation' (the title of Acheson's memoirs) and thus had the chance to create a new world order.[60]

Yet, as Glenn Kessler in his book on Rice's policies as Secretary of State convincingly demonstrates, she failed in her ambition to create a new international order. Instead Condoleezza Rice's foreign policy was largely characterised by reaction to emergency situations, such as the violence which repeatedly flared up in the Middle East during her tenure. Only seldom were constructive new initiatives developed in Foggy Bottom and of these which did see the light of day, many soon petered out. For instance the idea, much opposed by many experts, of democratising the Israel–Palestine conflict came from the State Department though Bush liked it a lot. Yet, it only led to the victory in the Palestinian parliamentary elections in January 2006 of Hamas, which the US still regarded as an illegal terrorist organisation. Hamas thereby greatly improved its respectability in the region and, amidst much intra-Palestinian violence, the outcome of the election resulted in a split in the Palestinian movement with Hamas controlling the Gaza strip and the Fatah party and the Palestinian President Mahmoud Abbas controlling the West Bank.[61]

The passive observer role which Rice and Bush assumed during the Israeli bombardment of the Lebanon in 2006 hardly showed a constructive and strategic approach to US foreign policy-making either. This sort of policy once again also estranged most of America's European allies from the Bush Administration. After all, Bush and his Secretary of State appeared to approve of the conflict when Rice referred to the short war as 'the birth pangs of a new Middle East', presumably a democratic one, which had to be endured.[62] Yet, this statement did not impress those on the ground who had no choice but to live in the war zone and see their families and businesses destroyed. Unwise phrases such as this contributed to discrediting both Israel and the US further in the eyes of the peoples of the Middle East who became increasingly radicalised and disaffected by Western attempts at mediation.

Both as National Security Adviser and in her first years as Secretary of State Rice largely followed President Bush's unilateralist instincts. Only during the last two years of her term in office did she develop a somewhat more independent stature. The increasing problems in confronting international terrorism which the administration was confronted with in Iraq, Afghanistan, Pakistan and elsewhere, the lack of credibility the Bush Administration enjoyed even among its allies but also Cheney's waning influence, Rumsfeld's replacement by Robert Gates in early November 2006 and the President's plummeting popularity ratings gave Rice the confidence to focus on the development of her own policy. Not least she paid more attention to guiding US foreign policy once again into a more cooperative multilateral direction, in particular with regard to transatlantic relations. Cooperation with Europe with respect to Iran, North Korea, the war in Afghanistan and not least in reacting to the Russian invasion of Georgian territory in

September 2008 improved considerably when compared to George W. Bush's first term in office.

Rice summarised her developing political philosophy in a wide-ranging article in *Foreign Affairs* in July/August 2008 and outlined the basic tenets of US foreign policy.[63] Above all she admitted that the 'new reality' of the post-9/11 world had led the Bush Administration to make 'some significant changes in our policy'. She explained that they had recognised 'that democratic state-building is now an urgent component of our national interest'. She also wrote that both US strength and American values – realism and idealism – were the basis of US foreign policy and fully recognised the 'importance of human rights' and the 'superiority of democracy as a form of government, both in principle and in practice'. While America's 'relations with traditional and emerging great powers still matter to the successful conduct of policy', she also admitted that the administration was now much more focused on 'how we view the relationship between the dynamics within states and the distribution of power among them'.[64]

In her essay Rice embarked on a wide-ranging review of America's geopolitical relations which hardly overlooked any country in the world. Not least she praised 'the endurance and resilience of the transatlantic alliance'. She even claimed that 'the United States does have permanent allies: the nations with whom we share common values'. While in her essay she looked at Africa and the Asia-Pacific region and briefly referred to the importance of climate change, energy sustainability and upholding human rights, above all she focused on reviewing relations with Russia and China and provided an analysis of how the conflict with Iran and the violence and tension in the broader Middle East might be overcome and how progress might be made in Iraq and Afghanistan. She emphasised that America still had the 'capacity for global leadership'. After all, 'the American character', based on both power and values, 'accounts for our unique role in the world'.[65]

Her solution to the manifold problems of the post-9/11 world can be summarised in the words 'democratic development'. Bringing economic and social development based on democratic freedoms to the world would ultimately overcome international terrorism and the conflicts of the present. 'An international order that reflects our values is the best guarantee of our enduring national interest', she wrote. 'It is our impatience to improve less-than-ideal situations and to accelerate the pace of change that leads to our most enduring achievements, at home and abroad'.[66] The Bush Administration's early missionary drive and the conviction that the world had to be re-made on the basis of the American model was still there, though perhaps in a somewhat more differentiated and perhaps even somewhat more humble form. Yet, there was no doubt in Rice's mind that America was still a powerful force for good in the world – never mind the illegal invasion of Iraq, the crass violations of human rights with, for instance, the administration's so-called 'extraordinary rendition' policy, the incarceration without trial and resource to due process of law of thousands of 'terrorists' at Guantanamo Bay on Cuba and the entirely self-inflicted plummeting international credibility of the United States almost anywhere in the world.

Conclusion

President George W. Bush's two Secretaries of State did not fulfil their potential. The greatly respected and highly experienced Colin Powell ultimately failed as he did not enjoy the President's confidence and trust. Moreover, Bush's preference for embarking upon the Iraq war and the 'war on terror' in a unilateral way ran counter to Powell's multilateral instincts. When Bush asked him to tender his resignation as he wanted to 'make a change' at the State Department, Powell's reputation was in tatters and his self-respect had suffered too. The man who had been much feted in the first half of the 1990s and who many had hoped would run for President in 1996 was widely regarded as a tragic failure when he left office in January 2005.

Powell's successor Condoleezza Rice enjoyed the trust and confidence of the President. Moreover, she did not have to dissipate her energies on fighting bitter battles and conflicts with the Pentagon and the Vice-President's office as Powell had to do. Yet, she failed too. On the whole it seems that Rice was not up to the job; she was out of her depth. Rice never managed to develop something approaching a coherent strategy for US foreign policy in the post-9/11 world. Hers was a piecemeal policy of largely reacting to emergency situations rather than creating something more profound and lasting.

However, ultimately neither Powell nor Rice were responsible for the difficulties they encountered in designing and 'selling' American foreign policy in the post-9/11 world. In the last resort, this was the responsibility of President Bush and the missionary zeal with which he pursued his unilateral foreign policy during most of his two terms in office. Paradoxically, towards the end of his presidency in the late summer and fall of 2008 the so-called 'credit crunch' and the almost fatal collapse of America's finance and banking system made it obvious that the days of the lone and unilateral superpower were numbered. The world of the future would be a multilateral one where America still would be a crucially important country within an elite club of five or six but the days of clear American hegemony, even dominance, were coming to an end. The unilateral President who had attempted to exploit America's 'unipolar moment' ended up presiding over a much weakened country that was dependent on cooperation and working with allies and foes in an increasingly multilateral world. In the world at large, this was welcomed. Even Washington's most loyal European allies breathed a sigh of relief when Bush and his underlings prepared to leave the White House and, not least due to a lack of other options, the prospect of a multilaterally inclined and cooperative America appeared on the horizon again. The election of Barack Obama as new American President was greeted with much initial enthusiasm.

Notes

1. See for example, Richard A. Posner, *Breaking the Deadlock: The 2000 Election, the Constitution, and the Courts* (Princeton, NJ: Princeton University Press, 2001).
2. James Mann, *Rise of the Vulcans: The History of Bush's War Cabinet* (London: Penguin, 2004).
3. Ibid., xv–xvi.
4. See Elisabeth Bumiller, *Condoleezza Rice. An American Life. A Biography* (New York: Random House, 2007); Glenn Kessler, *The Confidante: Condoleezza Rice and the Creation of the Bush Legacy* (New York: St Martin's Press, 2007); also Marcus Mabry, *Condoleezza Rice* (London: Gibson Square, 2007).
5. His successor, Condoleezza Rice, became the second one and the first African American woman in this position. For an interesting analysis, see Clarence Lusane, *Colin Powell and Condoleezza Rice: Foreign Policy, Race, and the New American Century* (Westport, CT: Praeger, 2006).
6. Powell did consider running for President in 1996. See Colin Powell, with Joseph E. Persico, *My American Journey* (New York: Ballentine Books, 1996), 599–602 (new afterword); Karen DeYoung, *Soldier. The Life of Colin Powell* (New York: Alfred A. Knopf, 2006), 263–84.
7. See Johanna McGeary, 'Odd Man Out', *Time*, 2 September 2001, http://www.time.com/time/printout/0,8816,173441,00.html.
8. See for example, the essays in Iwan W. Morgan and Philip J. Davies, eds, *Right on? Political Change and Continuity in George W. Bush's America* (Washington, DC: Brookings Institution Press, 2006), including my own essay on 'The Bush Administration and Europe', ibid., 75–91.
9. 'Ultimately', Kissinger wrote, 'a Secretary of State can succeed only if he or she is close to the President and is treated by him as the center of the policy process.' See Henry Kissinger,

'Condoleezza Rice: A New Panache in Foreign Affairs', *Time*, 2005, http://www.time.com/time/subscriber/2005/time100/leaders/100rice.html.

10. For all quotes, see DeYoung, *Soldier*, 295.
11. Ibid.
12. See Rice's article 'Promoting the National Interest', *Foreign Affairs* 79, no. 1, (January/February 2000), 9 (internet edition).
13. DeYoung, *Soldier*, 290–309, 310ff.
14. See for example, Dale R. Herspring, *Rumsfeld's War: The Arrogance of Power* (Lawrence: University Press of Kansas, 2008); Andrew Cockburn, *Rumsfeld: His Rise, Fall, and Catastrophic Legacy* (New York: Scribner, 2007); John W. Dean, *Worse than Watergate: The Secret Presidency of George W. Bush* (New York: Little, Brown, 2004).
15. This comes across clearly in the books by E. Bumiller and G. Kessler.
16. For a good account of neo-conservatism and its roots and impact on the Bush administration, see Tom J. Farer, *Confronting Global Terrorism and American Neo-conservatism: The Framework of a Liberal Grand Strategy* (Oxford, Oxford University Press, 2008); J. Micklethwait and Adrian Wooldrige, *The Right Nation: Conservative Power in America* (New York: Penguin, 2004).
17. 'The New Unilateralism', *Washington Post*, 8 June 2001. See also Krauthammer's original article 'The Unipolar Moment', *Foreign Affairs* (Winter 1990/1); and 'The Unipolar Moment Revisited', *National Interest* 70 (Winter 2002): 5–17. See also M. Hirsh, 'Bush and the World', *Foreign Affairs* (Sept./Oct. 2002); G.J. Ikenberry, 'America's Imperial Ambition', *Foreign Affairs* (Sept./Oct. 2002); also S. Mallaby, 'The Reluctant Imperialist: Terrorism, Failed States, and the Case for American Empire', *Foreign Affairs* (March/April 2002).
18. Quote from Canadian Broadcasting Cooperation News Online, 'Colin Powel. A Profile', 15 November 2004, http://www.cbc.ca/news/background/powell_colin/.
19. DeYoung, *Soldier*, 312ff.
20. Ibid., 358.
21. Ibid., 359–60.
22. See Dowling Campbell, ed., *A Bird in the Bush. The Failed Domestic Policies of the George W. Bush Administration* (New York: Algora Publishing, 2005), chapters 3, 4, and 5. The administration may have had Henry Kissinger in mind.
23. See Steven E. Miller, 'The End of Unilateralism or Unilateralism Redux?', *Washington Quarterly* 25, no.1 (Winter 2002), 15–29.
24. DeYoung, *Soldier*, 323–6.
25. See Gerard Baker, 'Not All Americans Now', *The Times* (London), 6 September 2006, http://www.timesonline.co.uk/tol/news/world/article628734.ece.
26. See for example, Bob Woodward, *Plan of Attack* (New York, Simon and Schuster, 2004), 24 ff.; Richard Clarke, *Against All Enemies* (New York, Free Press, 2004), 30 ff.; Ron Suskind, *The Price of Loyalty* (New York: Simon and Schuster, 2004), 184; DeYoung, *Soldier*, 348 ff.
27. For the State of the Union address, see http://www.whitehouse.gov/news/releases/2002/01/20020129-11.html.
28. For the strategy paper, see http://www.whitehouse.gov/nsc/nss.html.
29. T. Judd, 'Its Own Worst Enemy' [review of J. Nye, The Paradox of American Power], *New York Review of Books*, 15 August 2002, 3 (internet edition).
30. Salman Rushdie, 'A Liberal Argument for Regime Change', *Washington Post*, 1 November 2002, A35. The new administration appeared to behave 'like a sullen, pouting, oblivious, and overmuscled teenager'. For Bush's envisaged strategic vision, see John Lewis Gaddis, 'A Grand Strategy of Transformation', *Foreign Policy*, November/December 2002, 56.
31. Judt, 'It's Own Worst Enemy', 6–9 (internet edition).
32. See http://www.cnn.com/2005/WORLD/meast/08/19/powell.un/.
33. DeYoung, *Soldier*, chapter 19; for Powell's UN speech, see 446–52.
34. See DeYoung, *Soldier*, 510–11.
35. The crisis erupted in late August 2002 just before the German general election in September 2002.
36. See 'Mutual Incomprehension? U.S.-German Value Gaps over Iraq and Beyond', *Washington Quarterly* 26, no. 2 (Spring 2003): 23–42; William Shawcross, *Allies: The United States, Britain, Europe and the War in Iraq* (London: Atlantic Books, 2003); Philip H. Gordon and Jeremy Shapiro, *Allies at War: America, Europe, and the Crisis of Iraq* (New York: McGraw-Hill, 2004).

37. See Anne Applebaum, 'Here Comes the New Europe', *Washington Post*, 29 January 2003, http://www.washingtonpost.com/wp-dyn/articles/A57913-2003Jan28.html.

38. Roger Boyes, 'Germany: Deal on Iraq May End Steinmeier's Election Hopes', *The Times* (London), 11 September 2008, http://www.timesonline.co.uk/tol/news/world/europe/arti cle4727437.ece. For the original articles, see Uli Rauss and Oliver Schröm, 'Hat Steinmeier gelogen?', *Stern*, 11 September 2008, http://www.stern.de/politik/deutschland/638598.html; and Uli Rauss and Oliver Schröm, 'Die Bagdad-Protokolle', *Stern*, 24 September 2008, http://www.stern.de/politik/ausland/:Irak-Krieg-Die-Bagdad-Protokolle/639615.html.

39. For a good overview, see Stephen Szabo, *Parting Ways: The Crisis in German-American Relations* (Washington, DC: Brookings, 2004).

40. 'The German-American Alliance for the 21st Century. Joint Statement by President George W. Bush and Chancellor Gerhard Schroeder', 27 February 2004, http://www.whitehouse.gov/news/releases/2004/02/print/20040227-10.html.

41. Bush-Schröder, Joint Statement at the White House, 29 March 2001, http://www.presidency.ucs b.edu/ws/index.php?pid=45659.

42. Richard W. Stevenson, 'Bush and Schröder Laugh Over Lunch, but Not All Weekend', *New York Times*, 28 February 2004, http://query.nytimes.com/gst/fullpage.html?res=9C07E2DF1E3CF93 BA15751C0A9629C8B63.

43. Vincent Jauvert, 'Chirac-Bush. The Cordial Mistrust', *Le Nouvel Observateur*, 17 February 2005, 2.

44. Ibid.

45. Interview with Condoleezza Rice with Washington Post journalists on 25 March 2005.

46. For Bush's speeches when he visited Germany on 23 February 2005, see http://germany.usem bassy.gov/germany/bush_visit2005.html.

47. DeYoung, *Soldier*, 8–10.

48. See Bumiller, *Condoleezza Rice*, 79ff.

49. Ibid., 94–5.

50. Condoleezza Rice and Philip Zelikow, *Germany Unified and Europe Transformed: A Study in Statecraft* (Cambridge, MA: Harvard University Press, 1995).

51. See Russell Baker, 'Condi and the Boys' [review article], *New York Review of Books* 55, no. 5 (3 April 2008), http://www.nybooks.com/articles/21192.

52. As quoted by Mark A. Barabak, 'Not Always Diplomatic in Her First Major Post', *Los Angeles Times*, 16 January 2005, http://articles.latimes.com/2005/jan/16/local/me-rice16.

53. At least according to John A. Boehmer, Republican Congressman from Ohio, who knows both Bush and Rice well. See Richard T. Cooper and Tyler Marshall, 'Bush, Rice are Tightly Bound by Experience', *Los Angeles Times*, 17 November 2004, http://articles.latimes.com/2004/nov/17/nation/na-condi17.

54. Ibid.

55. See Clarke, *Against All Enemies*; and *The 9/11 Commission Report* (New York: Norton, 2003), 254ff.

56. See the documentation put together by the Washington based independent National Security Archive: http://www.gwu.edu/~nsarchiv/NSAEBB/NSAEBB147/index.htm; also Clarke, *Against All Enemies*, 237–8;

57. Elisabeth Bumiller and Philip Shenon, 'Threats and Responses: Political Memo', *New York Times*, 26 March 2004, http://query.nytimes.com/gst/fullpage.html?res=9F01E3DD1330F935A15 750C0A9629C8B63&sec=&spon=&pagewanted=print. For C. Rice's own testimony to the 9/11 Commission in May 2004, see http://www.cnn.com/2004/ALLPOLITICS/04/08/rice.transcript/.

58. See Kessler, *The Confidante*, 185–6.

59. See her own admission in Condoleezza Rice, 'Rethinking the National Interest. American Realism for a New World', *Foreign Affairs* (July/August 2008), http://www.foreignaffairs.org/20080701faessay87401-p0/condoleezza-rice/rethinking-the-national-interest.html, 9 (internet edition).

60. Kessler, *The Confidante*, 3–4.

61. See for instance, Steven Erlanger, 'Palestinian Split Poses a Policy Quandary for US', *New York Times*, 17 June 2007, http://www.nytimes.com/2007/06/17/world/middleeast/17assess.html.

62. Condoleezza Rice, 'Special Briefing [to journalists] on Travel to the Middle East and Europe', 21 July 2006, http://www.state.gov/secretary/rm/2006/69331.htm; see also Tony Caron, 'Condi in

Diplomatic Disneyland', *Time*, 26 July 2006, http://www.time.com/time/world/article/0,8599,1219325,00.html.

63. Her philosophy was however largely ignored by the media. See Rosa Brooks, 'National Disinterest in Condi', *Los Angeles Times*, 26 June 2008, http://articles.latimes.com/2008/jun/26/opinion/oe-brooks26.

64. See Rice, 'Rethinking the National Interest'.

65. Ibid.

66. Ibid.

President Clinton's Secretaries of State: Warren Christopher and Madeleine Albright

John Dumbrell

Department of Government and International Affairs, University of Durham, UK

An important thread in the story of recent US foreign policy-making involves the movement of authority from the State Department to the National Security Council (NSC), especially to the NSC staff and the National Security Adviser. Presidents tend to enter office – Richard Nixon did, Bill Clinton certainly did – with a stated commitment to a strong Department of State and a strong Secretary. Very often, however, this commitment breaks down. It did so very spectacularly in the case of President Nixon; but the same process has also affected other presidencies. This article offers a brief review of Bill Clinton's two Secretaries of State, Warren Christopher (1993–1997) and Madeleine Albright (1997–2001). It focuses particularly on their general orientation to the post, as well as their relationship with other foreign policy principals. The article additionally considers the roles of the two Secretaries in the context of key transatlantic developments in the 1990s, notably concerning the enlargement of the North Atlantic Treaty Organisation. By way of setting the stage for this discussion, let us remind ourselves of the particular bureaucratic difficulties faced by any recent or contemporary Secretary of State.

Being a successful Secretary of State in the 1990s

Many of the procedural problems of being Secretary derive from his or her lack of proximity to the president. The National Security Adviser is usually much closer to the keeper of power in the White House, both literally and in terms of being more intimately tied into the president's immediate political interests and fortunes. If nothing succeeds like success, as far as the National Security Adviser is concerned, nothing propinks like propinquity. To use the terminology of a 1984 study, co-written by Clinton's first National Security Adviser, Anthony Lake, the Secretary of State is a departmental 'baron' rather than a presidential 'courtier'.[1] By way of compensation, a successful Secretary must enjoy good presidential access and trust.

Besides the almost ontological rivalry with the National Security Adviser, the Secretary of State has a 'natural' bureaucratic antagonism with the Secretary of Defence. The clashes between Colin Powell and Donald Rumsfeld during the first George W. Bush Administration were unusual in their openness and intensity; they reflected fundamental differences in international policy outlook. However, the Powell–Rumsfeld tension also drew in inherent differences of bureaucratic perspective. It is also not unusual for a Secretary of State to experience poor relations with the White House political staff, a body, of course, even more intimately attached than the NSC staff to the presidential political and electoral interest. Successful Secretaries of State have to negotiate these various minefields. They also have to combine the job of departmental manager with that of foreign policy principal.

It is frequently observed that several of the most apparently successful and influential Secretaries of State, including James Baker under President George H.W. Bush, have actually made rather light of their departmental management responsibilities. A 'strong' Secretary may actually preside over a demoralised and uncertain Department. A 1989 article in the *Foreign Service Journal* by a former director of the Foreign Service Institute began: 'The Department of State has qualities of a second-rate organisation: a poorly articulated mission, ill-defined goals, unhappy employees ... and an apparent indifference to developing effective executives'.[2]

Clinton's two Secretaries of State faced deep-seated as well as more transitory difficulties in leading the Department. The State Department is regularly portrayed as prone to clientism. Another piece in the 1989 *Foreign Service Journal* recorded the 'negative stereotypes associated with the department', including the perception that Foreign Service Officers 'defend the interests of foreign countries better than those of their own country'.[3] As James McCormick puts it, the State Department is, in bureaucratic terms, 'at once, too large and too small'.[4] Policy recommendations have to traverse complex bureaucratic turf even before reaching the executive offices of the seventh floor at Foggy Bottom. Yet, as far as appropriations and the NSC interagency process is concerned, the State Department is often outgunned by the intelligence agencies and by the Department of Commerce.

Some particular features of the Clinton era should be noted. The early 1990s, of course, was the era of the 'Kennan sweepstakes'.[5] The race was on to find a pithy and sellable purpose for American internationalism, and not least for the future of Cold War alliance structures. The ending of the Cold War had called into question the prospects for existing policy and alliance architectures. Not only did a successful Secretary of State have to fight the Department's bureaucratic and budgetary corner, he or she had to argue the case for deeply engaged international diplomacy itself. A successful Secretary was required to transcend the, regularly breached but traditionally helpful, conceptual distinction between a 'thinking' NSC staff and a 'doing' State Department. 'Thinking', devising new theoretical underpinnings for US co-operative internationalism, to an unusual extent, was the job of Clinton's Secretaries of State. Above and beyond all this, the Secretaries had to contend not only with the rise of economic foreign policy, but also – at least during Warren Christopher's tenure – with President Clinton's preoccupation with domestic issues. During the post-Cold War era (let us say, roughly 1989 to 2001), it seemed as if, to quote Norman Ornstein in 1994, 'geoeconimcs drives geopolitics, compared to a Cold War agenda where geopolitics drove geoeconomics'.[6] Clinton's concern to reprioritise economic foreign policy had major implications for America's chief diplomatic agency. The president's early focus on domestic reform also set a less than auspicious context for his entire foreign policy team. Political commentator Elizabeth Drew offered the following distillation of instructions coming from the White House in 1993: 'Keep foreign policy from becoming a problem – keep it off the screen and spare Clinton from getting embroiled'.[7]

Public disputes between Secretary of State and National Security Council staff were not a major feature of the Clinton years. Certainly, procedural foreign policy cohesion was generally inferior to that prevailing under Clinton's immediate Republican presidential predecessor. However, the Clinton foreign policy team never exhibited the disarray of the Carter (Cyrus Vance versus Zbigniew Brzezinski) era, nor indeed of the first administration of George W. Bush. Clinton's two National Security Advisers, Tony Lake and Sandy Berger, remembered only too well how much the open Vance–Brzezinski split had harmed

Carter's operation. The weekly 'pickle' (PCL) meetings between William Perry (Defence Secretary, 1993–7), Lake and Christopher, were designed to head off any such damage. Yet there were still important personality clashes and bureaucratic snafus. State was severely, even humiliatingly, marginalised on occasion, as during the planning for the 1994 invasion of Haiti. In July 1994, the *Washington Post* reported the 'bitter tension' between the State Department and the White House political staff. White House counsellor David Gergen was transferred to Foggy Bottom, reportedly to provide State with 'political reality checks in the foreign policy arena'.[8]

If the early Clinton foreign policy-making context was defined to some degree by 'economics first' and by presidential immersion in domestic agendas, the political framework for the later years was established by the Republican legislative election victories of 1994. State, along with the entire foreign aid budget became a hunting ground for Republican budget-cutters, led by Senate Foreign Relations Committee chairman Jesse Helms. In 1995, Helms proposed to collapse the quasi-independent Agency for International Development, the US Information Agency and the Arms Control and Disarmament Agency (ACDA) into the State Department, pending a 'major re-examination of attitudinal, procedural and management issues within the department itself'.[9] Helms's initial plan was vetoed by Clinton, though the US Information Agency and ACDA were formally incorporated into the State Department in 1999. Though some of the reorganisation actually consolidated State's authority, Clinton's Secretaries of State had to fight hard for funding against a background of legislative assault and poor departmental morale. Warren Christopher informed Congress in 1996 that the US international budget had already been cut by half in real dollars since 1989. State Department employees began to display buttons bearing the slogan, 'JUST ONE PER CENT' – a reminder of the actual proportion of federal tax dollars devoted to non-military foreign spending.

Some 32 US embassies and consulates closed between 1993 and 1997. Under Warren Christopher and Madeleine Albright, the State Department was subject to constant and interminable reorganisations. In 1993, Vice-President Al Gore's 'reinventing government' plan called for the integration of State's 'policy, program and resource management processes' to suit its post-Cold War role and its 'increasingly limited resources'.[10] A 1996 report from former Secretary of State Lawrence Eagleburger and former Ambassador Robert Barry resulted in a major expansion in the role of undersecretaries, constituting a kind of 'corporate board' for the Secretary.[11] An internal report, State 2000, called for the radical integration of foreign and domestic policy, concluding: 'We must learn, in fact, to see them as two parts of the same whole'.[12]

The problems of the State Department during the Clinton era – problems of direction and purpose, uncertainties connected to new threats and new agendas abroad, as well as the politics of divided government in Washington – were also the challenges facing Clinton's foreign policy as a whole. How did Christopher and Albright measure up to them, particularly in the context of transatlantic relations?

Warren Christopher

Unveiling a portrait of Warren Christopher in 1999, President Clinton described his first Secretary of State as America's first diplomat in over 50 years to face 'the challenge of defining our foreign policy without a single, overriding threat to our security'. Clinton also noted: 'Chris has the lowest ratio of ego to accomplishment of any public servant I've ever worked with'.[13] For Madeleine Albright, Christopher was 'a lawyer's lawyer, who emphasized preparation, precision and perseverance'. Stories circulated about his mildness, his fastidiousness and his reluctance to express emotion. On a stopover visit in Ireland, Christopher famously ordered a decaffeinated Irish coffee with no alcohol. For Albright, he was 'the consummate team player'.[14] To his critics, he was 'Dean Rusk without the charisma'. For sceptical Democrats, he fell short of the job requirements for Secretary in the post-Cold War era. To quote David Halberstam: 'Christopher, they thought, was too much the functionary, a capable and highly competent bureaucrat, but probably a limited one, a man lacking originality and beliefs of his own'.[15]

Christopher had been a deputy to Secretary of State Cyrus Vance in the Carter Administration, known particularly for his work in coordinating the human rights policy at interagency level and for his role in the Iran hostage diplomacy of 1979–1980.[16] He worked on the Clinton transition team from his base in California. Leading candidates for the job of Secretary of State included Ed Muskie (for whom Christopher had worked following Vance's 1980 resignation), Zbigniew Brzezinski (National Security Adviser under Carter), and Senator Sam Nunn (Democratic chairman of the Senate Armed Services Committee). Compared to other candidates, Christopher was indeed a team player and this seems to have increased his attractiveness to Clinton. Warren Christopher formed a solid link to the previous Democratic administration, but one whose relatively low profile lessened the possibility of old conflicts being reignited. At 67, he was a Democratic 'grey-head'; several commentators pointed out that Christopher was precisely the same age as Clinton's deceased father (William Jefferson Blythe) would have been. During the transition Christopher was, according to Clinton, 'a whirlwind of activity'.[17]

Yet Christopher's effectiveness was hampered not only by Clinton's own unpredictable interventions, but also by his natural lack of forcefulness.[18] As a prospective Secretary of State, Christopher had the advantage of being considerably younger than Muskie and personally more amenable to Clinton than Sam Nunn.[19] Clinton seems, nevertheless, to have continued to regard Nunn as a species of Secretary of State-in-waiting, a situation which apparently prompted Christopher to offer his resignation in 1994. In due course, Clinton became reconciled to the Christopher style, valuing Christopher's reliability and dignified loyalty. According to Raymond Seitz (US ambassador to London), Christopher stood out in the early Clinton team 'like an adult in a kindergarten'.[20]

Warren Christopher's problems included the lack of guaranteed presidential access. To some extent this was connected to the new 'economics first' agenda. US Trade Representative Mickey Kantor seemed to have better access to Clinton. Christopher had major difficulties both in articulating a post-Cold War vision and in asserting his leadership at State. To some degree this was a matter of personality and style. Seitz recalled him advocating the 'lift and strike' policy in Bosnia in 1993 'with all the verve of a solicitor going over a conveyancing deed'.[21] For Sidney Blumenthal, Christopher had 'the appearance of gravity' but was 'without a vision'.[22]

Clinton's first Secretary of State also endured some damaging diplomatic calamities which undermined his reputation as a safe pair of hands. The European trip of May 1993 was actually acutely discomforting for Christopher. His role in the Haiti decisions of 1994 was minimal – a fact reflected in the omission of discussion of the invasion from his memoir, *Chances of a Lifetime*.[23] His subsequent visit to China, during which the authorities took the opportunity to arrest leading dissidents, also contributed to his reputation for ineffectuality.[24] Within State itself, Christopher had public disagreements with Undersecretary Peter Tarnoff over the viability of 'assertive multilateralism'. The appointment of long-standing Clinton friend Strobe Talbott to lead Russia policy at State also ruffled feathers at the Department and raised particular managerial difficulties for the Secretary. Clinton's shift to activism over Bosnia in 1995–6 additionally involved the recognition of Richard Holbrooke, rather than Christopher himself, as the effective leader of policy in this area.[25]

If Warren Christopher had his share of diplomatic embarrassments, his professional style generally saw him through. Even on the wider issue of 'vision', it can be argued that Christopher has been judged rather unfairly. Following the 'Kennan sweepstakes' agenda largely set by Tony Lake, Christopher made numerous efforts to construct a new rhetorical vision for American internationalism without the Soviet threat. He was certainly not helped but his own lack of personal forcefulness, yet others in the administration scarcely fared better. It may also be argued that the 'threat-less' early 1990s was not a propitious time for grand declaratory statements of internationalist purpose. The George H. W. Bush foreign policy team had provided a successful adjustment to post-Cold War conditions with little beyond the vague – and swiftly derided – 'New World Order' concept of 1990. 'Vision' can too often degenerate into rigidity, embarrassment and hot air. Yet to go too far along this line of argument would be to underplay unduly the need of the Clinton team to produce a meaningful successor to anti-communist containment as an integrating formula for the new foreign policy. The early notion of 'enlargement' (of markets and democracies) fitted the priorities of the Clinton Administration well enough. However, it achieved little wider credibility, and became hopelessly confused in the public consciousness with NATO enlargement.

Beyond 'enlargement', the early Clinton team vision for foreign policy centred on the global environmental agenda. Frequently denigrated, especially at NSC level as 'globaloney', global environmentalism had been given a formal ranking at State in 1993, when Congress was persuaded to create the new post of Undersecretary for Global Affairs. The first such undersecretary was former Senator James Wirth, whose brief encompassed much of what was to become the 'new security agenda' of cross-border threats of the later 1990s. Christopher is generally credited with little in the way of developing this agenda within State. He did have a commitment here, nevertheless. His concern for the environment ran back to his boyhood interests in North Dakota; he was influenced by Al Gore's environmental arguments and by the ideas of David Kennedy, a leading environmental campaigner and president of Stanford University. Christopher actually gave, at Stanford University in April 1996, what seems to have been the first ever speech by a Secretary of State devoted entirely to environmental concerns. He outlined the 'new threats' such as 'terrorism, weapons proliferation, drug trafficking and international crime', but went on to emphasise particularly 'the vast new dangers posed to our national interests by damage to the environment and resulting global and regional instability'.[26]

Christopher's orientation to the duties of Secretary was, in Sidney Blumenthal's word, 'lawyerly' rather than mission-driven.[27] His policy stances, especially towards the conflicts in the former Yugoslavia, were rooted in a caution which derived to some degree, no doubt, from his character, but also from internalised 'lessons of Vietnam'. For Dick Morris, Warren Christopher was insufficiently 'political'.[28] He certainly opposed some of the more incautious presidential departures in transatlantic policy, such as the issuing of a visa in 1994 to Sinn Fein leader Gerry Adams. Although embarrassed by the super-activism of his deputy Richard Holbrooke, Christopher was closely engaged in the diplomacy surrounding the 1995 Dayton Agreement. In some respects, Christopher was probably a poor choice as Clinton's first Secretary of State. In a difficult time for internationalist diplomacy, he lacked that reputation for policy effectiveness in Washington which is a precondition for success.

Madeleine Albright

The flamboyance of America's first female Secretary of State contrasted sharply with the style of her predecessor. Her appointment was aided by the support of Hillary Clinton. It was also assisted by the fact that, compared to her main rival, Richard Holbrooke – favoured by Vice President Gore as Christopher's successor – she was actually less inclined to grandstanding and freelancing. There were also indications that she was a Secretary of State who was broadly acceptable to the Republican leadership in Congress. She was confirmed by the US Senate, 1999–2000. The other main contender to succeed Christopher was Senate Majority Leader George Mitchell. Albright typically embarked on a Washington 'campaign' for the post. As she put it in her memoirs: 'I doubted that George Mitchell and Dick Holbrooke were sitting demurely at home waiting for the phone to ring'.[29] The key to her strategy lay in the development of a counter-network of Washington contacts and in finessing the gender issue. The key was to avoid any suggestion that the appointment be 'made a litmus test of the President's commitment to women's rights'. Clinton had already made numerous high-profile female appointments and was unlikely to respond positively to any attempt to railroad him into naming the first female Secretary of State. The Albright camp actually urged restraint upon women's groups in connection with the appointment; the idea of issuing a pro-Albright letter to female members of Congress was shelved.[30]

As US Representative to the United Nations during the first Clinton Administration, Albright had been associated with concept of 'assertive multilateralism'. The expansiveness of this early vision was quite swiftly undercut by the more restrained pragmatism put forward by Undersecretary of State Peter Tarnoff, as well as by Clinton's own Presidential Directive 25.[31] Albright's most celebrated comments as Secretary of State related to the view of America as 'indispensable nation' and to her description of her own 'mindset' as 'Munich not Vietnam'.[32] The 'indispensable nation' mantra was taken up by key administration figures. Introducing his new Secretary of State in December 1996, Clinton made a point of using the phrase. The 'Munich not Vietnam' motto was designed to fix the view of Albright as a principled doer rather than a pragmatic temporiser. It fitted in, of course, with her extraordinary family history. As Strobe Talbott later put it: 'More than any of the rest of us, she was literally a child of the cold war: she had been eleven in 1948, when a Soviet-instigated coup d'état forced her parents to gather up the family and flee their native Czechoslovakia'.[33] Brought up a Roman Catholic, Albright only discovered her Jewish origins following her appointment to Foggy Bottom. Opposing Christopher, Albright had strongly supported the invasion of Haiti in 1994. As Secretary of State she was in the vanguard of the administration's activist wing in relation to Balkans policy. Her own self-assessment was as a 'pragmatic idealist' – a Dean Acheson for the 1990s. For Thomas Lippman, she 'struggled throughout her tenure to reconcile her proud image as a tough-talking, straight-shooting "doer" with the administration's Candide-like belief in human improvement – that is, with its embrace of global meliorism'.[34]

Albright certainly seems to have seen herself as a counterbalance to the wider administration's tendencies both to naïve 'do-goodery' and to pragmatic wilting under pressure. Here was a Secretary of State who was manifestly not short on 'vision'. Numerous speeches – for example, her address in Prague of July 1997, her Harvard commencement address of June 1997 and her Henry Stimson Center speech of June 1998 – outlined her expansive, interventionist and anti-appeasement views. A former assistant to Zbigniew Brzezinski, Albright had, in David Halberstam's words, 'climbed the foreign policy establishment carefully and slowly'; yet, beyond her general reputation for hawkishness, 'no one associated her with any particular view or wing' of the Democratic Party.[35] As UN Representative, Albright had been prominent in broadening the US remit in Somalia and had argued without success for more activism on Bosnia. During the second administration, she wasted no opportunity to remind her listeners, often including the president himself, of the stated 'goal that America should remain the world's strongest force for peace, liberty, prosperity and security, so that we can build a future for the next generation free from the worries and plagues of the past'.[36] Her model was Dean Acheson. 'The test of our leadership, although far different in specifics', wrote Albright in 1998, 'is essentially the same as that confronted by Acheson's postwar generation'.[37] The task at hand was nothing less than the creation of a post-Cold war liberal world order, with American power as its fulcrum. The Clinton Administration needed to match the 'leadership and creativity' of the Truman/Acheson years. In some respects the con-temporary challenge was easier. 'In truth', Albright acknowledged, 'Acheson confronted a chorus of critics far fiercer than mine'.[38] Even the Congressional Republican leadership after 1994 did not attack Albright's basic loyalty in the way their predecessors had attacked Acheson's in the 1940s. In the 1990s, according to Albright, the danger was as much the post-Cold War ambivalence towards internationalism as political partisanship. 'We invest fewer resources in defense, diplomacy, and development. Since nations no longer need our protection from the Soviet Union, our international leverage, despite our strength, is not what it was in Acheson's day'.[39]

Albright's role as a policy advocate was seen most clearly in respect to the Balkans. By the time of her arrival at the State Department, Bosnian policy had already shifted, and Christopher-like caution was strongly out of fashion. Indeed, her appointment was itself an aspect of the Clinton Administration's shift on Bosnia. Her major substantive impact was on policy towards Kosovo in 1999. Clinton himself, Defence Secretary William Cohen and Sandy Berger were far from sure that force would work in Kosovo. At a Principals' meeting on 15 June, Albright's case for a strong line against Serbian leader Slobodan Milosevic was met by '"there goes Madeleine again" glances'.[40] Albright's reputation is closely bound up with what a *Time* magazine cover during the Kosovo bombing campaign dubbed 'Madeleine's War'. Defending US conduct in the approach to conflict, she later dismissed as 'nonsense' the view that, at the Rambouillet conference in February 1999, 'we missed signals from Belgrade that Milosevich was willing to sign an agreement'.[41]

Beyond the Balkans, Albright was a high-profile Secretary who was, in contrast to Christopher, relatively unconcerned about making enemies. She was the highest-ever ranking US diplomat to visit North Korea (October 2000). She supported and identified herself with the policy shifts of the second Clinton Administration, including intense bombing and the embrace of the doctrine of 'regime change' in Iraq.[42] The second Clinton Administration was also increasingly willing to countenance unilateral policy options. Indeed the Kosovo campaign, which was waged without UN authorisation, exposed a difficulty in working with the NATO allies which was to be reflected in later US caution about multilateral warfare.[43] Albright also played a central role in the various Middle East initiatives of 1997–1998 and 2000. The villain at Camp David in 2000 was, according to Albright, Yasser Arafat: the Palestinians 'wouldn't yield a dime to make a dollar'.[44] She wrote in 2006 that Arafat 'could have been the first president of an internationally recognised Palestine'. Instead, 'he chose ... the applause of supporters who praised him for refusing to sign away even a slice of "Arab land" or acknowledge the sovereignty of Israel over the Western Wall'.[45]

Albright was not devoid of pragmatism; her line on Kosovo in the early part of 1999, for example, was muted in face of the bureaucratic obstacles which then presented themselves.[46] However, as her account of the Camp David negotiations demonstrates, her approach to international questions was relatively straightforward, swift in identifying the 'bad guy', and rather short on nuance. In these respects she was the opposite of Christopher. Her enemies within the administration certainly included Defence Secretary William Cohen. She also clashed on occasion with Sandy Berger, though she appears to have recognised that the National Security Adviser frequently reflected the complex doubts, especially regarding Kosovo, of Clinton himself. Later on a major critic of the interventionist foreign policy of the George W. Bush Administration,[47] in some respects, she laid the foundations for it.

Christopher, Albright and NATO enlargement

The case for enlarging NATO in the early part of the first Clinton Administration was made within the State Department, not by Christopher, but in a widely circulated memo from Lynn Davis, Undersecretary for International Security. In August 1993, Davis and State Policy Planning head Sam Lewis formally put the case for enlargement to the Secretary of State. According to Davis and Lewis, the fudging of the enlargement issue, which had taken place under the George H.W. Bush Administration, should not continue. Further 'avoidance of this issue will undermine NATO by reinforcing the growing perception that the Alliance is only marginally involved in addressing Europe's new security problems'.[48]

Christopher generally accepted the line being urged upon him by his juniors at State, who were now being supported by Tony Lake at the NSC. The case against enlargement was presented to Christopher by some 15 senior diplomats, who anchored their case in the likely reaction in Moscow. Outlining an argument that was to be taken up by none less than George Kennan, the diplomats asserted that enlargement would isolate Russia. The project of integrating Russia into Western security, economic and political networks had been an important part of the late- and post-Cold War dynamic, and had brought success. Extending NATO up to the Russian border would engender perceptions of encirclement, marginalisation and even gratuitous humiliation.[49]

In June 1993, Christopher was prepared, at the Athens NATO summit, to hold open the prospect of enlargement though with little in the way of definite commitment. By early 1994, he was defending NATO expansion as a contribution to 'European stability and to transatlantic burden-sharing'.[50] The push for expansion was kept alive by the Partnership for Peace agreement with Moscow, announced in January 1994. Partnership for Peace, a compromise between the pro-expansion State Department (led in this policy area by Strobe Talbott) and the cautious Pentagon, represented an effort to ease Russian worries by bringing Moscow into a modulated consultative role with NATO. At this stage, Clinton also announced his own commitment to expansion – to a position not of 'whether' it would occur, but 'when'.

During 1994–1995, the key mover of the enlargement agenda at State was Richard Holbrooke, who was appointed as Assistant Secretary for Europe and Canada in September 1994. Holbrooke worked with an inter-agency bureaucratic coalition, with Nicholas Burns and Alexander Vershbow at the NSC. The split with the Defence Department became apparent with the issuing of the 'Perry principles' – Secretary Perry's conditions for accepting new NATO members – during 1995. While the Pentagon demanded progress towards democratic accountability and compatibility of armed forces between new and old members, Christopher became an important public advocate of the programme. In September 1996, with the Partnership for Peace now agreed with Moscow,

Christopher announced that the first invitations to join the new NATO would be issued in 1997. It was widely assumed that these invitations would go to Poland, Hungary and the Czech Republic. As the presidential election approached, however, Christopher's own bureaucratic standing slipped in the anticipation that he would no longer be in office after January 1997. Tony Lake issued his memo, 'NATO Enlargement Agenda Game Plan' in June 1996 and on his departure from office in January 1997, handed over the policy lead to the new National Security Adviser, Sandy Berger.[51]

Portrayed by Moscow as 'Madam Steel', Clinton's new Secretary of State was an unambiguous advocate for expansion. By this time, some of Moscow's more serious fears had been allayed, not only by the Partnership for Peace, but also by the apparently mutually agreeable settlement in Bosnia. Albright's Senate confirmation statement set the tone for her stance on NATO. Characteristically calling up the shade of Dean Acheson, she looked 'to do for Europe's East what NATO did 50 years ago for Europe's West: to integrate new democracies, defeat old hatreds, provide confidence in economic recovery and deter conflict'.[52] Strobe Talbott recalled her saying that she felt the case for admitting the Central European countries into NATO 'in my bones and in my genes'.[53]

Moscow's final reconciliation to expansion occurred at the Helsinki summit of March 1997 alongside new cooperative agreements. Russian President Boris Yeltsin was prepared to accept expansion provided no former Soviet states were included in the first accessions. Albright's role in all this was central. At Helsinki she developed working relationships with Yeltsin and with Russian Foreign Minister Yevgeny Primakov. Replying to Yeltsin's comments about her Cold War Czech background, she replied (as Strobe Talbott puts it 'rather sternly'): 'A new Russia has been born and it has nothing in common with the former Soviet Union, and that goes for Russian foreign policy as well'.[54] At the Sintra (Portugal) NATO meeting in May 1997, she persuaded the West Europeans to restrict the number of new entrants to Poland, Hungary and the Czech Republic. NATO's decision was finalised in Madrid in July.

Following the Madrid summit, Albright gave an emotional account of the enlargement process in Prague, talking of 'three journeys': her own journey to America, Europe's journey from war and communism, and the Czech Republic's journey to its 'rightful place in the family of European democracies'.[55] Her main priority now was to persuade the US Senate to ratify the new arrangements. Her successful campaign emphasised NATO adaptation and burden-sharing, as well as the march of democracy. The campaign went hand-in-hand with an assault on the forces of neo-isolationism and American introversion. At Harvard University in June 1997, for example, she urged her country not to forget 'what the history of this century reminds us, that problems abroad, if left unattended, will all too often come home to America'.[56] The new members were welcomed to the Washington NATO summit in 1999.

The story of NATO enlargement under Clinton puts into sharp focus the differences between his two Secretaries of State. Christopher worked slowly, reacting to the pro-enlargement bureaucratic consensus as it built. His style was rational, cautious and sometimes dilatory. Albright was emotional, utterly committed to the cause of NATO expansion, and also extremely effective, especially in dealing with NATO allies and with the US Senate in the ratification debate. In the first Clinton term, as James Goldgeier argues, Tony Lake was the enlargement 'conceptualizer' and Richard Holbrooke its 'enforcer'.[57] Yet the picture had changed by 1997. Albright did not have to develop new arguments, merely to run with the dynamic begun in the first administration. More generally, though she articulated a forceful case for committed American internationalism and greatly raised the profile of the State Department, she was unable to secure resources for American diplomacy commensurate with the role of 'indispensable nation'. The White House, rather than Foggy Bottom, remained in control of major foreign policy initiatives. Even at the end of the Clinton years, State remained a body which was struggling to come to terms with a world without the integrating Soviet threat.

Notes

1. I.M. Destler, Leslie H. Gelb and Anthony Lake, *Our Own Worst Enemy: The Unmaking of American Foreign Policy* (New York: Simon and Schuster, 1984), 114–15.
2. P. Bushnell, 'Leadership at State', *Foreign Service Journal* (September 1989): 30–1.
3. Vicki Huddleston, 'State's Image on the Hill', *Foreign Service Journal* (September 1989): 35.
4. James M. McCormick, *American Foreign Policy and Process* (Belmont CA: Thomson and Wadsworth, 4th edn, 2005), 351.
5. See Douglas Brinkley, 'Democratic Enlargement and the Clinton Doctrine', *Foreign Policy* 106 (1997), 111–27.
6. Norman J. Ornstein, 'Congress in the Post-Cold War World', in *Beyond the Beltway: Engaging the Public in US Foreign Policy*, ed. Daniel Yankelovich and I.M. Destler (New York: W.W. Norton, 1994), 107–30, 114.
7. Elizabeth Drew, *On The Edge: The Clinton Presidency* (New York: Simon and Schuster, 1994), 138.
8. A. Devrey, 'Christopher's Job is Said to be Safe Until the End of the Year', *Washington Post*, 3 July 1994.
9. See Congressional Record, 17 July 1995, S10086.
10. *Creating a Government that Works Better and Costs Less: National Performance Review: Department of State and US Information Agency* (Washington, DC: US Government Printing Office, 1993), 5, 14.
11. See Lawrence S. Eagleburger and Robert S. Barry, 'Dollars and Sense Diplomacy', *Foreign Affairs* 75 (1996): 2–8.
12. US Department of State Management Task Force, *State 2000: A New Model for Managing Foreign Affairs* (Washington, DC: State Department, 1992), 3. See also John Dumbrell, *The Making of US Foreign Policy* (Manchester: Manchester University Press, 2nd edn, 1997), 93–6.
13. Remarks by the President at Portrait Unveiling of Secretary Warren Christopher, 30 March 1999 (available on Clinton Presidential Library website).
14. Madeleine K. Albright, *Madam Secretary: A Memoir* (London: Macmillan, 2003), 132.
15. David Halberstam, *War in a Time of Peace: Bush, Clinton and the Generals* (London: Bloomsbury, 2003), 174–5.
16. See John Dumbrell, *The Carter Presidency: A Re-evaluation* (Manchester: Manchester University Press, 2nd edn, 1997).
17. Bill Clinton, *My Life* (London: Arrow Books, 2005), 447.
18. See Nigel Hamilton, *Bill Clinton: Mastering the Presidency* (London: Century, 2007), 30–1.
19. See Halberstam, *War in a Time of Peace*, 169–76.
20. Raymond Seitz, *Over Here* (London: Weidenfeld and Nicolson, 1999), 106.
21. Ibid.
22. Sidney Blumenthal, *The Clinton Wars* (London: Viking, 2003), 635.
23. Warren Christopher, *Chances of a Lifetime* (New York: Scribner, 2001); see also Hamilton, *Bill Clinton*, 311.
24. See Martin Walker, *Clinton: The President They Deserve* (London: Fourth Estate, 1996), 272, 283, 296–7.
25. See John Dumbrell, *American Foreign Policy: Carter to Clinton* (Houndmills: Macmillan, 1997), 183–6.
26. Thomas W. Lippman, *Madeleine Albright and the New American Diplomacy* (Boulder, CO: Westview, 2000), 278–80.
27. Blumenthal, *The Clinton Wars*, 635.
28. Dick Morris, *Behind the Oval Office: Getting Reelected Against All Odds* (Los Angeles, CA: Riverside Books, 1999), 254–6.
29. Albright, *Madam Secretary*, 217.
30. Ibid., 219.
31. See Dumbrell, *American Foreign Policy*, 184–5.

32. See Lippman, *Madeleine Albright and the New American Diplomacy*, 89.
33. Strobe Talbott, *The Russia Hand: A Memoir of Presidential Diplomacy* (New York: Random House Paperback, 2003), 223.
34. Lippman, *Madeleine Albright and the New American Diplomacy*, 335.
35. Halberstam, *War in a Time of Peace*, 386.
36. Remarks by the President and Secretary of State Madeleine Albright at Swearing-in Ceremony, 23 January 1997 (available on Clinton Presidential Library website).
37. Madeleine K. Albright, 'The Testing of American Foreign Policy', *Foreign Affairs* 77, no. 6 (1998): 11–16, 11.
38. Albright, *Madam Secretary*, 353.
39. Albright, 'The Testing of American Foreign Policy', 11.
40. Albright, *Madam Secretary*, 392.
41. Ibid., 427–8. See also M. Weller, 'The Rambouillet Conference on Kosovo', *International Affairs* 75, no. 2 (1999): 211–51.
42. See Scott Ritter, *Iraq Confidential* (London: I.B. Tauris, 2005).
43. See John Dumbrell, *Evaluating the Foreign Policy of President Clinton, Or Bill Clinton: Between the Bushes* (London: British Library, Eccles Centre for American Studies, 2005) on the second term policy shifts. On the Kosovo campaign, see Carl Cavanagh Hodge, 'Strategic Drift in the Expeditionary Era: NATO in the New World', *Journal of Transatlantic Studies* 5, no.1 (2007), 25–42.
44. Albright, *Madam Secretary*, 497.
45. Madeleine K. Albright, *The Mighty and the Almighty: Reflections on Power, God, and World Affairs* (London: Macmillan, 2006), 130. On the Camp David negotiations, see Dennis Ross, *The Missing Peace: The Inside Story of the Fight for Middle East Peace* (New York: Farrar, Straus and Giroux, 2004).
46. See Halberstam, *War in a Time of Peace*, 376.
47. See Madeleine K. Albright, 'Bridges, Bombs, or Bluster?', *Foreign Affairs* 82, no. 5 (2003): 17–24.
48. Ronald D. Asmus, *Opening NATO's Door: How the Alliance Remade Itself for a New Era* (Ithaca, NY: Columbia University Press, 2002), 36–7.
49. See Ibid. Also Ian Clark, *The Post-Cold War Order: The Spoils of Peace* (Oxford: Oxford University Press, 2001), ch. 4.
50. Warren Christopher, *In the Stream of History: Shaping Foreign Policy for a New Era* (Stanford, CA: Stanford University Press, 1998), 235 (December, 1994).
51. See generally, Asmus, *Opening NATO's Door* and James M. Goldgeier, *Not Whether But When: The US Decision to Enlarge NATO* (Washington, DC: Brookings Institution Press, 1999).
52. Asmus, *Opening NATO's Door*, 177.
53. Talbott, *The Russia Hand*, 223.
54. Ibid., 235.
55. Asmus, *Opening NATO's Door*, 178.
56. Ibid., 179.
57. Goldgeier, *Not Whether But When*, 11.

Ronald Reagan's and George H. W. Bush's Secretaries of State: Alexander Haig, George Shultz and James Baker

Michael F. Hopkins

Department of History, University of Liverpool, UK

When Ronald Reagan became American president in January 1981 the prospects for US–Soviet relations looked bleak. The administration of his predecessor, Jimmy Carter, had begun with a desire to build effective ties but had ended with the Americans imposing a grain embargo and a boycott of the 1980 Moscow Olympics in response to the Soviet invasion of Afghanistan. In addition, there were significant increases in US defence expenditure. Reagan's anti-communist rhetoric and arguments for even greater military spending only added to an atmosphere that led many to describe the 1980s as witnessing a new Cold War. All this put strains on American relations with their European allies. A decade later the world had been transformed with the fall of the Berlin Wall and the reunification of Germany, the collapse of communist regimes in Eastern Europe and the demise of the Soviet Union. The administrations of Ronald Reagan (1981–1989) and George H.W. Bush (1989–1993) played pivotal roles in these changes. Three secretaries of state served in this era: Alexander M. Haig (January 1981–July 1982), George P. Shultz (July 1982–January 1989) and James A. Baker (January 1989–August 1992). They were three very different men in talents, knowledge of international affairs and feel for diplomacy, and in their use of the State Department.

The Reagan Administration

When Ronald Reagan became president in January 1981 it was the culmination of an improbable journey. He was born in Tampico, Illinois in 1911, educated at Eureka College, spent a brief time as a radio sports journalist and then became a popular 'B-movie' actor. In 1947 he was elected president of the Screen Actors' Guild. He turned to politics in 1964 and simultaneously moved from the Democrats to the Republicans, serving two terms as Governor of California (1966–1974). He made three unsuccessful attempts to gain the Republican nomination for president in 1968, 1972 and 1976 before succeeding in 1980. He was a man of genuine charm with a gift for putting his ideas to the public in a simple, direct way. This was not, however, just the former actor's facility for performance. His speeches contained genuine conviction. He had a number of core views about the need to restrict the intrusions of government, to cut taxes, to act against communism and the Soviet Union in particular and to do so especially by building up the US military – all had formed parts of his successful presidential campaign. As Mervin says, 'These guiding beliefs can be criticized for being excessively simplistic, but they gave the Reagan administration a clear sense of direction, an important quality that other administrations have lacked'.[1]

Despite this clear vision for both domestic and foreign policy, his administrations did not display the same unity of purpose and coherence. Rather, they often appeared to be pursuing more than one policy on a given issue. Yet Reagan was seen as consistent. According to Gary Wills, this was mainly a result of his 'easy way of avoiding responsibility for mere facts, for accuracy or consistency' but also because of his 'refusal to become obsessed – or even involved – with the niceties of foreign policy'.[2] His administrations also witnessed a good deal of competition between individuals and agencies. Reagan treated his aides, whom he called 'the fellas' often because he could not recall their names, as interchangeable assistants. Martin Anderson, a long-term associate, explained that Reagan 'doesn't need people. Except for Nancy [his wife]. He's the most warmly ruthless man I've seen'; 'when he decided to get something done, you did not want to be in his way'. An illustration of this was his treatment of William Clark. After Clark left office in October 1983 Reagan never telephoned the man who had worked for him for 20 years. James Baker declared, 'He treats us all the same, as hired help'. His biographer has neatly captured the arrangement: 'The old actor was staff-dependent but not staff-driven'.[3]

Three men, sometimes called the troika or the triumvirate, were at the centre in the early days of the administration: James Baker, the White House Chief of Staff, Edwin Meese, a former California prosecutor who served as Counsellor and Michael Deaver, a California public relations man who had done much to enhance the governor's favourable public standing and who became Deputy White House Chief of Staff. As Robert Schulzinger says, 'The White House staff warred with the heads of the departments of State and Defense, who often were at each other's throats as well'.[4] According to Reagan's first Secretary of State, Alexander Haig, leaks were a way of life in the Reagan Administration. He characterised the president's closest aides as PR men. 'For the press it was a dream come true to get such access to the White House. It could not risk losing sources by offending them, so it wrote what was given'.[5] The turnover of staff working on national security affairs under Reagan was much higher than for preceding presidents and his successor, George H.W. Bush. There were six different occupants of the post of National Security Adviser. Two individuals served as Secretary of Defense, Caspar Weinberger (1981–7) and Frank Carlucci (1987–9). Haig concluded: 'The necessity of speaking with one voice on foreign policy … never took hold among Reagan's advisers'.[6]

Alexander Haig

Alexander Haig's term as Secretary of State was the briefest and least effective of the Reagan and Bush administrations. In many ways, it reflected the character of the first 18 months or so of the Reagan presidency. But Haig did not help matters – although he shared many of Reagan's views, he failed to grasp the nature of his way of governing. Haig was born in Philadelphia in 1924, educated at Notre Dame University and West Point, and enjoyed a distinguished military career, becoming a decorated soldier in both the Korean and Vietnam wars. In 1961 he took a master's degree in international relations at Georgetown University. He had experience of working in the Pentagon and as an aide to Cyrus Vance, who was successively Secretary of Army and Deputy Secretary of Defense in 1964–6. Haig worked as military aide to National Security Adviser Henry Kissinger in 1969–73. Haig served as Supreme Commander NATO forces in Europe in 1974–9.

He thus was familiar with the politics of defence policy, Haig also had experience of political activity when he served briefly (June 1973–August 1974) as Richard Nixon's White House chief of staff. He acted as foreign policy adviser during Reagan's presidential campaign in 1980. He possessed a character not ideally suited to his post: 'Indiscreet and volatile, knowledgeable and arrogant, Haig was ever ready to take offense at slights real and imagined'.[7] The Secretary of Defense, Caspar Weinberger, noted how Haig seemed unable to present issues without 'an enormous amount of passion and intensity' and displayed a 'deep suspicion of the competence and motives of anyone who did not share his opinions'.[8] Haig was, in Garthoff's view, the best informed on foreign affairs among the senior figures in the administration but this expertise was relative – he often displayed abysmal ignorance in the cases he cited so confidently.[9]

From the outset, Haig sought to establish himself as the dominant voice in foreign affairs – at times it seemed as if he wanted to be the sole voice. On inauguration day, 20 January 1981, he presented National Security Decision Directive 1 (NSDD1) to the president, which was an outline of lines of authority for the conduct of foreign policy that placed Haig and the State Department at the centre. He failed to secure Reagan's signature: Baker, Meese and Deaver dissuaded the president from signing what they took to be a power play by the secretary of state. Haig blamed the Troika, not able to grasp that they were acting at the president's bidding. The desire to exercise control was undoubtedly an element in Haig's thinking but he was also concerned to achieve an important goal – to avoid the danger of an absence of strategic leadership from Reagan. His experience of working for Henry Kissinger led him to recognise the need for co-ordination and for control of the mechanisms of policy-making and policy implementation. He seemed to be trying to emulate his mentor's move to sideline Nixon's Secretary of State, William P. Rogers. However, as Rubin points out, Kissinger was fulfilling Nixon's design while Haig was clearly not Reagan's alter ego.[10]

The Reagan Administration thus began without clear strategic leadership in foreign policy. Richard V. Allen served as National Security Adviser from January 1981 to January 1982. He was rather ineffectual in his role, which meant that Haig was alone in contesting the suggestions of the presidential aides.[11] Allen's departure did not improve matters for Haig, for the new Adviser was William Clark, who had proved a helpful Deputy Secretary of State. Without the protection of Clark, Haig faced Baker and Deaver who 'plotted like schoolboys to goad him into destroying himself with Reagan'.[12] Haig in his memoirs observed, 'Grand purpose fell victim to schoolboy scuffles for personal advantage'. As Secretary he struggled to obtain adequate access to the president. Not knowing his methods, system of thought and not having an opportunity to discuss policy in detail with him, Haig had to proceed on the assumption that their principles and instincts were the same. 'The President's aides in the first days appeared to believe that foreign policy did not matter that much'.[13] Moreover, many of these White House advisers had doubts about the State Department, regarding it as too prone to advocating liberal policies and enlisting the secretary to its cause.

Such circumstances might have hampered effective foreign policy but Haig's behaviour did not help. In March 1981 the Vice-President, George Bush, was appointed as coordinator for crisis management. Haig exploded with anger when he discovered this in the *Washington Post* of 22 March, accusing the president of reneging on his promise of 11 December 1980 that he Haig would be *the* spokesman on foreign policy. He drafted a resignation letter: – 'Members of your personal staff have consistently undermined your stated intention that the Secretary of State be your principal foreign policy adviser ... I hereby tender my resignation' – and then demanded to see Reagan. Haig telephoned Reagan and said that the Vice-President should have no foreign policy authority and that he was thinking of resigning. Reagan invited him to a meeting the next morning. He expected Haig to resign and thought he would need to try and persuade him not to do so, for a resignation so early in the administration would be embarrassing. Instead, however,

Haig was calm and requested a declaration from the president saying Haig alone was in control of foreign affairs. Reagan was unwilling to do that but did issue a statement acknowledging 'The Secretary of State is my primary adviser on foreign affairs'. At the same time he sent a memorandum to Baker and Meese: 'This is to confirm my prior verbal directive to you to attend all meetings of the National Security Council and to participate in such meetings and activities of the Council as representatives of the President'.[14] This incident did little to improve Haig's standing within the administration or with the public. Deaver and Baker circulated anti-Haig stories to the press. An editorial in the *New York Times* declared: 'So the single voice the Reagan administration intended to speak to the world has been saying nothing more urgent than "I quit". For a Secretary of State to threaten resignation eight or nine times in sixty-five days must be a record'.[15]

There were further worrying indications of Haig's temperament and ambitions in the same month. After the Cabinet meeting of 19 March 1981 Reagan spoke to Haig about Bush's suggestion that the Japanese be encouraged to introduce a voluntary reduction in automobile exports to the USA. In one of their first one-to-one meetings Reagan was disturbed by the intensity of the secretary's attitude. Haig pounded the desk, seeming ready to explode, and complained that White House people – Baker, Deaver, and Bush – were trying to take over his territory.[16] On 30 March 1981 there was an attempt to assassinate the president. Baker called a meeting in the White House Situation Room. Haig took charge. When he heard that Reagan was on the operating table, he said, 'the helm is right here. And that means right in this chair for now, constitutionally, until the Vice President gets here'. That was not constitutionally accurate. The 25th amendment of 1967 declared that the succession was first to the Vice-President, then the Speaker of the House and the President Pro Tempore of the Senate – all elected officials – followed by members of the cabinet in the order that their departments were founded, beginning with State. Military command authority, however, went from the President to the Vice-President, then the Secretary of Defense. Haig's prickly demeanour dissuaded Weinberger from challenging his claims. Richard Darman decided to act and remove prepared letters to the Speaker of the House, Thomas 'Tip' O'Neill of Massachusetts, and the President Pro Tempore of the Senate, Strom Thurmond of South Carolina. Although not authorised to do so, he put them in his safe. He knew that if they discussed the 25th amendment, the press would hear about it, thereby damaging Reagan's status as the man in charge. Meanwhile, the White House spokesman, Larry Speakes, held a press conference and answered questions about who was in charge. Feeling his answers were inadequate, Haig rushed to the press conference and claimed 'As of now, I am in control here, in the White House, pending the return of the Vice President and in close touch with him'. Reagan's other senior aides disagreed with the legal claims, were concerned about the push for power and, above all were stunned by Haig's febrile behaviour. 'Is he mad', asked Donald Regan.[17]

For all his erratic behaviour and assertive pursuit of control of foreign policy, the Secretary shared with the President a belief in the need to increase US power in the world and to adopt a tough attitude to the Soviet Union and communism.[18] Reagan, however, was more flexible than either Haig or his own rhetoric would have suggested. They agreed on the need for a major programme of defence spending – $1.6 trillion over five years. Many members of the Soviet leadership feared the Americans were trying to develop a first strike capability. In addition, the CIA received a boost to its funds, in particular to expand its covert activities. The next few years brought American aid to anti-communist guerrillas in Afghanistan, Angola and Cambodia and to Central America in particular – the El Salvador government had US military advisers, while Washington assisted the Contras in their conflict with the Sandinista regime in Nicaragua.

The tough attitude to the Soviet Union meant that there was no progress in relations, though the administration showed more flexibility on individual issues than its rhetoric might have suggested. The Soviet invasion of Afghanistan in 1979 had severely worsened US–Soviet relations, leading to the American boycott of the Moscow Olympics in 1980 and to the imposition of a grain embargo. In April 1981 the anti-Soviet Reagan administration ended the embargo and it was the anti-communist Reagan who pushed it through against Haig's objections. In December 1981 the communist government of General Jaruzelski introduced martial law in Poland in its battle with the independent trade union that was becoming a political force under Lech Walesa. Despite strong words of condemnation, neither Reagan nor Haig favoured retaliatory measures against Moscow which had clearly sanctioned Jaruzelski's actions. Furthermore, Reagan was also ready in April 1981 to write a personal letter to the Soviet leader, Leonid Brezhnev. Haig, however, objected, saying the State Department should draft it. As Reagan observed in his memoirs, Haig 'didn't want to carry out the president's foreign policy; he wanted to formulate it and carry it out himself'. The president did write to Brezhnev – he attached a personal note to an official message drafted by the State Department but both received 'an icy reply'.[19]

Reagan's robust approach to the Soviet Union was shared by the British Prime Minister, Margaret Thatcher.[20] The harmony of the transatlantic relationship was first challenged then vindicated in a major crisis for Britain in April 1982. Argentina invaded the Falklands Islands, a tiny island remnant of British colonial power in the South Atlantic, claiming it was their sovereign territory. It immediately posed a dilemma for the Americans who wanted to support their NATO allies in London while avoiding a break with one of their main allies in Latin America. The difficulties encountered in pursuit of these two goals in an administration not noted for its ability to follow a single consistent policy exposed the different priorities of the various members of the administration. The Americans, in public at least, were slow to back the British: Reagan told reporters that Washington would be ready to act as honest broker.[21] For Haig the crisis confirmed his view of the need for his directing influence. He was sympathetic to Britain and undertook 33,000 miles of shuttle diplomacy between Washington, New York, London and Buenos Aires. Jeanne Kirkpatrick, the US Representative at the UN, who wanted to retain Argentina as an anti-communist ally in Latin America, accused Haig and the State Department of being pro-British. Once the British began their fight to regain the Falklands, Reagan declared his support for them, saying 'armed aggression . . . must not be allowed to succeed'.[22] All the while Haig had been pursuing his global diplomacy, the American military had been aiding the British, confirming the depth of the special relations between the two navies. These efforts owed a great deal to the prompting of Weinberger, whose memoirs are critical of Haig's tardiness in backing Britain.[23]

Haig was convinced that his 'efforts in the Falklands ultimately cost me my job as Secretary of State'. Indeed, they were a major factor but not for the reasons he offered in his memoirs – that his image had suffered with the failure of his diplomacy. Rather, the crisis once again exposed the flaws in the way he conducted diplomacy and his continued failure to consult the president properly. One episode was symptomatic. Feeling no need to contact the president, he instructed Jeanne Kirkpatrick to abstain rather than veto a Security Council resolution calling for an immediate cease-fire in the Falklands war. The cease-fire, which the British opposed, was designed to save Argentina from a humiliating surrender. Kirkpatrick received the instruction three minutes after lodging her veto. Haig justified not telephoning her by saying 'You don't talk to the company commander when you have a corps and division in between'. Given the extremely bad relations between them, it is unlikely he would have wanted to call her.[24]

In the same month there was a further instance of Haig's inability to understand the correct relations with the president. It sealed his fate as secretary. In June 1982 the Israeli forces entered Lebanon. Reagan felt betrayed, since the Israeli prime minister, Menachem Begin, had suggested that this would not happen. In response, Haig acted without consulting Reagan. He sent a cable over the weekend with detailed guidance to the American 'special envoy' in Lebanon, Ambassador Habib, when Clark had told him to send it first to Camp David to be explored by the president. On Monday 21 June Haig met the president to discuss Israeli action and his sending of the cable. Reagan asked him what he would do 'if you were general and your lower commanders went around you and acted on his own?' 'I'd fire him, Mr President', replied Haig. 'No, I don't mean that', Reagan said, 'But this mustn't happen again. We just can't have a situation where you send messages on your own that are a matter for my decision'. 'There was no time for that, Mr President. It was too urgent', Haig replied and then launched into another litany of complaints about his treatment at the hands of Baker and Meese; and he now included Clark. At a further meeting on Thursday 24 June Haig returned to the theme, adding 'I simply can no longer operate in this atmosphere. It doesn't serve your purposes; it doesn't serve the American people'. The president told him that 'it's awfully hard for me to give you what you're asking for'. In the face of this, Reagan was coming round to the need to replace Haig. The next day, he decided to do so. In a meeting in the Oval Office he handed Haig a letter that read 'Dear Al, It is with the most profound regret that I accept your resignation'. He said he was going to speak to Shultz, whom he expected to accept. Haig asked for time to write his resignation letter, but Reagan immediately announced Haig's resignation and Shultz's nomination.[25]

For all the shock he felt, Haig ought not to have been surprised. Frequent threats to resign, complaints about the efforts of the president's staff to thwart his diplomacy and numerous instances of a failure to consult the president – all pointed to a breakdown in the relationship between secretary and president that must be the foundation for a successful term as Secretary of State. Haig's failure owed a good deal to the way the Reagan Administration worked in its first 18 months, and its focus on domestic affairs. Yet, Haig's unrealistic expectations and behaviour made a major contribution. His previous experience at MacArthur's headquarters during the Korean War and at the Nixon White House had seen him rewarded for his tough handling of rival voices to his bosses. He made the mistake of assuming he should do the same on his own behalf when he became Secretary of State but, as Rubin observes, 'a cautious, deferential style' was needed.[26] Above all, Haig failed to grasp that the role of the Secretary of State was not to be the person in charge of US foreign policy but to be the president's pre-eminent adviser on foreign affairs.

George Shultz

The new Secretary of State did not make the same mistake as Haig. As a member of the administration remarked, 'the whole secret of this administration is that the president is not to be humiliated. Whoever does this is dead. George Shultz never does it'.[27] Yet the same problems of competing counsels on foreign affairs confronted Shultz but he was much more able to cope with the situation.

George Pratt Shultz was born in New York City in 1920, studied economics at Princeton, served in the US marines in the Pacific during the Second World War, returned to complete a PhD in industrial economics at MIT, and then enjoyed a successful academic career, ending up as Dean of the Graduate School at the University of Chicago. He served in three cabinet posts for the Nixon Administration: Secretary of Labor, Director of the

Budget and Secretary of the Treasury. He then worked as president of the Bechtel Corporation, an international construction company, until he was appointed secretary. He thus had an unusual range of experience in government, university and business. A well-travelled individual who had met many world leaders, he had considerable knowledge of international economics but was less familiar with political and military issues. He brought patience, a calm approach, good judgment and a reputation for integrity to his work. Oberdorfer notes that he was politically adaptable but was 'absolutely unyielding on questions that struck him as matters of personal or public ethics'. He valued teamwork, understanding the importance of bringing as many people as possible into discussion and persuading them or, at least consulting, them on key decisions. His time as Labor Secretary taught him the importance of negotiations, during which he was persistent and undeterred by setbacks, since he always tried to view issues in the long term – he observed how his training as an economist had led him to deal with time lags, unlike the politician who sought instant results. A gift for effective organisation ensured that he and his officials usually worked well with presidential aides and other departments. On occasion, difficulties got the better of him and he sulked about an issue. Sometimes, he allowed clashes with individuals to cloud his view of their departments.[28]

Vital to his success would be a good relationship with the president. He took up his post aware of the tensions between the White House and the State Department and acted to remove them. At his first meeting with the president he declared, 'I consider myself to be part of the White House and of your team. I'm working for you, Mr President. I'll make use of the talent of the State Department to get our job done. I've always been able to work with career people in government, and I know they work hard for us if we give them leadership and involvement'.[29] Shultz held a favourable view of Reagan – they had met for dinner in July 1978 after which he had concluded that Reagan's 'views were real and ran deep'. Thereafter they enjoyed candid conversations. Shultz shared Reagan's view of the Soviet Union as an aggressive, economically bankrupt but militarily powerful state, but one with which they should be ready to negotiate constructively if the occasion arose. Shultz endorsed Reagan's basic principles and the focus of his foreign policy. Reagan was right to stress that economic progress would flow from free enterprise and an open trading system. The increases in defence spending were also appropriate and yielded the improved military strength and morale in the armed forces that was fundamental to effective policy. 'Power and diplomacy work together. Political pressures in Washington tend to push toward one extreme or the other; operating both at the same time would require great skill'. Shultz was confident, believing that the West was winning the ideological battle. The very things he had stressed in a speech at Stanford in 1979 were being realised. Time and will were needed 'to hold off the Soviet military threat long enough for America to regain its resolve internationally, to demonstrate how to use freedom and open markets as the organizing principles for economic and political development, and to do so long enough to allow communism's failures to be fully recognized and to play themselves out'.[30]

As Shultz moved into office he realised that Washington was very different from the Nixon era. Always astute about the bureaucratic framework in which he had to work, he noted a number of problems he would need to surmount. There was now a vast army of aides; the staffs of different agencies, supposedly following the same policy, were often in conflict; there appeared a cult of secrecy verging on deception. He appreciated how White House staff might overreach themselves unless the president and cabinet officers refused to let it occur. He was determined to ensure this did not happen to him and his department. The State Department had not been prominent under Haig, something Shultz wanted to change. He did not share the fear among so many members of the Reagan Administration that the department's officials were all bent on turning him to their liberal agenda.

Unlike Haig, Shultz had a high regard for its staff, and took care to establish an effective team in the State Department. The sheer volume of work facing the department made him realise the importance of having close contact with people who handled this flow of information. However, he wanted not only experts on the world's regions and various international issues but also people with political sensitivity. Given that the department would be helping to formulate and execute Reagan's foreign policy, it was important that they were on the same wavelength. He decided that his second in command, the Deputy Secretary, should be a political appointee. He chose a law professor, Kenneth Dam. But he retained Lawrence Eagleburger, who had been an important adviser to Haig, and a number of other senior figures.[31]

Shultz immediately confronted a crisis in Lebanon as a result of the Israeli invasion, aimed at halting attacks by the Palestine Liberation Organisation. American troops were despatched as part of a peacekeeping force, but an attack on the US Embassy in April 1983, killing 63, and a suicide bombing of the marines' headquarters in October, killing 241, caused the American commitment to waver, leading to the departure of troops by April 1984. The Middle East continued to be a problem throughout Reagan's presidency, made worse by the intifada, or uprising, that began among Palestinians in December 1987. The administration was also dogged by difficulties in Central America, as it pursued anti-communist policies. In November 1986 the Iran-Contra scandal broke when it was discovered that the Americans had sanctioned the supply of military spares to Iran in return for its aid in the release of US hostages in Lebanon; the money the Americans received in payment for the spares was then secretly siphoned to support the Contra movement who were trying to overthrow the Sandinista government in Nicaragua.

The main challenge for the Reagan Administration and the main concern of the Europeans was the US–Soviet relationship and arms talks in particular. There were two sets of discussions: the SALT negotiations, addressing intercontinental missiles, that Reagan renamed the Strategic Arms Reduction Talks (START); and the more pressing Intermediate Nuclear Forces (INF) discussions. The Americans were due to deploy Cruise and Pershing II missiles in Europe in response to the Soviet SS-20s. Moscow, however, had conducted a successful propaganda campaign in Europe against Carter's initial response to the SS-20s – the neutron bomb was abandoned in the face of protest in Western Europe. It now hoped to do the same against the Cruise and Pershing missiles. The risks of such a deployment by a strongly anti-communist American administration worried many in Europe. In late 1981 London, Bonn and Rome each saw marches that brought more than 250,000 people on to the streets. If the Soviets temporised, hoping the protests would weaken the commitment to the deployment, Reagan seemed equally reluctant to hold talks. He wanted to wait until his increased spending programme had restored US military might and until the Soviets adopted a more conciliatory attitude. So he only held his first meeting with the Soviet Ambassador, Anatoly Dobrynin, in February 1983, while the first discussions with the Foreign Minister, Andrei Gromyko, took place in September 1984.

Progress in the arms talks, Shultz realised, would require cohesion among NATO members, something difficult to achieve in what he appreciated to be the acrimonious atmosphere caused by US actions against European companies providing equipment and services for the Siberian pipeline. Shultz was concerned that this problem did not seem to be adequately appreciated by others in the administration. Even Margaret Thatcher, Europe's leading supporter of Reagan, expressed irritation with US action, pointing out how this came at a time when the Americans proposed to resume grain sales to the Soviet

Union. The claim that this would drain Soviet hard currency reserves did not convince, when it was clear that the sales were in the commercial interest of the US farmers. After some difficult negotiations, Shultz found a solution by allowing existing contracts for the pipeline to go ahead.[32]

Shultz inherited an impasse in the INF talks that had resumed in November 1981. While the Americans favoured a 'zero option', the Soviets argued that approximate parity already existed and the imminent deployment of Pershing and Cruise missiles would disturb this balance. The negotiating teams in Geneva produced a provisional agreement in July 1982, by which SS-20s would be limited to 75 and there would be 75 Cruise missiles and no Pershing missiles, but neither government pursued the proposal. Discussions on START, which had begun in June 1982, also failed to make progress.

Deadlock in 1982 was succeeded by serious tensions in 1983. On 23 March Reagan announced the Strategic Defence Initiative (SDI) programme, soon known as 'Star Wars', a network of lasers or particle beam weapons in space that would destroy incoming nuclear missiles. Most scientific opinion regarded it as an expensive fantasy. Shultz was not consulted as the speech was being prepared.[33] In the same month Reagan gave a speech in which he called the Soviet Union an 'evil empire' whose days were numbered.[34] In September a Soviet fighter shot down a Korean Airlines flight, KAL 007, which had mistakenly entered Soviet air space en route to Seoul, South Korea, killing all 269 people on board. The incident intensified anxieties in both Washington, which called it an 'act of barbarism', and Moscow, where Yuri Andropov, the new leader after Brezhnev's death in November 1982, spoke of the 'militarist course' of America.

The US invasion of Grenada in October to rescue Americans served to confirm Soviet fears. Then, in November, the NATO 'Able Archer' exercise caused Moscow to warn its missions abroad that American bases had been placed on alert. According to Oleg Gordievsky, who was working as a British double agent in the KGB, Andropov had believed since 1981 that the Americans were preparing for a nuclear war.[35] The NATO exercise coincided with the initial deployment of Cruise and Pershing II missiles. Mrs Thatcher's re-election in Britain in May 1983 and the election of Helmut Kohl and the Christian Democrats in West Germany in March, who were both committed to accepting the American weapons, ensured that the Soviet peace campaign against the missiles would fail. The Soviets quit both the INF talks and the START discussions. For the first time in 15 years the Americans and Soviets were not even talking to one another.

Yet in the following year the situation improved. American rhetoric was toned down, as Reagan and Shultz felt they enjoyed the position of strength from which they could negotiate. The president became more attuned to Soviet anxieties. He declared in his memoirs: 'Many people at the top of the Soviet hierarchy were genuinely afraid of America and the Americans. Perhaps this shouldn't have surprised me but it did ... Soviet officials feared us not only as adversaries but as potential aggressors who might hurl nuclear weapons at them in a first strike'. Moreover, he wanted to talk to a senior Soviet leader 'in a room alone and try and convince him that we had no designs on the Soviet Union'. He adopted a more understanding approach in public, referring in his 16 January 1984 speech to Jim and Sally and Ivan and Anya, two couples who both longed for peace.[36] The next day Shultz spoke in Stockholm about the need to 'reduce the risk of surprise attack, miscalculation, or misunderstanding ... we must never repeat the tragedy of 1914'.[37] On Reagan's orders, he created a small group within the National Security Planning Group with the task of opening new channels with the Kremlin.

On 24 September Reagan addressed the UN General Assembly and suggested a new framework for US–Soviet nuclear arms talks. He proposed that there should be three sets of discussions, addressing INF, START and, a new field, anti-satellite weapons (ASAT). On 28 September Reagan met Gromyko in Washington. The Soviet Foreign Minister was as 'hard as granite' in their 'three hours of give-and-take', unwilling to commit himself but giving the president the impression that the Soviets might return to discussions after the election.[38] Weinberger and William Casey, director of the CIA, were concerned about the meeting with Gromyko. They pushed, together with other hardliners, for the resignations of Shultz and the National Security Adviser, Robert McFarlane. Reagan was conscious of these pressures. His diary on 6 April 1984 noted that, though some members of the NSC were hard line and against any approach to the Soviets, 'I think I am hard line and will never appease. But I do want to try to let them see there is a better world if they'll show by *deed* they want to get along with the free world'.[39] After his re-election in November, the Soviets agreed to renewed talks. Shultz and Gromyko agreed, in January 1985, that these discussions should begin in March. That month, however, saw the death of Konstantin Chernenko, leader since Andropov's death in February 1984. The new General Secretary would be a younger, more energetic figure – the 54-year-old Mikhail Gorbachev.

Born in southern Russia in 1931, Gorbachev was a man of high intelligence and someone who was adept at bureaucratic politics – he secured the support of the old guard Gromyko in the vote for leader, only to remove him as Foreign Minister four months later. He had a reasonable understanding of Western Europe, thanks to his travels. During his rise through the party he had established a reputation for action. He faced major problems – from the costly war in Afghanistan to the crumbling economy to dissent within the Eastern Bloc countries. He appointed new reformist individuals and encouraged public discussion of issues, championing *glasnost* (greater openness) and promising *perestroika* (restructuring).

Gorbachev made an immediately favourable impression on the Americans. The Vice-President, George Bush, and Shultz met him at Chernenko's funeral. Shultz noted that he was 'articulate and spontaneous. He seemed to be thinking aloud', his 'free-flowing monologue showed a mind working at high intensity, even at the end of a long, hard day. He displayed a breadth of view and vigor, I thought, but his basic positions were ones we had heard before'. Here was an entirely different type of Soviet leader. 'He was quicker, fresher, more engaging, and more wide ranging in his interests and knowledge. The content of our meeting was tough and his manner was aggressive, but the spirit was different. He was comfortable with himself and with others, joking with Gromyko in a way that emerged from genuine confidence in his base of knowledge and in his political abilities'. The Secretary of State was 'genuinely impressed with the quality of the thought, the intensity, and the intellectual energy of this new man on the scene'.[40]

In July Gorbachev replaced Gromyko as Foreign Minister with Eduard Shevardnadze, First Secretary of the Communist Party in Georgia. The '[s]oft-spoken, invariably courteous' Shevardnadze shared Gorbachev's 'impatience with the way the Soviet system was operating'. Although he had no experience of foreign policy, he quickly adapted to his new role and came to play a vital part in Gorbachev's diplomacy. Shultz, later observed, 'The contrast between him and Gromyko was breathtaking. He understood there was more to the world than the United States, the Soviet Union, and Europe. He could smile, engage, converse. He had an ability to persuade and to be persuaded. We were in a real diplomatic competition now – we couldn't [*sic*] just sit around and say that the Soviet positions were "nothing new" or a "catastrophe for the free world". The Soviets were awake. We had to engage them'.[41] The presence of Gorbachev and Shevardnadze raised the real possibility of improvements in East–West relations. Nevertheless, the subsequent progress also owed a great deal to the Americans. Despite the tough rhetoric, Reagan wanted contact and had sent messages to each Soviet leader. By late 1984 he was willing to press for new arms talks. In all this he was aided and encouraged by Shultz.

Gorbachev immediately took the initiative. In April 1985 he suggested a temporary halt to the deployment of intermediate-range nuclear missiles in Europe, saying he would make it permanent if the Americans did the same. Washington, however, was not ready to accept a freeze that secured the current Soviet advantage in these weapons. In August he proposed a temporary moratorium on nuclear tests and invited the Americans to follow. They declined partly because of problems of verification but mainly because it would stop work on SDI. Next, he offered to meet the US president at a summit meeting. Discussions on a venue led, in May, to agreement to meet in Geneva. So in November 1985 Gorbachev and Reagan held polite and friendly talks in Geneva, though there were no breakthroughs on substantive issues.[42] Yet there was one positive outcome: they seemed to like each other and began to feel they could trust one another. Reagan, however, remained cautious, continuing to accept Weinberger's arguments for a tough line with Moscow.

For the next 11 months they maintained a regular correspondence, laying out their positions on arms talks and sometimes exchanging sharp words on other topics, such as Nicaragua, Afghanistan and human rights. But Gorbachev decided to make a concession, offering to drop the link between Soviet SS-20s and British and French nuclear weapons. Another summit was held in October 1986 in Reykjavik. The two leaders deepened their mutual understanding and even came close to reaching agreement to remove all ballistic missiles. The main obstacle, however, was Reagan's continued commitment to SDI.[43]

Thatcher was troubled by the prospect of eliminating strategic nuclear missiles, which she regarded as fundamental to peace and stability. She therefore encouraged Gorbachev and Reagan to focus on reaching a deal on the intermediate-range weapons.[44] Shultz undertook a series of tough negotiations with Gorbachev and Shevardnadze before reaching an INF agreement in September 1987 that removed all intermediate-range weapons from Europe, the so-called 'zero option'. Gorbachev had wanted the agreement to be conditional on American abandonment of SDI, which the Americans refused, but he went ahead, expecting Congress to reduce SDI funding, which it did indeed cut by a third. So, Gorbachev and Reagan signed one of the most significant arms treaties of the twentieth century at a summit in Washington – it eliminated a whole category of nuclear weapons. It involved the verified destruction of all ground-launched nuclear missiles with a range of 500–5500 kilometres in Europe and Asia. The INF Treaty, quickly ratified by the US Senate, saw the destruction of 1846 Soviet nuclear weapons and 846 US weapons in the next three years. This was verified through careful inspection of each side's nuclear sites, an unprecedented concession.[45]

At a further summit in Moscow in May–June 1988 Gorbachev and Reagan tried to produce a START treaty, exploring the possibility of a 50% cut in strategic nuclear missiles. The experts from both countries, however, could not resolve a number of questions, especially over sea- and air-launched cruise missiles. They expected to settle these differences but not before Reagan left office.[46] Despite the failure to reach an agreement on START, the final months of Reagan's administration saw continued progress in reducing tensions. Gorbachev told the UN on 7 December 1988 that the world was becoming less ideological and that 'force and the threat of force can no longer be … instruments of foreign policy'. He then said he would reduce Soviet conventional forces by 500,000 men.

The collaboration of Reagan and Shultz had produced extraordinary results. In his memoirs Shultz paid tribute to the efforts of the president 'to stick to his basic objectives, to maintain our strength and the cohesion of our alliances, and to be willing to recognise an opportunity for a good deal and a changed situation when he saw one'. Reagan, he added, 'had the courage of his conviction that Gorbachev represented a powerful drive for a different Soviet Union in its foreign policy and in its conduct of affairs at home'.[47] The president certainly played a central role in giving a sense of focus, but Shultz's contribution was also vital. As Oberdorfer observes, 'Reagan knew that he wanted a less dangerous relationship with the Soviet Union, but he did not know how to go about achieving it'. Shultz offered two vital assets for this task: his tenacious quest for practical goals and his talent for organising the often fractious elements in the US government to work together. 'Reagan wanted it to happen; Shultz was the key figure in his administration who made it happen'. Shultz was undaunted by frequent delays and other difficulties. 'Like the tortoise in the race with the hare, he just kept coming, moving slowly but relentlessly toward the goal'.[48] His strengths complemented some of Reagan's weaknesses. Shultz mastered details that bored Reagan, was resilient in negotiations, and had a keen appreciation of the need for consistency in overall policy. Reagan was masterly on a public platform.[49]

Shultz had also developed a remarkable partnership with Shevardnadze. The warmth of their understanding was evident to their delegations at the December 1987 summit: 'They briefly stood there in the spotlight, like two old friends. It was one of the most emotional and memorable moments at lunch, provoking a long round of enthusiastic applause.'[50] They also worked effectively to lessen the influence of the hawks in their own governments from derailing the progress. Shultz's achievements are all the more remarkable in that he had to operate in an often testy atmosphere in Washington, though his task was made easier by the reduction of the influence of the hardliners. Weinberger was succeeded in 1987 by Frank Carlucci, a more willing collaborator; and the Iran-Contra scandal undermined the credibility of the NSC in 1986.

The George H.W. Bush Administration

James Baker

The task of building on these substantial developments fell to a new president, Reagan's Vice-President, George Bush, who was very different from Reagan. Bush was born to a rich New England family in 1924, served as Navy pilot in the Pacific during the Second World War, and studied at Yale University prior to working in the oil industry for a decade. He then turned to government service, acting as US Ambassador to the UN, emissary to China, and director of the CIA before serving as Reagan's Vice-President for eight years. He therefore brought considerable experience of government and of foreign policy. Bush was a capable, honest, rather quiet individual with a sense of public duty, a knowledgeable man who was more interested in detail than in grand theories, a pragmatist who valued personal friendships and loyalty. His appointees were like-minded individuals, people who shared 'his penchant for low-key rhetoric and careful attention to details and the consequences of actions'.[51]

The new Secretary of State was James Baker, who was born in Houston in 1930, educated at Princeton and served in the US marines. After taking a law degree at the University of Texas, he worked as a lawyer in Houston before turning to politics. He served as Under Secretary and then Secretary of Commerce in the Ford administration, 1974–1977; and as White House Chief of Staff (1981–1985) and then Secretary of the Treasury (1985–1989) under Reagan. Baker was a smartly dressed, sharp-minded individual whose foreign policy experience was limited but who was a great political fixer with a firm grasp of the ways of Washington politics. He was a tough and dogged negotiator. His time as

White House Chief of Staff had taught him the importance of cultivating the press. Bush and Baker had been friends since 1959 and had similar political outlooks. Neither man was attracted to grand ideas.[52]

Dick Cheney, a straight-talking Congressman from Wyoming who had served as Chief of Staff to President Ford, was appointed as Secretary of Defense. The knowledgeable, experienced and self-effacing Brent Scowcroft became National Security Adviser, a post he had also held under President Ford. He saw himself as a foreign policy and national security manager who presented options to the president rather than being the initiator of a grand strategy. Baker, Cheney and Scowcroft proved to be a very effective team who worked well together, because, as Baker later observed, they liked each other. Baker was pre-eminent – Bush declared him to be his principal adviser – but he did not always prevail, since the president had his own views based on considerable experience in foreign affairs.[53]

Baker' style at the State Department was notably different from that of Shultz. He signalled his intent in a *Time* magazine interview, saying he intended to be the President's man at the State Department, not the State Department's man at the White House. Shultz had relied heavily on his officials and it had worked, according to Baker, because Haig before him had instituted the Reagan revolution in foreign affairs and the foreign service officials had adapted to the new policy. Baker believed that he faced the prospect of revolutionary changes in international affairs that would require new thinking, something bureaucrats find difficult. The change of administration would mean the departure of Reagan appointees and the development of a different strategy and this would require new people. He also wanted people more attentive to domestic audiences, not only on the Hill but also generally across the land, to try to restore a bipartisan policy after the bitterness of the election campaign. The 'institutional rigidity of the Foreign Service' would preclude the achievement of these tasks. So he established a small team of talented, loyal aides who could generate ideas and turn them into action. But he was wise enough to appoint the experienced Eagleburger as his deputy.[54]

This foreign policy team inherited a most favourable situation: East–West tensions had all but disappeared and there had been progress in reducing nuclear arms. However, Germany remained divided, two military alliances confronted one another and there were still two social and political systems in Europe. Reagan had established very effective co-operation with his European allies, especially Thatcher's Britain. The Bush Administration, however, chose to alter its focus, placing the relationship with Germany – rather than the 'special relationship' with Britain – at the centre. For Thatcher this was partly political, for Bush needed to distance himself from his predecessor, and partly personal, since, she learned later, Bush disliked her habit of talking nonstop when 'he felt he ought to have been leading the discussion'. She 'learned that I had to defer to him in conversation and not to stint the praise'. Bush put the issue differently in his memoirs: Reagan had often let her speak 'on their joint behalf' but he took the 'decision early on that there could be only one spokesman for the United States'.[55]

Bush and Baker were at first rather wary about Gorbachev, though not as sceptical as Cheney. In February they instituted a major review of US–Soviet relations, which meant that various bilateral talks were suspended. Arms negotiations did not resume until September 1989. At a speech in Texas on 12 May Bush outlined the findings of the review: the aim was to go 'beyond containment' to 'the integration of the Soviet Union into the community of nations'.[56] In the following months Europe witnessed a revolution. Free elections in the Soviet Union in March saw victories for liberals, radicals and Baltic and Caucasian nationalists. In June Solidarity, the independent trade union turned political movement, won the general election in Poland. There followed two months of crisis until

Gorbachev approved a compromise that brought the first non-communist prime minister in the Eastern Bloc in return for communist ministers of defence and the interior.

In Hungary the government allowed celebration of Imre Nagy, the hero of the 1956 uprising, and opened its borders. As a result, large numbers of East Germans found their way to the West German embassies in Budapest and Prague. As the German Democratic Republic (GDR) approached its 40th anniversary, Gorbachev encouraged it to reform rather than to instigate repression. The freedom to travel was a prominent demand. The new leader, Egon Krenz, granted this but the authorities failed to exempt Berlin (normally given special status). Gunter Schabowski, the GDR spokesman, then compounded the mistake by saying the new arrangements would apply immediately, when they needed to await approval by the East German legislature. In consequence, thousands arrived at the Berlin Wall, leaving the border guards unsure what to do. Reluctant to use force, they opened the wall on the night of 8–9 November and almost immediately people began to tear it down.[57] November 1989 also saw the 'Velvet Revolution' in Czechoslovakia. By the end of the year the regime in Romania had also fallen. In the space of a few months five states had witnessed the collapse of their pro-Soviet communist regimes. In mid-1990 the government in Bulgaria also collapsed. These developments were possible because Gorbachev had declared in July that he would not apply the Brezhnev doctrine of intervention to retain control. Indeed, his spokesman, Gennady Gerasimov, spoke of the 'Frank Sinatra Doctrine', letting them 'do it their way'.

This response persuaded Bush and Baker that they could work with Gorbachev. So when Bush visited Poland and Hungary in July he did not use triumphant rhetoric. He and Baker realised that it would only be with Soviet acquiescence that change could occur in Eastern Europe: there would be no gloating that might jeopardise that. An important component of better US–Soviet understanding was the very good relationship between Baker and Shevardnadze. They met regularly to address a vast array of issues – by the time of Shevardnadze's resignation in December 1990 they had held 25 meetings. The Gorbachev–Bush summit in Malta in December 1989 confirmed the new spirit of co-operation. They were acting as allies.[58]

The most challenging issue facing Baker was whether there should now be a united Germany. It was not the straightforward issue it might appear in hindsight. If the West German Chancellor, Helmut Kohl, was pressing for reunification, Thatcher and Mitterand had reservations. The Soviets also resisted. Shevardnadze said, 'We had paid an enormous price for it and to write it off was inconceivable. The memory of the war was stronger than the new concepts about the limits of security.'[59] But by January 1990 Gorbachev agreed to German reunification, recognising the collapse of the GDR and anxious to obtain Western economic aid. In February talks on economic and political union began between the two German governments. Baker adeptly pursued a strategy designed to satisfy all the parties. For once he made use of the State Department, which helped him devise the idea of 'two plus four' discussions that would see the two Germanys examine domestic issues while the four occupying powers, Britain, France, the Soviet Union and the United States, would tackle the international questions. Discussion between officials opened on 14 March 1990. The first ministerial meeting was in May. A crucial obstacle was the issue of whether the new united Germany would be a member of NATO. Soviet worries were overcome when the Germans agreed to fund the cost of the departure of the Soviet troops, which eventually totalled $9.5 billion, and to limit their army to 370,000. Germany also accepted its existing frontiers. In September 1990 a Soviet–German Friendship Treaty and the Final Settlement on Germany (ending four-power occupation rights) were signed. All-German elections were held in December and brought a victory for Kohl's CDU party.[60]

The achievement of German unification was succeeded by major arms agreements. A Treaty on Conventional Forces in Europe (as the MBFR talks were renamed in January 1989) was signed in November in Paris by 34 nations. It would apply to military equipment rather than numbers of troops. Each alliance would be allowed a total of 20,000 tanks, no more than 13,300 of them belonging to one country. The meeting also produced the Charter of Paris, a declaration of democratic rights and individual freedoms.[61] By July 1991 agreement was also reached on START in which Washington and Moscow pledged to halve their nuclear warheads to about 6000 by 1998.[62]

The unification of Germany and the CFE and START Treaties were great triumphs for US–Soviet diplomacy and for stability in Europe but contributed to a crisis in the Soviet Union. The Soviet elections in March 1989 saw defeats for many communist candidates. Gorbachev faced pressure for greater change from newly elected Baltic and Caucasian nationalists and from Russian radicals like the former communist Boris Yeltsin. At the same time, these developments and the collapse of communist rule in Eastern Europe worried old guard communists within the party and state bureaucracy, the military and KGB. Lithuania became a test case for the direction which Gorbachev would take when mass protests led to the election of nationalist leaders who announced independence. Military intervention was only avoided by the nationalists' decision to suspend their declaration. In January 1991 Gorbachev approved tough measures against Lithuania to deter Ukraine, Georgia and Armenia from following the Baltic example, but he equivocated between the wish to establish Soviet control and the desire to avoid bloodshed. He proposed a compromise 'Union of Sovereign States' which would allow some autonomy to the republics. This, however, angered the hardliners who launched a coup against him in August. It failed when Yeltsin, appointed Russian President in May 1990, rallied the people against it and persuaded the military not to back the plotters. When Gorbachev returned to Moscow he was the leader of a shell state, as the republics, except the Baltics and Georgia, established a Commonwealth of Independent States. Gorbachev resigned on 25 December and the Soviet Union ceased to exist.

If the disappearance of the USSR marked the definitive end of the Cold War, Baker's Middle East diplomacy in 1990–1 were the first major initiatives of the post-Cold War era, as he succeeded in enlisting Moscow support. He secured Soviet backing for UN condemnation of the Iraqi invasion of Kuwait in August 1990 and for military action in January 1991. In addition, he organised the first direct peace talks between Israel and all its major Arab adversaries. Invitations to the first round of talks, which began in Madrid in October 1991, were issued jointly by United States and the Soviet Union. Further meetings in Washington and Moscow helped to develop the outlines of a Middle East settlement.

Baker stepped down as secretary in August 1992 to take charge of Bush's faltering presidential campaign. The new Secretary of State was Lawrence Eagleburger who served until January 1993 when Bill Clinton took office after defeating Bush in November.

Conclusion

The performances of Haig, Shultz and Baker as secretary reveal the importance of individual talents, personal relations and the mechanisms for policymaking in a successful foreign policy. All three men shared a view of the need to be strong in the face of the Soviet threat, while being ready to negotiate, though Haig seemed to set higher hurdles than Shultz and Baker. Haig did not enjoy good relations with Reagan. He never quite escaped a belief that he understood the problems better than the president, though his grasp was not as great as he imagined. His prospects for a successful term were handicapped by bitter infighting between presidential aides, the NSC, Defense Department and the State Department. Shultz's personal relations with Reagan were much better but he too suffered from the lack of co-ordination in foreign policy-making. Yet he possessed more skill in coping with the inter-agency and personal disagreements and had a real ability for negotiating with the Soviet Union. His achievements are all the more impressive for being accomplished in such difficult domestic circumstances. He had a talent for converting Reagan's general goals into practical agreements, achieving this through adept use of the considerable expertise of the State Department. Shultz and Shevardnadze developed a remarkable level of co-operation. The result was a transformation in international affairs. By 1988 the Cold War was practically over, epitomised by Reagan's statement in Moscow that the 'evil empire' belonged to 'another time', and there had been a major reduction in nuclear arms with the INF agreement and START was almost settled.

Baker's term was also very successful, thanks to the best personal relationship with the president, the most effective foreign policy team, and a talent for deal making. In general, he eschewed reliance on State Department officials, though he benefited from his departmental officials in the negotiations for Germany's unification. He too worked well with Shevardnadze. He might have inherited a favourable situation but built on it very effectively. Tactful diplomacy with the Soviet Union ensured the peaceful collapse of the regimes in Eastern Europe. An equally thoughtful approach resulted in German unification. Baker and Bush were able to go beyond Cold War rivalries and engage the Soviet Union in multilateral diplomacy on Kuwait and the Arab–Israeli question. The achievements of Baker and Shultz, and the limitations of Haig, point to the central importance of a harmony of outlook between president and secretary for successful diplomacy. Reagan and Shultz and Bush and Baker were vital partnerships in one of the most momentous eras in twentieth century international affairs.

Notes

1. Richard Reeves, *Ronald Reagan: The Triumph of Imagination* (New York: Simon & Schuster, 2005), xv; David Mervin, *Ronald Reagan and the American Presidency* (London: Longman, 1990), 217.
2. Gary Wills, *Reagan's America* (London: Heinemann, 1988), 350.
3. Reeves, *Reagan*, 14, 503–4n.
4. Robert D. Schulzinger, *American Diplomacy in the Twentieth Century*, 3rd edn (New York: Oxford University Press, 1994), 333; Alexander Haig, *Caveat: Realism, Reagan, and Foreign Policy* (London: Weidenfeld & Nicolson, 1984), 19.
5. Haig, *Caveat*, 17, 19.
6. Haig, *Caveat*, 269.
7. Reeves, *Reagan*, 111.
8. Caspar Weinberger, *Fighting for Peace* (New York: Warner Books, 1991), 29.
9. Raymond L. Garthoff, *The Great Transition: American-Soviet relations from Nixon to Reagan* (Washington, DC: Brookings, 1994), 21n.
10. Christopher Simpson, *National Security Directives of the Reagan and Bush Administrations* (Boulder, CO: Westview Press, 1995), 9, 19, cited in Reeves, *Reagan*, 30; Garthoff, *The Great Transition*, 16; Haig, *Caveat*, 74–94, 355; Barry Rubin, *Secrets of State* (New York: Oxford University Press, 1985), 206.
11. Rubin, *Secrets of State*, 209.
12. Reeves, *Reagan*, 113.
13. Haig, *Caveat*, 355–7.
14. Reeves, *Reagan*, 31–2; Ronald Reagan, *An American Life* (London: Hutchinson, 1990), 255–6; Haig, *Caveat*, 12, 142–9.
15. Reeves, *Reagan*, 32; *New York Times*, 27 March 1981.
16. Reagan, *American Life*, 254.

17. Haig, *Caveat*, 150–66; Weinberger, *Fighting for Peace*, 81–99; Reeves, *Reagan*, 38–40; Rubin, *Secrets of State*, 209–10.
18. See, for example, Haig's speeches: 'A New Direction in US Foreign Policy', 24 April 1981, in *Department of State Bulletin* 81, no. 2051 (June 1981): 5–7; and 'American Power and Purpose', 27 April 1982, in *Department of State Bulletin* 82, no. 2063 (June 1982): 40–4.
19. Reagan, *American Life*, 270–3 (quotation at 270); Haig, *Caveat*, 110–14.
20. See Geoffrey Smith, *Reagan and Thatcher* (New York: W.W. Norton, 1991).
21. Reagan 'Question-and-Answer Session with Reporters on Foreign and Domestic Issues', 5 April 1982', in Public Papers of the Presidents: Ronald Reagan, 1982, available online at www.reagan.utexas.edu/archives/speeches/1982/40582c.htm.
22. Reagan 'Remarks to a Question-and-Answer Session with Editors and Broadcasters from the Midwestern States', 30 April 1982, in Public Papers of the Presidents: Ronald Reagan, 1982, available at www.reagan.utexas.edu/archives/speeches/1982/430826.htm.
23. Weinberger, *Fighting for Peace*, 203–17.
24. Reeves, *Reagan*, 107; Haig, *Caveat*, 261–302 (quotation at 298); Reagan, *American Life*, 359–62.
25. Reagan, *American Life*, 361; Haig, *Caveat*, 311–15.
26. Rubin, *Secrets of State*, 205.
27. Ibid., 212.
28. Don Oberdorfer, *From the Cold War to a New Era* (Baltimore, MD: Johns Hopkins University Press, 1998), 44–6, 480; Jack F. Matlock, *Reagan and Gorbachev* (New York: Random House, 2004), 25, 321; George P. Shultz, *Turmoil and Triumph* (New York: Charles Scribner's, 1993), 7–37 passim.
29. Shultz, *Turmoil and Triumph*, 9.
30. Shultz, *Turmoil and Triumph*, 6, 8, 10.
31. Shultz, *Turmoil and Triumph*, 12–13, 33–4, 37.
32. Shultz, *Turmoil and Triumph*, 31, 135–45; Margaret Thatcher, *The Downing Street Years* (New York: HarperCollins, 1993), 256.
33. 'White House Announcement on the Development of a Defensive System Against Nuclear Ballistic Missiles', 25 March 1983, www.reagan.utexas.edu/archives/speeches/1983.32583d.htm; Shultz, *Turmoil and Triumph*, 261–4, 266–7; Matlock, *Reagan and Gorbachev*, 61.
34. 'Remarks at the Annual Convention of the National Association of Evangelicals', Orlando, FL, 8 March 1983, www.reagan.utexas.edu/archives/speeches/1983/30883b.htm; Reagan, *American Life*, 568–70.
35. Christopher Andrew and Oleg Gordievsky, *KGB* (London: Hodder & Stoughton, 1990), 488, 501.
36. Reagan, *American Life*, 588–9; 'Address to the Nation and Other Countries on United States-Soviet Relations', 16 January 1984, www.reagan.utexas.edu/archives/speeches/1984/11684a.htm.
37. Shultz, 'Statement at the CDE', Stockholm, 17 January 1984, in *Department of State Bulletin* 84, no. 2084 (March 1984): 34.
38. 'Address to 39th Session of UN General Assembly', New York, 24 September 1984, www.reagan.utaxas.edu/archives.speeches/1984/92484a.htm; Reagan, *American Life*, 605.
39. Matlock, *Reagan and Gorbachev*, 101–02; Reagan, *American Life*, 572.
40. Shultz, *Turmoil and Triumph*, 529–32.
41. Matlock, *Reagan and Gorbachev*, 130–1; Shultz, *Turmoil and Triumph*, 702.
42. See National Security Archive Briefing Book No. 172, Geneva 1985, www.nsarchive.org.
43. See National Security Archive Briefing Book No. 203, Reykjavik 1986, www.nsarchive.org; Reagan, *American Life*, 642–79.
44. Thatcher, *Downing Street Years*, 465–6, 471.
45. National Security Archive Briefing Book No. 238, Washington 1988, www.nsarchive.org.
46. National Security Archive Briefing Book No. 251, Moscow 1987, www.nsarchive.org; Reagan, *American Life*, 705, 713–14.
47. Shultz, *Turmoil and Triumph*, 1015.
48. Oberdorfer, *Cold War to New Era*, 480.
49. Matlock, *Reagan and Gorbachev*, 321.
50. Igor Korchilov, *Translating History* (London: Aurum, 1997), 109–10. See also the jocular exchanges at the Moscow summit: NSA Briefing Book No. 251, document 21, Memorandum of Discussion, 31 May 1988.

51. David Mervin, *George Bush and the Guardianship Presidency* (Basingstoke: Macmillan, 1998), 21–2; Philip Zelikow and Condoleezza Rice, *Germany Unified, Europe Transformed* (Cambridge, MA: Harvard University Press, 1995), 20–1.
52. Zelikow and Rice, *Germany Unified*, 21–2; Mervin, *Bush*, 160–2; James A. Baker, *Work Hard, Study ... and Keep Out of Politics* (New York: G.P. Putnam's, 2006), 17–26, 283; George Bush and Brent Scowcroft, *A World Transformed* (New York: Knopf, 1998), 18.
53. Baker, *Work*, 281–3; Oberdorfer, *Cold War to New Era*, 336.
54. James A. Baker, *The Politics of Diplomacy* (New York: G.P. Putnam's, 1995), 29–32; Baker, *Work*, 284.
55. Thatcher, *Downing Street Years*, 783; Bush and Scowcroft, *World Transformed*, 69–70.
56. Oberdorfer, *Cold War to New Era*, 348.
57. Zelikow and Rice, *Germany Unified*, 81–99.
58. Baker, *Politics of Diplomacy*, 167–71; Bush and Scowcroft, *World Transformed*, 160–74.
59. Thatcher, *Downing Street Years*, 783–4, 792; Jacques Attali, *Verbatim III* (Paris: Fayard, 1995), 241; Robert McMahon, *The Cold War* (Oxford: Oxford University Press, 2003), 166.
60. Baker, *Politics of Diplomacy*, 195–216, 230–2, 237–47, 250–4; Bush and Scowcroft, *World Transformed*, 182–204, 232–78, 281–3, 290–301.
61. Text at www.osce.org/documents/doclib/1990/11/13752_en.pdf. See also Baker, *Politics of Diplomacy*, 473–4.
62. Text at http://dtirp.dtra.mil/tic/START/start1.htm.

The scholar statesman: Henry Kissinger

Dieter Dettke

Georgetown University, Washington, DC, USA

Statesmen become statesmen as much by the power of their office and the force of their personality and vision as by the circumstances and conditions of their time. Rarely does history allow men to join the rank of statesman from a position of derivative power. Metternich, Castlereagh, Bismarck and Disraeli, the great statesmen of the nineteenth century, whose policies Henry Kissinger had studied and admired so much, were able to act on their own visions and perceptions of the *raison d'état* from positions of great authority without major domestic concerns. They were less restricted by their respective domestic environment and public opinion at home and abroad than statesmen of the first and the second half of the twentieth century. When Kissinger arrived in the corridors of power in Washington in the late 1960s, American foreign policy was in a profound crisis over Vietnam. Initially very little attention was paid to the country's policies towards Europe and Washington's relations with its transatlantic allies. After all, the global power configuration had begun to shift to the disadvantage of the United States. The more US military forces appeared to be bogged down in Indochina, the more American global pre-eminence was challenged politically as well as economically. Mutual vulnerability became the defining condition for diplomacy in the nuclear age. Regional and local conflicts generated more dilemmas than opportunities and both superpowers saw their freedom to act militarily beyond their borders severely limited.

Kissinger's greatest achievement under these conditions was the statesmanship he demonstrated in spite of the Vietnam War and in particular with regard to East–West relations in Europe and elsewhere. He received the Nobel Peace Prize for the Paris Peace Agreement. But what he achieved through negotiations was hardly the comprehensive peace in Indochina he attempted to bring home from Paris. The agreement barely covered the unilateral nature of the US withdrawal and it did not prevent the communist takeover of South Vietnam, Laos and Cambodia. His most important contribution to modern statecraft in the twentieth century was the profound transformation of great power relations at a time of fierce political competition and ideological conflict, the creation of principles to reduce the risk of nuclear war between the United States and the Soviet Union and other agreements with the Soviet Union as well as with China at a critical stage in the development of East–West relations. Indirectly, he thus contributed to a peaceful end of the Cold War.

War, domestic upheaval and limited authority

That Henry Kissinger, as a German-born Jew who fled the Nazi regime with his parents in 1938 when he was 15 years old, would ever become a prominent scholar, let alone a Secretary of State was extremely unlikely. Never before in American history had a foreign-born US citizen become Secretary of State. Nixon left no doubt that he planned to be his own foreign minister. 'I have always thought', he declared in an interview in 1967 before he became President, 'this country could run itself domestically without a President. All you need is a competent Cabinet to run the country at home. You need a President for foreign policy; no Secretary of State is really important; the President makes foreign policy.'[1]

What propelled Kissinger into a unique political role first in the Nixon and then in the Ford Administration and ultimately into statesmanship was not the office he occupied. There were not many US Secretaries of State who history has recognised as statesmen. Among the 55 US Secretaries of State before Henry Kissinger, probably only Thomas Jefferson, James Madison, James Monroe and John Quincy Adams are recognised as America's finest. They all became Presidents after serving as US Secretary of State. George C. Marshall and Dean Acheson also stand out as chief architects of the post-Second World War international order. Truman had no difficulty allowing them to take on prominent roles of their own and grant them full authority. Kissinger's relationship with President Nixon was more complicated. By any standard it was a very special relationship and propelled Kissinger as Nixon's chief foreign policy adviser into a position of great power and influence precisely at the time when the President began to lose support and credibility over the Watergate scandal. As a result of the loss of presidential authority and without trying to benefit from Nixon's downfall, Kissinger moved into a position of extraordinary influence over the entire foreign policy decision-making process. This was accomplished in spite of his initial dependency on the President he served as an adviser. It is very likely that without Watergate and with a full two-term presidency, Nixon would have overshadowed any other foreign policy-maker in his administration. As a result of Watergate and against Nixon's intentions and desires,[2] Kissinger's role was catapulted into prominence and ultimately pre-eminence to the same degree that Nixon's authority decreased.[3]

In his memoirs Kissinger opened the chapter about becoming Secretary of State with a revealing discussion of the crisis of the executive at the start of Nixon's second term:

> One of the more cruel torments of Nixon's Watergate purgatory was my emergence as the preeminent figure in foreign policy. Richard Nixon wanted nothing so much as to go down in history as peacemaker. He had organized his government so that he would be perceived at the front of foreign policy, in conception and execution. To this end he had insisted on launching all major international initiatives from the White House; he had excluded the State Department and Secretary of State William P. Rogers relentlessly, and at times humiliatingly, from key decisions.[4]

Of course, Kissinger benefited from this arrangement in a major way and he was no slouch himself when it came to bureaucratic infighting. In his role as National Security Adviser he had unique access to the President. His office cleared all the cables instructing diplomats abroad.[5] 'All this', Kissinger wrote, 'placed Secretary Rogers in an impossible position. If he approved a telegram or option before it was passed to the White House, he might see his judgment overruled in full view of his own subordinates. If he waited until I had stated my view, he was in the position of either rubber-stamping or challenging what for all he knew had already been approved by the President.'[6] In the relationship between Kissinger and Rogers the conflict was built-in and Kissinger was in the stronger position. It was a matter of time before Rogers gave up, opening the way for Kissinger to take over.

Nixon's strong interest in foreign policy made Kissinger not only a logical but also a necessary choice.[7] In a way Kissinger had already passed the zenith of his power when he moved from the White House to the State Department but remained in control of his White House office in order to avoid the bureaucratic stalemate that had characterised the Kissinger-Rogers relationship. In Kissinger's own perception and as he described it in his memoirs, he appeared to be an ideal National Security Adviser for Nixon insofar as he seemed 'ideally suited for a role behind the scenes. As a Harvard professor, I was without a political base; as a naturalised citizen, speaking with an accent, I was thought incapable of attracting publicity; in any event, since I was a member of the President's entourage, my access to the media could be controlled by the White House.'[8] With no political base of his own and no special access to the President through friendship or previous close cooperation he appeared to be destined for a role as supporting actor at best and not the star that he later became. Kissinger was much closer to the Governor of New York, Nelson Rockefeller, who represented the liberal wing of the Republican Party and was not a political soul mate but a political rival for Nixon. Kissinger was quite critical of the ardent and ultimate anti-Communist Richard Nixon, at one time even characterizing him as 'paranoic' and 'dangerous'.[9] And yet Nixon, as President Elect in 1968, hit it off well from the beginning after he first met with Kissinger in preparing his foreign policy agenda.

Nixon took over the presidency from Lyndon Johnson with the determination to reform what he saw as a dysfunctional system of foreign policy decision-making. He wanted a new decision-making structure with the White House at the centre and the rest of the administration in a supporting role. Kissinger's writings pointed in the same direction. Already in his book *A World Restored* he saw the spirit of policy and that of bureaucracy as 'diametrically opposed'[10] and he continued: 'The essence of bureaucracy is its quest for safety; its success is calculability. Profound policy thrives on perpetual creation, on a constant redefinition of goals.'[11] In his book *The Necessity for Choice*, Kissinger depicts the bureaucracy even more pointedly as an obstacle to creativity.[12]

Kissinger and Nixon had a similar preference for keeping foreign policy decisions out of the hands of the bureaucracy and with the smallest possible number of participants. He made no secret of his preference for keeping decisions secret and the only way he thought 'secrecy can be kept is to exclude from the making of the decision all those who are theoretically charged with carrying it out'.[13] As a bureaucrat himself and in the Office of National Security Adviser he did not hesitate to put his theoretical insights into practice and created a highly centralised and hierarchical bureaucratic structure under the NSC system. The new system not only assured the full White House authority over the foreign policy-making process; it also institutionalised Kissinger and his NSC as the centrepiece of the American foreign policy apparatus, eloquently characterised by an insider as a system where 'Everybody reports to Kissinger, and only Kissinger reports to the President'.[14]

In his famous interview with Oriana Fallaci Kissinger added another dimension to his and Nixon's preference for secrecy: the necessity to 'act alone', the lone cowboy image which subsequently caused much criticism, particularly from Jimmy Carter when he was running for President. The image of lonesome foreign policy decision-making ran deep against the fundamental American principle of openness and transparency. The other issue was human rights. Kissinger took a very cautious position on human rights towards the Soviet Union most visibly demonstrated in Ford's refusal to meet Alexander Solzhenitsyn in the White House. In retrospect, Kissinger saw the decision not to schedule a meeting with the writer he admired deeply as a mistake.[15] Détente was now being castigated as appeasement in the US domestic debate giving Carter a popular issue for his campaign in the 1976 presidential elections.

Much of the criticism levelled against Kissinger had its origin in his and Nixon's preference for this secrecy. In fact, the first question Senator Fulbright as Chairman of the Committee on Foreign Relations asked Kissinger at his nomination hearing was not about a substantive foreign policy issue but about his role in the White House wiretapping between early 1969 and 1971. Kissinger's answer was that the system was put in place by the FBI and the Attorney General because of the many leaks that occurred from White House sources on major policy issues. In his defence he argued that as far as he was able to judge the procedure met the legal requirements for such action.[16] In spite of the extraordinary length of time of the nomination hearings – six hearings between 7 September and 17 September 1973 – Kissinger's Senate confirmation went rather smoothly ending with a strong bipartisan support for his nomination. In the nomination Hearing report the Senate concluded that 'Mr. Kissinger's role in the wiretapping of 17 Government officials and newsmen did not constitute grounds to bar his confirmation as Secretary of State'.[17]

A cloud of suspicion remained and although Kissinger managed to keep himself out of the centre of the Watergate scandal, his image did not benefit from the violation of public trust the scandal brought into the open. In fact rumours that it was Kissinger himself who ordered the wiretapping on some of his associates – Anthony Lake, Morton Halperin and Helmut Sonnenfeldt were among those mentioned most often in the media in the summer of 1974[18] – were partially stimulated by remarks attributed by White House Counsel John Dean III to President Nixon. Based on a recording obtained by the House Judiciary Committee with a passage that was deleted by the White House, Nixon allegedly said that 'I know that he asked that it be done. And I assumed that it was.'[19] Hard evidence about Kissinger's direct implication was never found including in the legal suits brought against him by Morton Halperin and Anthony Lake.[20]

Kissinger's real problem was not the degree of his legal entanglement in wiretapping. It was the burden that he had to carry as the President's alter ego in foreign policy. As much as the media admired Kissinger as a 'prodigiously intelligent, articulate, talented, witty, captivating, and imposing man',[21] as the New Yorker magazine put it, they could not separate the grand design and the diplomatic creativity of the man who, as many acknowledged, had 'the makings of a great Secretary of State' from the secret actions of the Nixon Administration that the Watergate scandal revealed in the middle of an agonizing debate over Vietnam. Nixon's breach of public trust became Kissinger's burden, too. The *New Yorker* magazine article argued:

> Together, they had established relations with China, improved our relations with Russia, and successfully completed the first phase of SALT – and for these immense achievements most Americans are grateful. Together, also, they had planned the undisclosed bombing of Cambodia in 1969 and 1970; they had initiated the unauthorized wiretapping of members of Kissinger's staff and of newsmen in 1969; they had planned the invasion of Cambodia in 1970; they had planned the use of American air power to support the invasion of Laos in 1971; in 1971, too, they had 'tilted' in favor of Pakistan in the India-Pakistani War, though at the time Pakistan was carrying out mass murder of Bengali subjects in East Pakistan; in early 1972, they had planned the mining and blockade of North Vietnamese harbors; later in 1972 they had planned the 'Christmas bombing' of North Vietnam – all this done in secrecy, and without congressional consent.[22]

There was an enormous admiration – some even spoke about a Kissinger cult – for the man who provided American power with a sense of purpose at a time of profound political divisions and self-doubt. His new grand design of launching an 'era of negotiations' and engaging the Soviet Union and China in a dialogue was extremely popular. Because of him, foreign policy lost some of its earlier elitist character. His bold vision of a new 'structure of peace' that included America's ideological opponents electrified the American people and freed them of their sense of frustration about a distant war that had lasted for too long. But even those who were sceptical that Kissinger's policies would achieve their stated aims, for example, Hans Morgenthau, conceded that 'they have brought about a drastic transformation of world politics'.[23] Morgenthau saw in Kissinger 'the best endowed Secretary of State the United States has had since Dean Acheson ... and one of the six or so best Secretaries of State the United States has had altogether'.[24]

Kissinger's foreign policy philosophy

No one could question Henry Kissinger's foreign policy credentials when he first became President Nixon's National Security Adviser in 1969 and then the 56th US Secretary of State on 22 September 1973 serving until January 1977 when Jimmy Carter moved into the White House. Immediately after the Nixon administration took over from its Democratic predecessors and had forged an unprecedented relationship with America's Cold War opponent on the basis of wide ranging treaties including an Agreement on the Prevention of Nuclear War (PNW), National Security Advisor Kissinger had already negotiated limitations on nuclear strategic arms with the Soviet Union (SALT). He had also opened a surprisingly warm political dialogue with China creating a new triangular relationship in an effort to allow the United States to extricate itself from Vietnam. Based on these initiatives Kissinger then conducted peace negotiations with North Vietnam that ushered in the Agreement on Ending the War and Restoring Peace in Vietnam on 27 January 1973.

By the time Kissinger was sworn in as Secretary of State he already had such an unusually high standing as the key foreign policy-maker in the eyes of the media and the American public in general that as Kissinger saw it 'both Nixon and I knew there was no other choice'.[25] *Time* magazine had made Nixon and Kissinger 'Men of the Year' in the first issue of 1972 and given the profound unpopularity of the Vietnam War both in the United States as well as in Europe and the rest of the world, Kissinger's diplomacy provided the last best hope for America to make up for the loss of prestige – if not even power – as a result of the morass that the war effort had created.

Kissinger was a historian and political scientist first before he became a statesman. He came into office with more experience and in theory better prepared to exercise power than most secretaries of state before him. What also prepared him for the monumental tasks before him was that he was a big thinker conceptualizing the international system in terms of overarching structures of peace and conflict and defining the role of statesman guided by the example of Bismarck as the 'genius who proposed to constrain the contending forces, both domestic and foreign, by manipulating their antagonisms'.[26]

Deeply interested in history and philosophy and intimately familiar in particular with the writings of Hegel and Kant but also with classical philosophy in general, Kissinger was comfortable with the broad concepts of power, justice, order and legitimacy. It speaks volumes about the profound ambitions of Kissinger as a thinker to take on a subject such as 'The Meaning of History: Reflections on Spengler, Toynbee and Kant' as his undergraduate thesis at Harvard University. In academic circles he was mostly known as a realist in the tradition of Hans Morgenthau. But he was often misunderstood as just a realist and not enough as someone who would also be capable to embrace the other great tradition of American foreign policy thinking: idealism. It was not only, as suggested by Walter Isaacson, a morally questionable diplomacy based on European style power politics that drove Kissinger's foreign policy thinking.[27] What is not always understood is his profound commitment to achieve a synthesis between idealism and realism.

In essence he wanted to create a better balance between acceptance of the status quo, on the one hand, and the transcendence of its limits, on the other.[28] Kissinger concluded from Bismarck's foreign policy that the best use of power is to create incentives for restraint in your opponent's behaviour. Taking Bismarck's cautious policy as a model he would argue, for example, that 'the nemesis of power is that except in the hands of a master, reliance on it is more likely to produce a contest at arms than self-restraint'.[29] Conversely, in the same line of dialectical thinking it was his firm belief that 'Whenever peace – conceived as the avoidance of war – has been the primary objective of a power or a group of powers, the international system has been at the mercy of the most ruthless member of the international community.'[30] In the end both left and right remained sceptical as the tension between his willingness to accept realities while at the same time trying to transcend their limits was never fully clarified. In a Hegelian sense, of course, it cannot be clarified; it can only be reconciled on a higher level of development which in his thinking would be the creation of a new legitimate system of stability. And this was precisely what he was trying to achieve with the concept of a 'new structure of peace'.

Kissinger's core beliefs reflect not only Metternichian conservatism as many falsely concluded from his Harvard dissertation and masterwork on Metternich and Castlereagh. It is also Bismarckian activism, creativity and the will to change the status quo that served as his historical model and that he highlighted in his study on Bismarck published under the title *The White Revolutionary: Reflections on Bismarck*.[31] For him these two strands of statecraft can be reconciled in a legitimate order of stability. Legitimacy is key in Kissinger's thinking. As he pointed out in *A World Restored*, stability does not result 'from a quest for peace, but from a generally accepted legitimacy'.[32] 'Legitimacy should not be confused with justice. It means no more than an international agreement about the nature of workable arrangements and about the permissible aims and methods of foreign policy.'[33] Simply put, the normative implication of this concept of stability was behaviour in support of a common international framework such as an understanding to prevent a nuclear Armageddon.[34] In this respect Kissinger followed Kant and saw nuclear war as the *summum malum* and the prevention of a nuclear holocaust as the highest moral imperative.[35] He never believed that goodwill alone could transform a revolutionary power into a status quo power and often warned against the 'false atmosphere of euphoria and trust'.[36]

The proper lesson for Vietnam for him was that 'ending the war honourably is essential for the peace of the world. Any other solution may unloose forces that would complicate the prospects for international order.'[37] Munich and the disastrous consequences of appeasement were still on his mind even as he was willing to ratify the nuclear status quo with America's Cold War opponent and to accept Mao's China as a new pillar of international security.

Here his own thinking converged with that of Richard Nixon. Just like Nixon, Kissinger assumed that for a long time one of the legacies of Vietnam for US foreign policy will be a deep reluctance to become involved again in any major regional intervention. But both were willing to invest American military power and economic resources in demonstrating to the Soviet Union and China that America would not simply give up its foreign policy commitments. Withdrawing unilaterally from Vietnam would send the wrong signal to US allies everywhere and more importantly, it would embolden the Soviet Union and China in their revolutionary drive to create more Vietnams. Kissinger firmly believed that without insisting on a negotiated settlement for Vietnam, his position vis-à-vis the Soviet Union and China would become weaker. The result would be less willingness on their part to engage in the new 'structure of peace' that he had in mind.

In his first Report to Congress on US Foreign Policy, Nixon outlined the new structure of peace:

> The post war period has ended ....Western Europe and Japan have recovered their economic strength, their political vitality, and their national self-confidence .... Once many feared that they would become simply a battleground of cold war rivalry and fertile ground for Communist penetration. But this fear misjudged their pride in their national identities and their determination to preserve their newly won sovereignty .... The power of individual Communist nations has grown, but international Communist unity has been shattered ... by the powerful forces of nationalism.

And finally the report mainly authored by Henry Kissinger said that 'Both the Soviet Union and the United states have acquired the ability to inflict unacceptable damage on the other, no matter which strikes first. There can be no gain and certainly no victory for the power that provokes a thermonuclear exchange'.[38] Nuclear weapons had changed the equation for a classical game of power politics. The new element for superpower rivalry was that hostilities could spin out of control and take on a catastrophic dimension that needed to be contained in the interest of all parties concerned. In Kissinger's view the US, the Soviet Union and China had

> to deal with the root fact of the contemporary situation – that we and the Soviet Union, and we and the Chinese, are ideological adversaries, but we are bound together by one basic fact: that none of us can survive a nuclear war and therefore it is in our national interest to try to reduce those hostilities that are bureaucratic vestiges or that are simply not rooted in overwhelming national concerns.[39]

The evolution of a new foreign policy concept: triangulation and the Nixon Doctrine

In its most elementary form the Nixon Doctrine was a doctrine of devolution, a concept of encouraging regional assertiveness within the framework of American security alliances. It was not a 'retreat from empire',[40] but an attempt to adjust alliance structures to the reality of political multipolarity. Kissinger's thinking shaped the Nixon Doctrine just as much as the man whose name it carries. Long before he joined the Nixon Administration when he was still Governor Rockefeller's foreign policy adviser he argued that

> the United States is no longer in a position to operate programs globally; it has to encourage them. It can no longer impose its preferred solutions; it must seek to evoke it. In the forties and fifties, we offered remedies; in the late sixties and seventies our role will have to be to contribute to a structure that will foster the initiative of others. We are a superpower physically, but our designs can be meaningful only if they generate willing cooperation. We can continue to contribute to defense and positive programs, but we must seek to encourage and not to stifle a sense of local responsibility. Our contribution should not be the sole or principal effort, but it should make the difference between success and failure.[41]

On the basis of this analysis the key question was, of course, how to restore American power. The basic principle of withdrawal was already established by the Johnson administration and the electoral mandate of the 1968 elections was clear in one respect. Whoever would be in power after the elections had one paramount objective: to bring the Vietnam War to an end. Nixon's and Kissinger's advantage over their Democratic predecessors was that they had a better chance to chart out a new course of American foreign policy. Most importantly, they were willing to give the Soviet Union and China a stake in the new post-Vietnam world order they were about to initiate. Where Johnson's summit diplomacy had failed in the ill-conceived 1967 Glasboro Summit in New Jersey,[42]

Nixon and Kissinger could start all over again once the negative repercussions of the Soviet intervention in Czechoslovakia in August 1968 began to fade.

Clearly the most striking phenomenon was the changing level of strategic forces between the US and the Soviet Union. Between early 1967 and late 1969 the strategic offensive force level of the United States basically remained stable with 1054 ICBMs and 656 SLBMs; the number of strategic bombers even slightly declined from 650 to 525 and the number of SLBMs had grown moderately from 576 to 656. On the other hand the number of Soviet offensive nuclear weapons increased dramatically: ICBM's from 500 in 1967 to 1140 in 1969 and SLBMs from 100 to 185. Only the number of strategic bombers remained stable with 145 in 1969 as opposed to 150 in 1967, but the overall number of Soviet nuclear weapons doubled from 750 in 1967 to 1470 in 1969.[43]

The Soviet Union in spite of its impressive nuclear achievements had its own reasons to engage in superpower diplomacy. One was to shake off the stigma of the use of force against its own ally Czechoslovakia; another, more important one, to seek Western economic and political cooperation in its growing competition with China. Fighting between Soviet and Chinese forces along the Ussuri River in early 1969 unveiled a profound split within the communist world that also diminished, at least indirectly, Soviet power and prestige within its alliance system. In fact, the Soviet leadership more than once in the 'era of negotiations' tried to effectively achieve a US–Soviet condominium over Europe and Asia. In Vladivostok, Breshnew aimed in that direction suggesting to President Ford that 'we should become allies in the field of nuclear weapons, and then everything else would fall into place . . . . Then there would be no problem about nuclear weapons since we would be allies and our respective allies would also be reassured.'[44] From Kissinger's perspective a superpower condominium would have deprived American diplomacy of a crucial asset in influencing Soviet behaviour and could have even be used as a carte blanche for the Soviet Union to deal with the growing threat from China by taking out its nuclear potential.

Two other crucial developments in the strategic relationship between the two superpowers added concerns about the future of stability in the nuclear age: the development of missile defence systems, on the one hand, and on the other, as far as offensive nuclear systems were concerned, the potential of MIRV technology. Flight testing for MRVs on Minuteman III ICBMs and the Poseidon SLMBs began in mid August 1968 and already at the end of August the Soviet Union followed with MRV tests of its SS-9 ICBMs.[45] The ability to put up to 10 times as many and more warheads on each intercontinental missile in the arsenal of nuclear weapons of each superpower would amount to a massive increase of offensive nuclear capabilities. Unrestrained such a development could bring the world closer to what the scholar Henry Kissinger considered to be the danger of a nuclear Armageddon. The technologically logical solution to this problem was missile defence and both superpowers proceeded with the missile defence technology available at the time: the United States with its preparations for deployment of Sentinel and the Soviet Union with its Galosh system.[46]

Sentinel, originally a nationwide missile defence concept was later changed to Safeguard, a system to protect America's land based intercontinental missiles as the heart of America's nuclear power from a possible Soviet first strike capability. Such a theoretical possibility could have resulted from Soviet advances in multiple warhead technology. For Kissinger and Nixon Safeguard was the safest way to enhance US deterrence capability without threatening the retaliatory capability of the Soviet Union.[47] The fundamental problem they were facing was the danger of a political stalemate between the United States and the Soviet Union and possibly also the loss of the diplomatic initiative on a regional level at a time of increasing strategic instability as a result of technological developments. Under these conditions it was particularly Kissinger's thinking that helped to overcome the growing limitations of American power through diplomatic creativity. What he recognised and understood better than most other foreign policy and military experts at the time was that in order to address both the risk of strategic instability between the United States and the Soviet Union as well as the danger of losing the diplomatic initiative, it was necessary to transform the antagonistic character of the superpower relationship. During the Cuban Missile Crisis both countries came close to a full-blown nuclear confrontation and realised how quickly this situation could have degenerated to include Berlin and even into a global confrontation. Kissinger saw an opportunity in the emerging commonality of interests – albeit for different reasons – in limiting strategic arms competition. He was willing to move both superpowers towards a distinct bilateralism that could be used as an instrument to bring about a more advantageous regional diplomatic constellation for America's growing dilemmas in Indochina and in other areas.

Key to the success of this strategy was what became known as 'triangulation': the management of relations with the Soviet Union under the conditions of nuclear parity with an aim of reducing or preventing possible Soviet actions in regional conflicts such as Vietnam or the Middle East while at the same time using the growing Soviet concern over China's rise to great power status on the basis of the Chinese nuclear ambitions and China's considerable economic dynamism to consolidate cooperation. With the benefit of hindsight Kissinger's critics pointed out that détente might have artificially prolonged the life of the Soviet Union. Robert Kagan, for example, charges that Kissinger in reality assumed the Soviet Union would be the permanent superpower opponent and did not even try a winning strategy in the Cold War.[48] In Kagan's view only Ronald Reagan turned things around with a clear policy of confrontation and won the Cold War. In reality, Kissinger's own thinking was less accommodating and Ronald Reagan's policy was not only confrontational either. Reagan went quite far in his arms control policy and efforts of nuclear risk reduction. For Kissinger détente was 'designed to control a relationship conceived as adversarial'.[49] It was not, as he later emphasised, 'to conjure up a nirvana from which all tensions had automatically been removed'.[50] Kissinger's right-wing enemies, therefore, could not be more off the mark.[51] Nuclear parity should not be confused with weakness. As much as Kissinger ultimately wanted to transcend the Cold War, he remained convinced that the communist system was clearly inferior and that the West had the better chances in a competition between the systems. 'If performance is any criterion, the contest between freedom and communism .... has been won by the industrial democracies'[52] he declared in 1976.

In his view the crucial instrument to direct détente policy in the right direction from a Western perspective was 'linkage'. 'Linkage' politics in the context of a new global understanding between the United States, on the one hand, and the United States and China, on the other, became necessary first and foremost as a result of domestic expectations. But it was also an in-built mechanism in the sense that détente required mutual adjustment of behaviour. This has been most forcefully expressed in the 'Basic Principles of US–Soviet Relations' signed on 29 May 1972.[53] Key stipulations of these principles were:

> that there is no alternative to conducting ... mutual relations on the basis of peaceful coexistence;
> that they will do their utmost to avoid military confrontations and to prevent the outbreak of nuclear war;
> that they will always exercise restraint in their mutual relations, and will be prepared to negotiate and settle differences by peaceful means.

It is important to note that détente did indeed generate a number of agreements with the Soviet Union on a bilateral level as well as multilateral agreements. In addition to SALT and the Basic Principles it is foremost the ABM treaty that must be seen as a cornerstone of nuclear stability between the United States and the Soviet Union for a number of years. Although no longer in force today, it was a useful instrument to curb potentially aggressive nuclear ambitions of the Soviet regime before its demise. The larger question whether détente helped in the process of implosion of the Soviet system in the end or whether it artificially prolonged the life of a system that was condemned to failure by history anyway, is an open question. Only history can make that judgement. It is clear – and dissident movements in the former Soviet Union would acknowledge this – that as a result of détente (in particular on the basis of the Helsinki process which resulted from the CSCE Agreements), greater access of the West and Western institutions to communist regimes in Eastern Europe did generate and encourage internal pressure of peaceful change. Détente could well have made the difference between a largely peaceful implosion of the Soviet Empire as it unfolded before and after the fall of the Berlin Wall, as opposed to a potentially much more violent explosion.

For many Europeans, in particular for Germans, it is an article of faith that détente paved the way for German unification as a peaceful process. 'Linkage politics' worked here in the sense that without détente on the superpower level there would have been no chance to improve inner German relations and the situation in the divided city of Berlin. It was not unusual at the time to argue that with all the bilateral and multilateral East–West treaties such as Ostpolitik, the inner German treaties, the German treaties with Poland and Czechoslovakia, the ABM Treaty, MBFR, later named CFE, CSCE, later named OSCE, the Berlin Agreement, SALT I and SALT II, the Agreement on the Prevention of Nuclear War, detente amounted to the equivalent of a peace agreement.[54] Even if the effect in historical terms was more a 'time out' in the long struggle between East and West rather than a permanent structure of peace, it allowed the West to put together a better foundation for the time left in the struggle between East and West.

The linkage between Ostpolitik and SALT and between Ostpolitik and the Berlin Agreement was in many ways essential for the success of both American and European detente: In political terms SALT ratified the nuclear status quo between the superpowers and Ostpolitik – also in political terms, not legally, because the right of peaceful change was explicitly preserved – ratified the territorial status quo in Europe.[55] It was necessary to recognise both in order to be able to transcend the limitations of the stalemate that had previously existed. Nothing was given up in the act of recognition that wasn't already given up in reality as a result of the military confrontation and the great danger of unacceptable damage and devastation should war ever break out again over territorial demands. Kissinger was seriously concerned about the explosion of technology and the number of warheads on both sides if there would be no arms control agreement following the SALT I Agreement with its limited duration of five years. He doubted that 'the tendency to measure the strategic balance by numbers of delivery vehicles in a period when the numbers of warheads on both sides were much more worrisome'[56] would help to maintain stability in the nuclear age. This caused him to exclaim after Vladivostok: 'What in the name of God is strategic superiority? What is the significance of it, politically, militarily, operationally, at these levels of numbers? What do you do with it?'[57] Kissinger was more radical in his thinking about nuclear weapons and as we know today, he was willing to consider a world without nuclear weapons.[58]

For the Soviet Union détente policy was not only arms control and the basic principles of restraint and cooperation; it was access to Western technology. The crucial instrument from the Soviet perspective was Most Favored Nation Status on the basis of American trade legislation as it was envisioned in the US–Soviet Trade Agreement. The American Congress and in particular Senator Henry Jackson put enormous emphasis on tying MFN status for the Soviet Union to an increased number of Soviet Jews being able to leave the Soviet Union. The fact is that Moscow, under Congressional pressure and US government persuasion, changed its emigration policy and step by step increased Jewish emigration from approximately 400 in 1968 to nearly 35,000 in 1973.[59] When the expectation of emigration was finally made official policy by Congressional legislation, the delicate deal with the Soviet Union that Kissinger had put together collapsed. The Soviet Union finally rejected the very trade agreement it was seeking because of the Jackson–Vanik amendment and Jewish emigration decreased dramatically.[60] It turned out to be impossible to keep linkage politics free of contradictions.

Extricating America from Vietnam

Vietnam is in many ways the most problematic legacy of Kissinger's diplomacy. The war in Vietnam led to a profound political and moral crisis in America. Toward the end of the Johnson Administration America appeared to be divided as a nation and exhausted as a society by a war that the American people were no longer willing to support. Nixon and Kissinger believed that the crisis emanated primarily from a 'collapse of confidence'[61] at home and abroad rather than a lack of resources. In order to restore American power the liquidation of the Vietnam conflict was not only unavoidable; it was prerequisite. Kissinger always thought that it was a mistake and an aberration of the policy of containment to make the outcome of the Vietnam conflict a test case for the overall confrontation between East and West. In his essay on 'Central Issues on American Foreign Policy' for the 1968 edition of the Brookings Institution's Agenda for the Nation he criticised America's 'undifferentiated globalism' in the past and argued in favour of a concept that would correspond to the new reality of a world that was bipolar militarily but multipolar politically.[62] He wanted to remain focused on the central issue of preserving American power in the long run and winning the ultimate test of American power: the political, military, economic and ideological struggle between East and West.

Paramount in any effort to conceive a new approach in American foreign policy-making was the task to put an end to the Vietnam conflict. But such an end as both Nixon and Kissinger saw it had to be achieved without humiliation. 'Our defeat and humiliation in South Vietnam without question', Nixon declared, 'would promote recklessness in the councils of those great powers who have not yet abandoned their goals of world conquest.'[63] Writing before he joined the US administration Kissinger had also warned that 'However fashionable it is to ridicule the terms "credibility" or "prestige", they are not empty phrases; other nations can gear their actions to ours only if they can count on our steadiness.'[64] In his article in *Foreign Affairs* in January 1969 written well before the Nixon Administration took over from the Johnson Administration on 20 January 1969, Kissinger also emphasised how important it was for the United States that a solution to the Vietnam conflict had to be the result of a negotiated agreement with North Vietnam and at the same time the beginning of new international environment, a new 'structure of peace' as he liked to call it scholarly, that would give the Soviet Union and China a stake in maintaining the stability of the international system of the future. 'Ending the war honorably is essential for the peace of the world. Any other solution may unloose forces that would complicate the prospects for international order.'[65]

The main strategic concept to achieve an honourable peace was 'Vietnamization'. But 'Vietnamization' as a strategy was never a credible way to an autonomous South Vietnam not to speak about the democratic legitimacy of the South. That America was on its way out was no secret to North Vietnam and Kissinger's task as a statesman was further undermined by the beginning of American troop reductions while the negotiating process was still in its initial phase. The only bargaining power left in the hands of the United States was 'to make continuation of the war a greater risk than a settlement would be'.[66] Under these conditions the American assumption was that peace in the end would be the result of a process between North and South Vietnam. But that South Vietnam would be able to survive as an American ally was anything but realistic. Kissinger knew that this objective was unobtainable and it was clear to him as well as to his North Vietnamese counterpart that given the domestic environment in the United States, American military power on the ground had little currency at the bargaining table no matter how artful the negotiating strategy was conceived. He acknowledged himself that during the peace talks it became obvious that North Vietnam had no intention of withdrawing its own forces from the South. For North Vietnam the only issue was the withdrawal of American forces from the South and from Indochina altogether. In other words, Hanoi 'would be satisfied only with victory'.[67]

The Vietnam peace agreement was not meant to be a guarantee for the future of South Vietnam as an independent country.[68] Only if the United States would have been willing to do what it ultimately wanted to avoid: to prop up the South indefinitely, could South Vietnamese independence have been maintained. What the American people were not willing to do was to guarantee the existence of a regime that lacked democratic legitimacy and would be unable to protect itself in the future. Kissinger's main argument in defence of his own Vietnam strategy was that the US Congress was to blame for the collapse of the Paris Peace Treaty and the ultimate failure of the US commitment in Vietnam.[69] The problem is that foreign policy decision-making can not be withdrawn from the democratic process of decision-making. The difference between the nineteenth-century doctrine of the 'primate of foreign policy' and foreign policy decision-making in a democracy is precisely the subjection of foreign policy to the democratic process.

It is true, Congressional unwillingness to provide the necessary funding for the support of South Vietnam was the decisive factor in the downfall of the South. Congressional cut-offs of military aid and operations were also critical in enabling the Khmer Rouge to take over power in Cambodia. What followed was the establishment of a regime that waged war on its own population, committing genocide and unspeakable acts of terror. After the fall of South Vietnam Kissinger himself in a memorandum to President Ford about the lessons of Vietnam stated that the American people would have been prepared to 'support a policy that would have saved South Vietnam if such an option had been available to use'.[70] From the beginning, the point of negotiations was that such an option was not available for domestic reasons alone. But also from a regional perspective Kissinger's own insight was that Vietnam could hardly be stopped to dominate Indochina and he knew that Vietnamese nationalism would be unstoppable in its drive to unite with the South. He defended the American commitment simply with the argument that 'our efforts, militarily, diplomatically and politically, were not in vain. We paid a high price but we gained ten years of time and we changed what then appeared to be an overwhelming momentum. I do not believe our soldiers or our people need to be ashamed.'[71] Kissinger was convinced that the American decision to save South Vietnam in 1965 'prevented Indonesia from falling to communism and probably preserved the American presence in Asia'.[72]

Not all Vietnam related policy decisions were Kissinger's decisions only. In spite of his tremendous popularity as the Nixon Administration's preeminent foreign policy figure head he lacked true autonomous power. In general, Kissinger shared the 'domino theory' which became official US policy in 1952,[73] but he saw a number of flaws in the way containment policy was shaped and implemented beginning with the Truman Adminis- tration. For one, as he saw it, 'the defense of Indochina ran head-on into America's tradition of anti-colonialism'.[74] More importantly, he never saw the Vietnam conflict as part of a central US commitment in winning the Cold War.

Although clearly the most urgent aspect of American foreign policy for the Nixon Administration, Vietnam was only one aspect of the much more complex dilemma the Nixon Administration had to face attempting to preserve America's preeminent role in the world. There were six components that best describe his and President Nixon's strategy to achieve the goal of restoring American power:

> to extricate the United States from Vietnam under honorable conditions;
> to confine the dissent of the protest movement to Indochina;
> to seize the high ground of the peace issue by a strategy that demonstrated to the American public that, even while pursuing the Cold War, the administration would its utmost to control its dangers and gradually to overcome it;
> to broaden the diplomatic chessboard by including China in the international system;
> to strengthen our alliances; and, from that platform
> to go on the diplomatic offensive, especially in the Middle East.[75]

Marginalizing the Soviet Union in the Middle East

Kissinger's greatest diplomatic accomplishment was to outmanoeuvre the Soviet Union in the Middle East and to establish the United States as the dominant power in the Middle East. The decisive change and the opening for this opportunity came with Sadat's expulsion of Soviet troops from Egypt in 1972. Kissinger did not hesitate to exploit this unique opportunity. In his memoirs Kissinger surmised that the troop pull out might have been prompted by the fact that the American–Soviet agreements in May did not take a key Arab interest into consideration: Israel's withdrawal from the occupied territories.[76] On the other hand, in spite of détente US support for Israel grew stronger and Sadat, realizing that the only way to influence Israel was not through reliance on the Soviet Union but through Washington, opened up a secret channel to the United States.[77] Kissinger sensed, of course, that a seminal opportunity 'to bring about a reversal of alliances in the Arab world'[78] was in the making and took up the Egyptian initiative but did not follow up immediately. The Paris peace negotiations, particularly in view of the 1972 elections, clearly demanded priority and the contacts with Egypt only resumed in February 1973, after the Paris Peace Agreements of January 1973.

The Yom Kippur War started on 6 October 1973 less than a month after Kissinger became Secretary of State. It was his first test in office with the authority of the key cabinet member to advise the President at a time of dramatic developments in the unfolding of the Watergate crisis. As the Middle East crisis reached its peak, the US Presidency began to sink to its lowest point of authority. The impeachment process was now a distinct possibility. This situation put Kissinger fully into the centre of decision-making and he approached the crisis determined 'to use the war as an extension of diplomacy'.[79] Convinced that in spite of the Egyptian–Syrian surprise attack Israel would win, he approached the crisis convinced that the United States was in a good position to dominate events.[80] Kissinger assumed that Europe and Japan might dissociate themselves from

America's diplomatic actions and that the Soviet Union would try to 'manoeuvre warily',[81] but avoid active involvement. Still, he believed that an assertion of American leadership would mitigate these factors and enable the US to 'induce Soviet caution by threatening the end of détente while assembling the means for a confrontation, should diplomacy fail'.[82] Kissinger's approach to the Middle East war was not universally shared. Particularly his cautious handling of the Soviet Union in spite of its massive military support for Egypt and Syria during the war raised concern in the media as well as in the general public.

After all, he did not hesitate to initiate UN Security Council Resolution 338 in conjunction with the Soviet Union calling for a cease-fire and immediately after that to start negotiations aimed at establishing a just and durable peace in the Middle East. But Kissinger's aim was not to engage the Soviet Union as an equal partner in the peace process following the war. When the Soviet Union proposed to 'dispatch to Egypt the Soviet and American military contingents to insure the implementation of the decision of the Security Council'[83] and threatened to send troops unilaterally if the US refused, Kissinger used the opportunity not only to reject the Soviet proposal but to take rather dramatic countermeasures should the Soviet Union follow through with the threat of a unilateral dispatch of troops to Egypt. What followed was not only a DefCon III alert, basically an increase of readiness though without the determination that war is likely, but also the dispatch of American naval forces to the region.[84] The move bolstered Kissinger's tough diplomacy and convinced the Soviet leadership that they had to give in. Kissinger's political approach to the crisis had won and the United States could now act from a much superior position for its Middle East diplomacy. The US position not to accept the sending of a joint Soviet–United States military contingent to the Middle East could only be interpreted as a diplomatic victory and sent a clear signal of American assertiveness to the region. The Soviet position in the Middle East was weakened permanently.

Conclusion

Kissinger's *realpolitik* will always remain controversial. He became the object of countless conspiracy theories, not only in the case of Chile but also in the case of the Turkish invasion of Cyprus, his role in the war between India and Pakistan, his treatment of the Kurdish issue in Iraq and his responsibility for the secret wars in Indochina including the Pol Pot genocide.[85] There were even suggestions that Kissinger should be tried for war crimes, crimes against humanity and other offenses such as conspiracy to commit murder, kidnap and torture.[86] According to other conspiracy theorists Kissinger was a Soviet agent.[87]

Kissinger once mentioned that power is a great aphrodisiac. One should add that power also stirs up extremism, facilitates conspiracy theories and breeds fantasies. Détente will always remain popular in Europe. It became the object of much criticism in the US, particularly after the Soviet invasion of Afghanistan. For many conservative Americans, détente was a policy course on the wrong side of history. This will not pass as the final judgment about the era of détente in Europe. But there were other issues, for example the 1973 Middle East War and the oil crisis following the war that drove Europe and the United States apart. The 'Year of Europe' that Kissinger proclaimed in April 1973 did little to stop the erosion of the Atlantic alliance. Germany even refused to provide logistical facilities for US supply operations for Israel. For the French leadership the notion that Europe was just a regional power and – as Kissinger saw it – had only regional interests while the United States, as a global power, had to pursue global interests, did not go down well. In theory the Nixon doctrine should have pushed the transatlantic dialog in the direction of greater European independence within the Atlantic Alliance and greater European defence efforts, but what Kissinger really had in mind was greater alliance cohesion at a time of new Soviet challenges for the US. This was impossible to achieve at the time. France was more interested in putting the EEC/EC as an international player on the map than to demonstrate Atlantic unity. In the end, Kissinger simply lost patience with the slow EEC/EC decision-making process. When more than a year after the proclamation of the 'Year of Europe' a Declaration of Atlantic Relations was finally accomplished, the idea Kissinger concluded 'had been drained of its moral and psychological significance by a year of bickering'.[88]

In one respect there is little controversy about Kissinger's extraordinary role in American foreign policy: it was the brilliance of his mind, his capacity to anticipate the opportunities as well as limitations of the use of power and the capacity to get to the bottom of even the most complex issues that took him to the heights of power, influence and statesmanship. There is also little disagreement about the outstanding quality of his work as a historian, as a political scientist and as one of the most profound strategic thinkers of his time. Judged by the enormous amount of literature and the public discourse about him, no other National Security Adviser or US Secretary of State achieved as much prominence, media coverage and attention as a public persona than he did. Yet at the same time, he had to suffer much opposition, rivalry, personal attacks and public controversy. Conspiracy theories about his actions and his great achievements are never likely to go away. Kissinger will remain controversial but history may well see him in a largely positive light.

Notes

1. Quoted in Robert S. Litwak, *Détente and the Nixon Doctrine. American Foreign Policy and the Pursuit of Stability, 1969–1976* (Cambridge: Cambridge University Press, 1984), 49.
2. See Kissinger's own account in *Years of Upheaval*, 415.
3. Ibid.
4. Ibid., 414.
5. Ibid., 418.
6. Ibid.
7. See for example, Robert Dallek, *Nixon and Kissinger. Partners in Power* (New York: Harper Collins, 2007), 99.
8. Kissinger, *Years of Upheaval*, 414.
9. Quoted in Litwak, Détente and the Nixon Doctrine, 49.
10. See Henry A. Kissinger, *A World Restored. Metternich, Castlereagh and the Problems of Peace 1812–22* (London: Weidenfeld and Nicholson, 1957), 326.
11. Ibid.
12. See Henry A. Kissinger, *The Necessity for Choice. Prospects of American Foreign Policy* (New York: Harper and Brothers, 1961), 356.
13. Henry A. Kissinger, Bureaucracy and Policy Making: The Effects of Insiders and Outsiders on the Policy Process, as quoted in Litwak, Détente and the Nixon Doctrine, 65.
14. Quoted in Litwak, Détente and the Nixon Doctrine, 70.
15. See Henry Kissinger, *Years of Renewal* (New York: Simon and Schuster, 1999), 648–52.
16. See Nomination of Henry A. Kissinger, Hearings before the Committee on Foreign Relations, United States Senate, Ninety-Third Congress, First Session, Part 1, US Government Printing Office, Washington, 1973, 13.
17. See Dr Kissinger's Role in Wiretapping, Hearings before the Committee on Foreign Relations, United States Senate, Ninety-Third Congress, Second Session, US Government Printing Office, Washington, 1974, V.
18. See the collection of news articles on this issue in the Special Hearing on Kissinger's role in wiretapping, 29-37.

19. Ibid., 29.
20. See for more details of the wiretapping issue, Walter Isaacson, *Kissinger. A Biography* (New York: Simon and Schuster, 1992), 212–33.
21. See the article of the *New Yorker* magazine, 'The Talk of the Town', 17 September 1973 as reprinted in the Senate Hearing on Kissinger's role in wiretapping, 352.
22. Ibid.
23. See Hans J. Morgenthau, 'Henry Kissinger, Secretary of State. An Evaluation', *The Encounter* XLIII, no. 5 (November 1974), 59.
24. Ibid., 60.
25. Kissinger, *Years of Upheaval*, 4.
26. Quoted in Isaacson, *Kissinger*, 16.
27. See Isaacson, *Kissinger*, 15, 16.
28. This aspect of Kissinger's realism is well argued by Litwak, *Détente and the Nixon Doctrine*, 58.
29. Ibid.
30. See Kissinger, *A World Restored*, 1. See also Henry Kissinger, *White House Years* (Boston, MA: Little, Brown, 1979), 70.
31. See Henry A. Kissinger, 'The White Revolutionary: Reflections on Bismarck', Daedalus, Journal of the American Academy of Arts and Sciences, Philosophers and Kings: Studies in Leadership (Summer 1968): 888–924.
32. See Kissinger, *A World Restored*, 1.
33. Ibid.
34. See Litwak, Détente and the Nixon Doctrine, 62.
35. Ibid.
36. Ibid.
37. See Henry A. Kissinger, 'The Vietnam Negotiations', *Foreign Affairs* 47, no. 2 (January 1968), 234.
38. See Richard Nixon, US Foreign Policy for the 1970s: A New Strategy for Peace, Report to Congress, 18 February 1970, Washington, DC, 2–3.
39. See Litwak, Détente and the Nixon Doctrine, 84.
40. See Henry Brandon, *The Retreat of American Power* (New York: Doubleday, 1973).
41. See Henry Kissinger, 'Central Issues in American Foreign Policy', in *Agenda for the Nation*, ed. Kermit Gordon (Washington, DC: Brookings Institution, 1968), 612.
42. See http://history.sandiego.edu/GEN/20th/LBJ/glassboro1.html for the results or lack thereof at Glasboro, NJ, June 1967.
43. See *SALT Handbook, Key Documents and Issues 1972–1979*, ed. Roger P. Labrie (Washington, DC: American Enterprise Institute for Public Policy Research, 1979), 11.
44. See Kissinger, *Years of Renewal*, 294.
45. Ibid., 9.
46. Ibid.
47. Ibid.
48. See Robert Kagan, 'The Revolutionist: How Henry Kissinger Won the Cold War, or So He Thinks', *The New Republic* 220, no. 25 (21 June 1999), 38–48.
49. Ibid.
50. Ibid.
51. For example, Frank A. Capell, *Henry Kissinger: Soviet Agent* (Zarepath, NJ: Herald of Freedom, 1974).
52. Henry Kissinger, 'Between the Old Left and the New Right', *Foreign Affairs* 78, no. 3 (2004), 99–116, here 105.
53. See the text of the Basic Principles in *SALT Handbook*, 50–52.
54. See Francois Duchene, 'SALT, Ostpolitik und die Liquidierung des Kalten Krieges', *Europa Archiv* 17 (1970), 639.
55. On this issue, see in particular Dieter Dettke, Allianz im Wandel. Amerikanisch-Europaeische Sicherheitsbeziehungen in Zeichen des Bilateralismus der Supermaechte, Schriften des Forschungsinstituts der Deutschen Gesellschaft fuer Auswaertige Politik, Reihe: Ruestungsbescharaenkung und Sicherheit, Band 12 (Frankfurt am Main: Alfred Metzner Verlag, 1976), 37–57.
56. See Kissinger, *Years of Upheaval*, 1176.
57. Ibid., 1175.

58. See the article by George Shultz, William Perry, Henry Kissinger and Sam Nunn on 'A World Free of Nuclear Weapons', *The Wall Street Journal*, 4 January 2007, A 15, available at: http://www.fcnl.org/issues/item.php?item_id =2252&issue_id =54.
59. See Kissinger, *Years of Upheaval*, 249.
60. See in particular, Kissinger, *Years of Renewal*, 302–09.
61. See Seyom Brown, The Crises of Power. An Interpretation of the United States Foreign Policy during the Kissinger Years (Ithaca, NY: Columbia University Press, 1979), 2.
62. See. Kissinger, 'Central Issues in American Foreign Policy', 590.
63. Richard Nixon, The Pursuit of Peace in Vietnam, Department of State Bulletin, No. 1587, 24 November 1969 as quoted in Brown, *The Crises of Power*, 49.
64. Henry Kissinger, 'The Vietnam Negotiations', *Foreign Affairs* 47, no. 2 (January 1969), 218/19.
65. Ibid., 234.
66. See Barbara Tuchman, 'Book Review of Kissinger's "White House Years"', *New York Times Book Review*, 11 November 1979.
67. See Kissinger, *White House Years*, 283.
68. Ibid., 276.
69. See in particular Henry Kissinger, Ending the Vietnam War. A History of America's Involvement in and Extrication from the Vietnam War (New York: Simon and Schuster, 2003), 536.
70. Memorandum for the President from Henry A. Kissinger on Lessons of Vietnam, without date, reprinted in Berman, *No Peace, No Honor*, 279.
71. Ibid., 283.
72. Ibid., 282.
73. See Kissinger, *Ending the Vietnam War*, 18.
74. Ibid., 17.
75. See Kissinger, 'Between the Old Left and the New Right', 104.
76. This point is made by Jussi Hanhimaeki, *The Flawed Architect, Kissinger and American Foreign Policy* (Oxford: Oxford University Press, 2004), 305.
77. See Kissinger, *White House Years*, 1293.
78. Ibid., 1300.
79. See Litwak, Détente and the Nixon Doctrine, 158.
80. See Kissinger, *Years of Upheaval*, 467.
81. Ibid.
82. Ibid., 468.
83. Text of the Soviet proposal in Kissinger, *Years of Upheaval*, 583.
84. Ibid. for the nature of the DefCon III alert.
85. See in particular the anti-Kissinger material at: http://www.thirdworldtraveler.com/Kissinger/HKissinger.html.
86. Ibid. and his book, *The Trial of Henry Kissinger*, first published in *Harper's* magazine, March 2001 under the title 'The Case Against Henry Kissinger'.
87. See Capell, *Henry Kissinger, Soviet Agent*.
88. Kissinger, *Years of Upheaval*, 193.

The quiet man: Dean Rusk and Western Europe

Christian Nuenlist

University of Zurich, Switzerland

'Mr Secretary' – Introduction

Dean Rusk, the sole cabinet member President John F. Kennedy addressed as 'Mr Secretary', was one of the few secretaries of state who directed American foreign policy for two full administrations – only Cordell Hull served longer. Yet, Rusk remains an enigmatic figure, primarily for two reasons. First, his working methods and his deep respect for confidentiality obscured the extent of his contributions to the formation of US foreign policy. Rusk later claimed that he provided the bulk of his advice to the president during private talks. He explained that 'the extensive documentary record cannot tell the whole story. Documents are surrounded by much discussion among those handling policy, and these discussions are, of course, nowhere in the record'.[1] Rusk was very secretive and believed that 'there are some things that history does not deserve to know'. He never dictated memoranda of conversations with the president and he ended the practice of having someone from the State Department listening in on his telephone conversations with the president and transcribing the discussion for the record. Rusk's view was that 'a president was entitled to have a completely private conversation with his secretary of state' – a nightmare for archive-eating diplomatic historians! 'I felt it was my role to stand as a buffer between the president and the bureaucracy with respect to matters of considerable controversy', Rusk later explained.[2] During crucial meetings, Rusk often scribbled a short plea on note paper and slipped it to the man next to him. The message: 'Don't make a decision now, Mr. President. Let me see you later.'[3] All of this means, as Thomas Buckley states, that 'it is not an easy task to pin down what advice Rusk gave, when he gave it, and whether it was followed'.[4]

Second, Kennedy's 'court annalist' Arthur M. Schlesinger, Jr, shaped an influential, but inaccurate image of Rusk and his relationship with Kennedy. Ever since *A Thousand Days* was published in 1965, Rusk has been stigmatised as a bland, unimaginative, and wooden bureaucrat. Schlesinger attacked him as 'Buddha-like' and 'irrevocably conventional' and said that Kennedy, unhappy with his secretary of state, would have replaced him in 1965 – an unfair accusation, as Rusk had made it clear to JFK at the time of his appointment that, because of financial reasons, he would only serve four years.[5] Thomas Schoenbaum believes that Rusk had a difficult working relationship with Schlesinger, whom he regarded as a windbag who was soft on communism. While Rusk ignored him as much as he could, Schlesinger had his revenge in 1965.[6]

Recently, the study of Kennedy's and Johnson's policies towards Europe has flourished. Critical evaluations of Kennedy's foreign policy are being replaced by more balanced analyses, which recognise the 'little détente' of 1963 and the preservation of the transatlantic alliance.[7] Such revisionism applies even more explicitly to the Johnson years:

Thomas Schwartz and several European scholars have heralded a positive view of LBJ's foreign policy 'beyond Vietnam'.[8] Their analyses confirm early statements by veterans that Johnson's policy towards Europe was a success.[9] Building on these studies, this essay re-evaluates the role of Dean Rusk in shaping US foreign policy towards Western Europe. Different from Schlesinger's 'grumpy stranger in the Kennedy White House', the 'quiet man' comes across as a trusted key advisor in both the Kennedy and Johnson administrations.[10]

The hidden builder among the best and brightest

Rusk was probably one of the best-prepared US secretaries of state in history. As a former professor and dean at Mills College in California, Rusk – not Henry Kissinger – was the first academic at the top of Foggy Bottom. In 1961, Rusk took office rather self-assured. He told his brother: 'If I don't take the job, all that experience will be wasted'.[11] While he had become an expert on Asia during the Second World War, Rusk's biography also reveals several links with Western Europe.[12] In college, he learned German because his mother was born in the Black Forest region. Rusk was gifted in languages and also studied Greek, Latin and French. In the 1930s, he spent three years at Oxford University and took university courses in Hanover and Hamburg, where he witnessed the rise of Nazi Germany. In 1947, Secretary of State George Marshall appointed Rusk director of the Office of Political Affairs in the State Department. As an Asian specialist, however, he was on the fringes within the Foggy Bottom establishment. In addition, his legalistic approach (he graduated from the Berkeley Law School in 1940) and his support for a strong United Nations became secondary with the rise of the Soviet threat. In 1952, he became president of the Rockefeller Foundation in New York; internationally, he served as co-chairman of the US participants in the 'Bilderberg Group', a group of leading Americans and Europeans that meets regularly to discuss transatlantic issues.[13]

When Kennedy assembled his cabinet in late 1960, Rusk was not his first choice for secretary of state. He was more of a compromise solution: Kennedy felt that Adlai Stevenson, William Fulbright and Chester Bowles were too progressive and too liberal; David Bruce, the former US ambassador to Paris and Bonn, seemed 'too European' for the job. When Robert Lovett suggested Rusk for the job, Kennedy remarked: 'Who the hell is Dean Rusk?' Yet, Rusk had few enemies and the reputation of being a loyal subordinate. Loyalty was an important factor for Kennedy, who wanted to be his own foreign-policy leader. Biographer Thomas Buckley thus characterises the 'hard-working, competent, unassuming Rusk' as a perfect choice for Kennedy: 'The president would be the famous architect and the secretary of state would be the hidden builder'.[14]

In early 1961, news editorials praised Rusk for his competence, energy, intelligence and practical experience in diplomacy and foreign policy. He appeared on the cover page of *Time* magazine, which regarded him as the key appointment of the new administration.[15] The *New York Times* also praised Kennedy for 'an absolutely first-rate appointment' and called Rusk 'a figure of tremendous ability, character and intellect, an excellent choice'.[16] Rusk, however, started his job in a delicate position between an opinionated, strong president and opinionated, strong subordinates like Bowles, Stevenson or Averell Harriman, who had not been picked by Rusk but imposed by Kennedy. Competition also arose with the White House, with National Security Advisor McGeorge Bundy and his NSC staff – soon dubbed the 'little State Department' – in particular.

After Kennedy's assassination, Rusk told President Lyndon B. Johnson of his intention to retire at the end of 1964 as planned. Johnson, however, begged Rusk to stay on and overwhelmed him with constant praise.[17] Johnson had already liked him in 1960. 'He's a damn good man. Hard working, bright, and loyal as a beagle. You'll never catch him working at cross purposes with the president.'[18] In 1964, Rusk's status and influence as foreign policy advisor increased under the fellow Southerner as president.[19]

Keeping the Europeans on board during the Berlin Crisis

In 1961, Europeans were anxious to learn more about the intentions of the Kennedy administration and to get to know the new US secretary of state. In the mid-1950s, they had become disappointed in the lack of US leadership in the alliance and the growing trend towards superpower bilateralism, as evidenced at the 1959 superpower summit in Camp David.[20] Yet, most Europeans were even more worried by the worldviews of Kennedy, Rusk and Bowles, which seemed to be significantly less Europe-centred than the ones of Dwight D. Eisenhower, John Foster Dulles and Christian Herter. The NATO ministerial meeting in May 1961 was the first opportunity for most Europeans to get to know the new US foreign minister. Rusk dominated the five-day meeting in Oslo. His effort 'to encourage effective consultation by talking less about how to consult and just starting consulting' was well received. 'NATO's old timers' praised Oslo as 'the most open and intimate political discussion in NATO within their memories'.[21] Despite Rusk's priorities in areas beyond Europe, his focus soon came to centre on the traditional central Cold War battleground – Germany.

In Oslo, Rusk expected increased tensions with the Soviet Union over Berlin in the near future.[22] Meeting Kennedy in Vienna, Soviet leader Nikita Khrushchev renewed his Berlin ultimatum. Rusk went to Paris to brief French President Charles de Gaulle and NATO about the summit. He circulated copies of the Soviet aide-memoire and felt that the West had 'a formidable issue in prospect with heightening of tension and perhaps even grimmer problems before long'.[23] According to Schlesinger, Kennedy was soon fed up with Rusk's handling of the Berlin Crisis. The president apparently was 'exasperated' that State delayed a reply to Khrushchev's aide-memoire for six weeks. In addition, Schlesinger wrote, Kennedy was disappointed that Rusk did not come up with a clear US negotiating position.[24] In reality, however, the delay was not caused by Rusk's shop, but by the White House itself. First, it lost the State Department's draft reply, and once it was resent, a White House aide had put it into his office safe and left for a two-week holiday.[25]

Schlesinger's statement that 'no one quite knew where Rusk stood' in the Berlin Crisis[26] is also contradicted by the archival record. Like Dean Acheson – Kennedy's special Berlin advisor – Rusk initially felt that Berlin was no place for compromise. He emphasised US contractual rights and obligations in Berlin. His views were supported and influenced by his 'Europeanists' – George McGhee, Foy Kohler, William R. Tyler, J. Robert Schaetzel, and Martin J. Hillenbrand – all of whom had shaped Eisenhower's policy towards Europe and now recommended to stay the course.[27] In mid-July, during the crucial debates in Washington, Rusk advised a tough stance – including a military build-up – but he also hoped to defuse tensions through exploratory talks with Moscow.[28] Kennedy decided for a compromise between the hard-line course recommended by Acheson and a more conciliatory approach recommended by his White House advisors – in essence, the line Rusk recommended in a memorandum on 17 July.[29] On 25 July, Kennedy presented his new Berlin policy in a landmark speech.[30]

Prior to JFK's decision, Rusk had avoided discussions with the European allies – despite promises to the contrary in Oslo. He was 'deeply disturbed by the restlessness on the part of NATO Secretary-General Dirk Stikker and the NATO Council members about consultations on Berlin'. Rusk felt that 'if NATO members are impatient about delay, they should reflect upon the fact that the Berlin crisis involves the gravest possible issues and that the problem requires serious and intensive study'.[31]

As tasked by Kennedy, Rusk submitted his first substantial plan for Berlin negotiations with Moscow on 2 August. He advised Kennedy to avoid formal negotiations until after the elections in West Germany in mid-September, although he endorsed a 'quiet approach' of informal discussions with Khrushchev concerning the problem of access to the city.[32] In August, Rusk travelled to Paris and met with the foreign ministers of Britain, France and West Germany. France was vehemently opposed to direct talks with Moscow.[33] After a visit to the NATO Council, he was surprised by the unity within NATO, as he had expected complaints from the Europeans about the lack of consultations in June–July.[34]

Talking the issue to death after the building of the Berlin Wall

Rusk did not think that the erection of the Berlin Wall on 13 August 1961 was a reason to go to war with Moscow and advised Kennedy to remain calm and steadfast.[35] While the White House took an activist position and proposed a variety of new US concessions – for example, the recognition of the Oder-Neisse line, a partial recognition of the German Democratic Republic (GRD), or a non-aggression treaty with Moscow – Rusk was not prepared to yield an inch. He was more or less satisfied with the status quo ante in Berlin – the Soviets had been the ones who changed the rules of the game. Therefore, as he saw it, the US should 'sit tight, talk the issue to death and hold the line'.[36] In a meeting with German Chancellor Konrad Adenauer on the shores of Lake Como, Rusk said that his greatest ambition was 'to pass the Berlin question on to my successor'.[37]

On JFK's urging, Rusk began to meet his Soviet counterpart Andrei Gromyko to determine whether a basis for negotiations existed.[38] Rusk still questioned the necessity of these explorations. Before the US Congress, he stated: 'Our basic position is that these fellows ought to leave us alone and leave our rights alone'.[39] After three meetings with Rusk, the Kremlin was ready to delay its deadline if the Kennedy administration was serious about negotiations. Rusk thus informed Kennedy that the real problems did not arise from superpower tensions, but intra-West troubles. France, which still categorically dismissed negotiations, and the West German government, not wanting to risk the elections, prevented a common Western front, although the other 13 NATO countries all favoured negotiations over Berlin with Moscow.[40]

Contrary to the story told by Schlesinger, Rusk had won Kennedy's trust during the Berlin Crisis. He saw the president several times a week, often three to four times a day. Because of his cautious and un-dramatic approach – a significant contrast to the fear displayed among the young 'action intellectuals' in the White House who were ready to offer Moscow significant concessions – Rusk's influence within the administration had grown. In the autumn of 1961, the press reported that Rusk had emerged 'beyond any doubt as the president's principal advisor on foreign affairs'.[41] Kennedy came to appreciate that Rusk's 'war of words' had contributed to the avoidance of both a dangerous confrontation in the heart of Europe and a similarly risky policy of appeasement and, as a result, a possible rift within NATO.[42] Rusk understood that it was not possible to achieve a real solution of the Berlin and German problems without a deterioration of US relations with Bonn and Paris. Unlike several of Kennedy's White House aides, Rusk recognised the danger of NATO disintegration resulting from bilateral superpower negotiations.

Dealing with Europe on an almost daily basis was, however, the exception rather than the norm for Rusk. He appeared at NATO meetings, paid homage to European leaders like Adenauer or de Gaulle, and maintained a warm friendship with Western leaders such as Harold Macmillan and Alec Douglas-Home in Britain and Paul-Henri Spaak in Belgium, but his deputy George Ball dominated day-to-day relations with Europe. Economic issues bored Rusk – and he generally left policies concerning European integration to Ball as well.[43] Europe only returned to the top of Rusk's agenda again when Kennedy wished to move towards a superpower détente with Moscow in 1963 – once more at the expense of the European allies.

Sceptical towards an East–West détente in 1963

Rusk was not comfortable with the thaw in East–West relations after the Cuban Missile Crisis and was never as optimistic about ending the Cold War as Kennedy and his White House aides were. In late 1962, Kennedy's White House advisors wanted America to assume leadership within NATO: 'We'll never be in a better position to bring our allies along with anything we want', they urged.[44] Rusk, however, remained sceptical. He reacted with concern to the news from Paris that 'euphoria' had broken out in NATO after the peaceful conclusion of the Cuba crisis. Rusk felt that NATO 'should accelerate, not relax' its defence efforts. He was concerned about a 'certain division of opinion' within the alliance about the desirability of broad East–West negotiations.[45] His fears were proven right at the NATO meeting in Paris in December, when several European leaders expressly wished that the West now move quickly to negotiate with Moscow from a position of strength to reach a *modus vivendi* in Europe.[46]

At the next NATO meeting in Ottawa in May 1963, Rusk promised consultation and full participation of the alliance in further East–West talks.[47] When Rusk was asked if Washington would consider a deal with the Soviet Union behind the back of NATO, he replied: 'Well, I don't quite see how an agreement could contribute to peace if it turned out to be at the expense of our European NATO allies'.[48] Yet, in 1963, Kennedy was keen to grasp the chances for an arms control arrangement with Moscow. A breakthrough should not be prevented anymore by a French-German veto.[49] In contrast to JFK's peace rhetoric and the excitement in Europe about the 'little détente' that seemed to blossom after the conclusion of the Limited Test Ban Treaty (LTBT) in late July, Rusk insisted in his public statements that the Soviet–American relationship could not yet be characterised as in a state of 'détente'.[50] Walt Rostow, the creative head of Rusk's Policy Planning Council (PPC), also warned Kennedy that his policy of détente carried great danger for the alliance with Western Europe. He warned that the LTBT negatively impacted Washington's recently 'refreshed' relations with West Germany – and bluntly advised Kennedy that his policy of détente might also cause him political harm in the election year of 1964.[51] JFK, however, decided to throw Rusk's caution to the wind. 'I have some cash in the bank in West Germany', he allegedly said, 'and I am prepared to draw on it'.[52]

In the aftermath of the LTBT, the French and West Germans felt sidelined by the Anglo-Saxons' push for détente – as foreseen by Rusk and Rostow.[53] Rusk now had to repair the damaged relations with Bonn. On short notice, he flew to Bonn and assured the West Germans that the US would not recognise the GDR – despite its accession to the LTBT. His mission was successful – West Germany also signed the LTBT.[54] Similarly, when

Kennedy authorised a substantial withdrawal of US troops from Western Europe, Rusk had to reassure the Germans in a speech in Frankfurt that America would leave six divisions in Germany 'as long as they were needed'.[55]

At the same time, Rostow began to draft a new US policy towards Eastern Europe, favouring a 'peaceful engagement in Eastern Europe' over the stabilisation of the territorial status quo in Central Europe. He suggested carrying discussions about détente into NATO.[56] For Rostow, the key towards a European settlement was the integration of Germany into US détente policy. He suggested rethinking the push for a bilateral détente that had led to fundamental disagreements with West Germany. Instead, he opted for multilateral arrangements – playing the 'Eastern game' should be a 'planned Atlantic effort [...] with the Europeans out front', particularly West Germany, that would unify rather than fragment NATO.[57]

While Rusk reluctantly went along with Rostow's visionary strategy, he was surprisingly passive and reserved when discussing any possible future multilateral détente agreements at the next NATO ministerial in December 1963. His wording and tone clearly reflected his misgivings towards the euphoria surrounding détente. Rusk stated that the first small steps made towards a relaxation of East–West tension did not constitute a genuine policy of détente, particularly as so many disputes – such as those in Berlin, Laos, Vietnam, or Cuba – remained unresolved. He concluded: 'At most, what we have today is a license to search for a détente.'[58]

Interestingly, however, the foreign ministers of Britain, Italy, Belgium and Canada felt that the international situation had improved considerably since the last ministerial meeting. They saw NATO's negative stance towards a non-aggression pact and ground observations posts in August–September 1963 as a missed opportunity and regretted that the implementation of these follow-up agreements to the LTBT had been successfully blocked by West Germany and France during NATO's détente debates.[59] The most remarkable speech at the NATO meeting was new West German foreign minister Gerhard Schröder's review of Bonn's tentative efforts for a normalisation of relations with its Eastern neighbours. Schröder's speech, with its focus on an 'inner-German détente', symbolised a radical departure from the rigid Adenauer line.[60] Thus, with even West Germany supporting a normalisation of relations with the East, Rusk ultimately reported a fragile NATO consensus on the desirability of 'exploring avenues for possible future discussions with the Soviets on outstanding East-West issues'.[61] This new trend towards a multilateralisation of Western détente policy was not lost upon the other side. The Soviet Union officially praised the NATO communiqué of its December meeting as 'very interesting'.[62]

Getting the balance between alliance and détente right again

After Kennedy's assassination, Johnson left foreign policy mostly to Rusk. Unlike JFK, LBJ did not want to be his own secretary of state.[63] Rusk's department gained more influence over American foreign policy than it had had under Kennedy. Together with European experts George Ball and Bill Tyler, Rusk succeeded in emphasising alliance solidarity and transatlantic integration over détente policies with the Soviet Union – the preferred option of Bundy and the White House. For a moment, Kennedy's close advisors in the White House lost their influence on US policy-making. Johnson's 'anti-intellectualism' strained his relations with JFK's 'egg heads'. As a result, American détente policy and disarmament policies stagnated under LBJ in 1964, even though Johnson, Bundy and

McNamara wished to continue Kennedy's policy of détente.[64] Already in December 1963, Bundy complained to Johnson that Rusk tended to be 'more rigid' than Kennedy had wanted with regard to the next steps towards détente.[65] Rusk, however, prevailed in shaping Johnson's policy towards Europe in 1964. He shifted the balance away from Kennedy's unilateral détente policy in 1963 and towards more consideration of Washington's European allies, West Germany in particular. Yet, more and more Rusk found himself absorbed by the escalating war in Vietnam. As a consequence, he left US policy towards Europe to a large extent to his deputy Ball.[66]

Rostow's concept of a 'policy of movement' – instead of a hardening of the status quo in Europe – was further developed in the State Department in early 1964. The new policy towards Europe was now called 'bridge-building' and in essence stated that German reunification was only achievable through a rapprochement between East and West Germany.[67] In April, Rostow produced a sharp analysis of the interdependence between détente and alliance policy. In a memorandum for Rusk, he complained that the erosion of the Western alliance resulting from the LTBT was worse than the prospect of additional Soviet missiles. He urged Rusk to take the security interests of West Germany seriously and to come up with new arms control proposals only in tandem with NATO.[68] Johnson publicly announced the 'bridge-building' concept in May.[69]

Rusk, however, did not yet think that the time was ripe for bridge-building in Europe. First, Gaullist France was still radically opposed to negotiations with the Soviet Union and Eastern Europe in the first half of the year. Second, détente was a delicate issue in America in 1964, an election year. Third, the Soviet Union was against bridge-building because it interpreted it as another US strategy aimed at driving a wedge between Moscow and its East European satellites.[70] Fourth, and most importantly, an early success of bridge-building would have depended upon Washington's pressure on West Germany. In 1964, Rusk was not ready to pressure Bonn. Johnson agreed: 'We can only go as far as the Germans are prepared to do'.[71]

In the shadow of Vietnam: Rusk and the MLF

Germany also created problems with regard to the Kennedy and Johnson administration's goal of preventing further nuclear proliferation. To meet the needs of the continental European allies for a voice in NATO's nuclear strategy, the US had proposed the creation of a nuclear Multilateral Force (MLF) in 1960. Rusk, however, he was absolutely opposed to giving up the US veto over the use of nuclear weapons. He knew that both the US Congress and the Soviet Union would be outraged if the Germans were given control over, or access to, nuclear weapons.[72] When Johnson made it clear that he wanted to make a decision on the future of the MLF in April 1964, Rusk was unable to attend the crucial meeting. Writing down his position in advance, he argued that both the negotiations with the European allies as well as recent briefings with members of Congress, in his view supported making an attempt to reach the signatory stage of the MLF negotiations by the end of the year.[73] Rusk's recommendation did anticipate the result of the meeting and Johnson's decision. The main problem with the MLF was that the project was incompatible with the Nuclear Non-Proliferation Treaty (NPT) to be signed with Moscow. The Soviet Union opposed an NPT that did not exclude the MLF (and a German finger at the nuclear trigger).[74]

After the first Chinese nuclear test, Rusk, Bundy and Johnson in December 1964 decided to cancel the MLF project and shifted their priorities in favour of achieving a NPT, but did not tell this to the European allies. In fact, Rusk saw advantages in the efforts of Britain to continue discussions about the MLF in the form of London's proposal for an Atlantic Nuclear Force (ANF). Plans for nuclear sharing thus remained on the US–European agenda in 1965. Ball and other 'MLF theologians' continued with their campaign for a nuclear sharing solution. And even Rusk, in his dealings with European foreign ministers, deliberately kept the MLF–ANF proposal alive as a possible way to solve NATO problems. In effect, however, the US decision of December 1964 marked the end of the MLF. Without US leadership, no solution was possible. The NATO Nuclear Planning Group (NPG) in 1965 satisfied some of West German demands, but the NPT in 1968 definitely sealed Bonn's (and Rome's) non-nuclear status.[75]

Rusk's behaviour in the MLF controversy frustrated a number of European allies and colleagues within the US government – both supporters and opponents of the concept. They were not sure which exact position Rusk had recommended to Johnson. Looking back to the MLF episode about 25 years later, Rusk recalled: 'This was never an American proposal for which Kennedy, Johnson and I wanted to bleed and die'.[76] But if Rusk was sceptical, why did he allow Ball to press so hard? If he did not support the idea, why did he let it float so long? Why did he allow so much of State's energy to be expended? The official rationale, as emphasised by Ball, was that it was meant to avoid the danger of perpetuating discrimination against West Germany and to give Bonn a legitimate role in the defence of NATO, albeit 'on a leash'.[77] In retrospect, Rusk confessed that he did not want to offend the sensibilities of George Ball, for whom he had a high regard. Rusk seems to have underestimated the momentum Ball could generate in the MLF debate. In addition, he believed that the MLF was useful as a basis for discussion among the NATO allies. As long as the (illusionary) project was on the table, it prevented more dangerous alternatives, namely German insistence on an independent nuclear weapon. Washington's European allies wanted something. 'Let them discuss the MLF, see how complicated and costly the proposals were, and turn them down', was Rusk's attitude. The US would not be denying European aspirations and the whole problem might fade away – as it actually did.[78]

Neglecting and isolating Charles de Gaulle

De Gaulle's challenge to US leadership within the Western alliance dominated US–European affairs during Rusk's tenure, in particular in 1965–1966.[79] For Rusk, communications with de Gaulle were 'a little bit like climbing on your knees up a mountainside to talk to the oracle'.[80] In 1961, Rusk had tried to ignore de Gaulle as much as possible. Yet, from mid-1962, Rusk sent alarming messages to Kennedy about the rapprochement between de Gaulle and Adenauer. He feared that French–German cooperation might be extended to the nuclear field and warned that de Gaulle might 'seduce' Adenauer. 'I cannot help but share the fear that the Chancellor will not stand up well, if the two statesmen do much business alone', he cabled from Europe.[81] Rusk recommended the launch of a new US initiative to strengthen the transatlantic partnership – Kennedy's 'Grand Design' presented on 4 July 1962 – to neutralise de Gaulle and to offer West Germany an alternative to French leadership in Europe.[82] In October, Rusk asked Kennedy to sound out Foreign Minister Maurice Couve de Murville on French intentions. 'We know as yet very little about the nature of these proposals but it seems evident that they are closely related to UK entry [into the European Common Market] and that intensified French–German cooperation is designed to serve as a counter weight to the UK', Rusk speculated. Yet, he also tried to reassure Kennedy: 'As long as we are not confronted with a closed

French–German system (and there is at present no reason to assume that we are), we should welcome this development because intimate French–German relations are a sine qua non for greater European integration'.[83]

In 1963, de Gaulle formed a close partnership with Adenauer – feeding rumours in Washington of secret provisions on a nuclear bilateral cooperation. Rusk was concerned – but not shocked like Ball – about the Franco–German friendship treaty and the parallel French 'no' to Britain's entry into the Common Market.[84] To offer an alternative to de Gaulle's vision of a Europe under French leadership and to avert a new NATO crisis, Rusk flew to Paris in April and warned NATO ministers of the historical 'ghosts haunting in the corridors of the Alliance'. He particularly referred to the following 'ghosts':

> Doubts that the US would meet its commitment to defend Europe in the event of an attack; the assertion that the US wished to dominate NATO; the accusation that the US was seeking a settlement with the Soviet Union at the expense of Europe; the idea of Europe becoming a third force capable of defending itself by its own means and adopting a neutralist attitude; the doubt that Europe would fight for its own defence; suspicion in Germany that France would make an agreement with the Soviet Union at Germany's expense; etc.[85]

The US policy of isolating France and concentrating its efforts on the continent instead on West Germany might have worked fairly well up until mid-1964. But when le général embarked on a rapprochement with Moscow, the turnaround in French Ostpolitik directly challenged the Johnson administration. Rusk faced a serious policy dilemma: The US could not go much further in its détente policy than the West Germans were prepared to go; but it increasingly ran the risk of losing the initiative to de Gaulle.[86] At this crucial moment, a planning session of key State Department officials on how US leadership should be played out in the 1960s reveals fascinating insights into the differences in Rusk's and Ball's thinking on the US–European relationship. Ball criticised the fact that the US was 'reluctant to exercise the kind of leadership needed, turning away from its broader based responsibilities and resorting to the easier and less useful and effective bilateral track'. Ball emphasised that 'leadership requires that we lead – the alternative is chaos'. Rusk offered a radically different viewpoint. It seemed to him that this 'Ball doctrine' played directly into de Gaulle's hands. He joked that he sometimes wondered whether 'the reason we did not like de Gaulle was that we were essentially Gaullist ourselves'. Rusk felt that the Europeans had a legitimate role to play in international affairs. 'The situation now called for a proportionately smaller US input and greater proportionate US exertion', the secretary of state said and concluded: 'Why not let the Europeans come to us sometimes?' Ball replied that the Europeans would never do anything by themselves and Henry Owen chimed in that the Europeans were 'like inexperienced teenagers who knew what to do once they were told, but were incapable on their own of deciding what was right or necessary'. Rusk insisted that it was important to 'draw a clear line between leadership and hegemony' and concluded that he was convinced that the requirements of leadership in the 1960s and 1970s were not the same as in the 1940s and 1950s.[87] Unlike Ball, Rusk seemed ready to move NATO towards a less hierarchical alliance.

Crisis and opportunity: coping with the French withdrawal from NATO

In May 1965, Rusk learned on the basis of anonymous French sources that de Gaulle already was preparing plans to completely withdraw France from NATO after the presidential elections in December. Instantly, he ordered his European experts to draft a report on the future of NATO without France.[88] Yet, despite the grim prospects for the Western alliance, Rusk decided that a real crisis in the Dominican Republic was more important than rumours of a French withdrawal from NATO. For the first time, he decided not to attend a NATO meeting. While Rusk was trying to manage the crisis in the Caribbean, Ball travelled to the ministerial meeting in London. The NATO gathering was dominated by Washington's search for moral, financial and military support from its European allies for the escalating Vietnam War,[89] but Ball also tried to counter de Gaulle's hinted exit from NATO. Ball proposed the launch of a serious alliance-wide debate on the future of NATO, to be discussed again at the next high-level meeting in December.[90] In the meantime, Rusk had realised that his presence was urgently needed in Western Europe and flew from the Dominican Republic to London to join the rest of the NATO meeting after all. In side-meetings, he agreed to jumpstart contingency planning for a NATO without France. 'When husband and wife talk of divorce, it is already too late to fix the marriage', he quipped and advised NATO Secretary-General Manlio Brosio to begin preparations for the worst case scenario.[91]

Still heavily preoccupied with the Vietnam War, Rusk left the harmonising of allied positions on how to deal with a French defection from NATO once more to his deputy. In autumn, Ball toured European capitals to promote a 'policy of neglect' towards de Gaulle and to multilateralise US contingency planning.[92] In late September, the State Department formulated its strategy for the expected confrontation with de Gaulle. The remaining 14 allies – NATO minus France – should continue a policy of integration and multilateralism. The US should follow a middle way between inactivity – which would call US leadership within NATO into question – and an overly hasty, aggressive approach to de Gaulle – which might alienate some of the European allies.[93]

When de Gaulle finally announced the withdrawal of all French forces from NATO officially in March 1966, the Johnson administration could rely on the results of several months of internal and transatlantic contingency planning directed by Ball. Still, de Gaulle's final step provoked a serious re-evaluation of US policy towards Europe and split the Johnson administration into two camps. Rusk was outraged and wanted Johnson to take a tough stance against de Gaulle's designs and to punish the French. Relations were so strained at one point that in a famous conversation between de Gaulle and Rusk, de Gaulle stated that every US soldier must leave France. Rusk, known for his *bon mots*, asked the general: 'Does that include the dead Americans in military cemeteries as well?'[94]

Johnson, much wiser in this case, ignored Rusk as well as Ball, Acheson and US Ambassador to France Charles Bohlen. Listening to White House aides Francis Bator and Bob Komer instead, LBJ treated de Gaulle with respect and restrained his advisors from criticising de Gaulle or the French.[95] Yet, the differences of viewpoints between the Rusk-Ball-Acheson and the Bator-Johnson camps were not about substance, but rather confirmed the old saying: 'It's not what you say but how you say it'. Johnson's cool-headed, polite and friendly reaction in retrospect appears as the perfect course of action – de Gaulle's decision to withdraw from NATO's military command did have a few practical consequences, but was rather a symbolic step.[96]

In the end, the NATO crisis served as a catalyst for the Johnson administration to move on with its European initiatives that had been blocked by de Gaulle. Rusk already called NATO the 'Family of 14' when all NATO allies (minus France) decided to remain together in June 1966.[97] By 1968, Rusk's final year as secretary of state, the US had secured NATO acceptance (minus France) of its military strategy of Flexible Response; found a solution to the offset and force level problem through the US–UK–West German Trilateral Talks; and revitalised Rostow's policy of movement and bridge-building concepts.[98] In July 1966, Johnson had authorised Rusk to 'actively develop' – in consultation with Washington's European allies – 'areas of peaceful cooperation' with the Soviet Union and East European nations.[99] LBJ made public his new policy towards Europe on 7 October 1966, calling for a step-by-step East–West 'environment improvement'.[100] Johnson's approach was made NATO policy in late 1967, when the Western alliance adopted the so-called Harmel Report. NATO governments codified the coordination of the 'Eastern policies' as one of two major tasks of the alliance, making deterrence and détente the two guiding principles for the 1970s.[101]

During the 1967 Harmel exercise, Rusk had warned of French obstruction and hoped that – despite the danger of a French exit from NATO's political structure as well – the allies should not allow themselves to be 'blackmailed' by de Gaulle.[102] When France reluctantly decided to subscribe to the Harmel Report – preferring 'the embarrassment of compromises to the risk of rejection' – this transformed the seemingly-futile Harmel exercise into a 'triumph of American diplomacy' (Tom Schwartz).[103] De Gaulle, however, did not need to fear that NATO's newly found priority of searching for détente would materialise into a series of East–West agreements. While the signing of the Non-Proliferation Treaty (NPT) on 1 July 1968 marked another major foreign policy success of the Johnson administration in the shadow of Vietnam, the Soviet military invasion in Prague in August ended the hopes for a more comprehensive East–West détente. In July, Rusk had told Soviet Ambassador Anatoly Dobrynin that any Soviet action would have very negative effects on US–Soviet relations and felt that the real crisis was over after his warning. When Moscow nonetheless sent tanks to Prague, Rusk bluntly remarked to Dobrynin that it was like 'throwing a dead fish in the president's face'.[104]

Conclusion

Dean Rusk's misfortune was that he directed US foreign policy at a time when the power of the US was in decline, when the influence of the State Department was being nibbled away by Bundy's NSC staff, and President Kennedy wanted to act as his own secretary of state. The personal contacts between Rusk and Kennedy were always strictly official, or in Rusk's own words, 'I never played touch football with the Kennedys – I never got pushed into their swimming pool'.[105] Yet, after a shaky start, the working relationship between the president and his secretary of state improved immensely during 1961. In the Kennedy years, Rusk succeeded in keeping the delicate balance between alliance solidarity within NATO and détente with the Soviet Union. Washington's relations with key European allies were strained at times, but the Western alliance was maintained. Compared with the frequent complaints of Western Europeans about the Eisenhower administration's neglect of Europe, Rusk successfully restored US leadership in NATO, with the notable exception of Gaullist France, and he renewed the American commitment to the defence of Western Europe. At the same time, the Kennedy administration succeeded in creating the 'little détente' of 1963 and in establishing a direct dialogue with Nikita Khrushchev.

In the Johnson years, Rusk found himself progressively more absorbed by the Vietnam War and left US policy towards Western Europe to his deputy George Ball. Yet, despite the war in Vietnam, Rusk achieved some notable successes in his European policies during the Johnson administration. His cautious approach towards the Soviet Union, while ensuring that West Germany was on board with Western détente policy, became a huge success. To be fair, the visionary 'policy of movement' and 'bridge-building' was not Rusk's brainchild, but originated in his Policy Planning Council. Initially, Rusk had in fact been rather sceptical of Walt Rostow's proposal to multilateralise the bilateral détente and, in 1963–4, he slowed down the détente euphoria that reigned in the White House. Rusk accepted the price of a stagnation of superpower détente, which was based on the acceptance of the status quo in Europe, for a long-term vision of an alliance-wide multilateral détente policy, which was intended to transform the status quo and ultimately bring about the reunification of Germany.

During Rusk's tenure, it also became increasingly clear that America could no longer maintain the benign hegemony it had provided since 1945. By 1961, Western Europe had become richer and stronger and demanded to be treated more like a partner than a dependent ally. Rusk thus had the great opportunity to fashion a new style of leadership, a post-hegemonic style – and the fascinating discussion between Rusk and Ball on this subject in early 1965 proves that Rusk had more empathy for Western Europe than the leading 'Europeanist' in his department. Rusk had played 'devil's advocate' for Washington's European allies since mid-1961 – and thus balanced the eagerness of Kennedy, Bundy and his NSC staff to reach a bilateral superpower arrangement even at the cost of the allies. And despite the rivalry with Bundy – there was a lot less bureaucratic infighting between the White House and the State Department from 1961 and 1969 than during most US administrations since Johnson.

Looking back to Johnson's policy towards Western Europe and Rusk's role in shaping this policy, his contribution still remains mixed. In retrospect, it seems that his strategy towards the MLF worked quite well. By keeping the MLF option on the table through Ball's enthusiasm, West Germany and Italy were kept busy until the US signed the Non-Proliferation Treaty in 1968 – and precious time was won during which Bonn and Rome did not try to come up with a national or European nuclear program (something they had desired since the mid-1950s). With regard to the de Gaulle challenge, however, Johnson rejected the advice of Rusk, who had suggested a tough line and public confrontation in the 1966 crisis. Instead, he chose to listen to the more moderate advice given by the White House, and Deputy National Security Advisor Francis Bator in particular.

Despite a number of real achievements during both the Kennedy and Johnson administrations, particularly with regard to Western Europe, Rusk will – like other of Kennedy's 'best and brightest' (David Halberstam) – forever be stigmatised by the failure of Vietnam. This remains the real tragedy of Dean Rusk, because fact is, as this essay looking at Rusk's policies towards Western Europe has tried to demonstrate: Rusk was the kind of secretary of state you wanted to have if you were president – 'hard-working, bright and loyal as a beagle'.

Acknowledgements
I would like to thank Thomas Gijswijt for his very helpful insights, comments and suggestions and Sean Mullan for his excellent editorial assistance.

Notes
1. Dean Rusk, *As I Saw It* (New York: Norton, 1990), 12.
2. Rusk, 'A modest note for future archivists, historians, and other scholars' (13 January 1975), Lyndon B. Johnson Library, Austin, TX (LBJL).
3. *Time*, 9 August 1982, http://www.time.com/time/magazine/article/0,9171,925631,00.html (accessed 21 June 2008).

4. Thomas H. Buckley, 'Dean Rusk', in *American Statesmen*, ed. Edward S. Mihalkanin (Westport, CT: Greenwood Press, 2004), 443–9, 445.

5. Arthur M. Schlesinger, Jr, *A Thousand Days* (Boston, MA: Houghton Mifflin, 2002, [1965]). See 'The Enigma of Dean Rusk', pp. 432–7.

6. Thomas J. Schoenbaum, *Waging Peace and War: Dean Rusk in the Truman, Kennedy, and Johnson Years* (New York: Simon & Schuster, 1988), 285f.

7. Marc Trachtenberg, *A Constructed Peace: The Making of the European Settlement, 1945–63* (Princeton, NJ: Princeton University Press, 1999); Christian Nuenlist, *Kennedys rechte Hand: Der Einfluss des Nationalen Sicherheitsberaters McGeorge Bundy auf die amerikanische Aussenpolitik, 1961–63* (Zurich: CSS, 1999); Christof Münger, *Die Berliner Mauer, Kennedy und die Kubakrise: Das westliche Bündnis in der Zerreissprobe, 1961–63* (Paderborn: Schöningh, 2003); Christian Nuenlist, 'Eisenhower, Kennedy, and Political Cooperation in NATO: The Western Alliance and Khrushchev's Foreign Policy, 1955–64', PhD thesis, University of Zurich, 2005; Andreas Daum, 'Atlantic Partnership or Simply A Mess?', in *John F. Kennedy and the Thousand Days*, ed. Manfred Berg and Andreas Etges (Heidelberg: Winter, 2007), 17–38.

8. Helga Haftendorn, *NATO and the Nuclear Revolution* (Oxford: Oxford University Press, 1996); Thomas Schwartz, *Lyndon Johnson and Europe* (Cambridge, MA: Harvard University Press, 2003). See also Pascal Morf, 'Building Bridges: Die amerikanische Deutschlandpolitik unter Lyndon B. Johnson zwischen Allianzpolitik und Détente, 1963–69', MA thesis, University of Zurich, 2001; Andreas Wenger, 'Crisis and Opportunity: NATO's Transformation and the Multilateralization of Détente, 1966–68', *Journal of Cold War Studies* 6, no. 1 (2004): 22–74; Anna Locher, 'Crisis – What Crisis? The Debate on the Future of NATO, 1963–66', PhD thesis, University of Zurich, 2006; Andrew Priest, *Kennedy, Johnson and NATO: Britain, America and the Dynamics of Alliance, 1962–68* (London: Routledge, 2006).

9. Rusk, Oral History Interview (OHI), LBJL, p. 18f.; Francis M. Bator, 'Lyndon Johnson and Foreign Policy: The Case of Western Europe and the Soviet Union', in *Presidential Judgment: Foreign Policy Decision Making in the White House*, ed. Aaron Lobel (Cambridge, MA: Hollis, 2001), 41–77.

10. *Time*, 6 December 1963.

11. Rusk, *As I Saw It*, 195.

12. The following paragraphs are based on Warren I. Cohen, *Dean Rusk* (Totawa, NJ: Cooper Square, 1980), 1–92; Schoenbaum, *Waging Peace*, 1–262; Thomas W. Zeiler, *Dean Rusk: Defending the American Mission Abroad* (Wilmington, VT: Scholarly Resources, 2000), 3–22; and Buckley, *Rusk*, 443f.

13. Thomas Gijswijt, 'Uniting the West: The Bilderberg Group, the Cold War and European Integration, 1952–66', PhD thesis, University of Heidelberg, 2007.

14. Buckley, *Rusk*, 445.

15. Schoenbaum, *Waging Peace*, 263.

16. Quoted in Cohen, *Rusk*, 96.

17. Cohen, *Rusk*, 218f.

18. Sam H. Johnson, *My Brother Lyndon* (New York: Cowles, 1970), 117.

19. Buckley, *Rusk*, 447.

20. See e.g. Klaus Larres, 'Eisenhower, Dulles und Adenauer', in *Deutschland und die USA im 20. Jahrhundert*, ed. Klaus Larres and Torsten Oppelland (Darmstadt: WBG, 1997), 119–50.

21. Foreign Relations of the United States (FRUS) 1961–3: 13, no. 104.

22. NATO Council (NAC) Meeting, 8 May 1961, C-R(61)16, NATO Archives, Brussels (NA).

23. Finletter to Department of State (DoS), 5 June 1961, US National Archives, College Park, MD (USNA), RG 59, Central Decimal File (CDF), 740.5.

24. Schlesinger, *Thousand Days*, 383f. See also Sorensen, *Kennedy*, (New York: Harper & Row, 1965), 322. Schoenbaum also mentions that Rusk was 'a very difficult man to work for', that 'aides complained that Rusk was reticent, shy, and uncommunicative' and that 'no one ever knew what he was thinking'. Schoenbaum, *Waging Peace*, 273.

25. Schoenbaum, *Waging Peace*, 339.

26. Schlesinger, *Thousand Days*, 383.

27. Adrian Schertz, *Die Deutschlandpolitik Kennedys und Johnsons* (Cologne: Böhlau, 1992), 55.

28. On the bureaucratic debates in Washington, see Nuenlist, *Kennedys rechte Hand*, 95–100.

29. Foreign Relations of the United States (FRUS) 1961–3:14, 207–9.

30. http://www.presidency.ucsb.edu/ws (accessed 21 June 2008).
31. Christian Nuenlist, 'Die NATO und die Berlinkrise von 1958–61, in *Krisen im Kalten Krieg*, ed. Bernd Greiner et al. (Hamburg: HIS, 2008), 240–69.
32. Bundy to Kennedy, 2 August 1961, John F. Kennedy Library, Boston (JFKL), National Security Files (NSF), Box 88.
33. FRUS 1961–3:14, 269–81 and 312–6. On Rusk's talks in Paris, see also Rolf Steininger, *Der Mauerbau* (Munich: Olzog, 2001), 249–60.
34. Memorandum of Conversation (MemCon) Rusk-Adenauer, 10 August 1961, USNA, RG 59, CDF, 396.1-PA.
35. Rusk, *As I Saw It*, 233.
36. Ibid., 221. See e.g. MemCon Rusk-Gromyko, 19 October 1961, JFKL, NSF, Box 186. On the differences between Rusk and Bundy, see Nuenlist, *Kennedys rechte Hand*, 103–12.
37. Quoted in Schoenbaum, *Waging Peace*, p. 342.
38. Famously, JFK let Rusk know on 21 August that he wanted to take a 'stronger lead on Berlin negotiations' and that the European allies 'must come along or stay behind'. FRUS 1961–3: 13, 359f.
39. Cohen, *Rusk*, 143. See also Rusk, *As I Saw It*, 224–8; Andreas Wenger, *Living with Peril: Eisenhower, Kennedy and Nuclear Weapons* (Lanham, MD: Rowman & Littlefield, 1997), 234ff.
40. Rusk to Kennedy, 15 September 1961, JFKL, NSF, Box 220.
41. Quoted in Cohen, *Rusk*, 105.
42. Zeiler, *Rusk*, 48f.
43. Ball, OHI, LBJL, 27. See also Cohen, *Rusk*, 194.
44. Komer to Bundy, 29 October 1962, JFKL, NSF, Box 36.
45. FRUS 1961–3:13, 449, 463. See Anna Locher and Christian Nuenlist, 'What Role for NATO? Conflicting NATO Perceptions in View of Détente, 1963–6', *Journal of Transatlantic Studies* 2, no. 2 (2004): 185–208.
46. NAC Meetings, 13 December 1962, C-R(62)58, 59, NA.
47. NAC Meeting, 23 May 1963, C-R(63)29, NA.
48. CBS Interview Rusk, 24 May 1963, USNA, RG 59, Conference Files (CF), Box 334, CF 2266.
49. Cyrus Sulzberger, *The Last of the Giants* (New York: Macmillan, 1970), 985.
50. Cohen, *Rusk*, 161f.
51. Rostow to Kennedy, 5 July 1963; Rostow to Kennedy, 8 July 1963, both in JFKL, NSF, Box 265. Kennedy had triumphantly visited Berlin in June 1963.
52. Schlesinger, *Thousand Days*, 904. See also FRUS 1961–3:7, no. 320.
53. Rusk, OHI, JFKL, p. 225. See Kendrick Oliver, 'West Germany and the Moscow Test Ban Treaty Negotiations, July 1963', in *Controversy and Compromise*, ed. Saki Dockrill (Bodenheim: Philo, 1998), 151–71; Maurice Vaïsse, 'La France et le Traité de Moscou, 1957–63', *Revue d'Histoire Diplomatique* 107 (1993): 41–53.
54. George McGhee, *At the Creation of a New Germany* (New Haven, CT: Yale University Press, 1989), 91f.
55. *New York Times*, 28 October 1963.
56. Rostow to Harriman, 30 July 1963, JFKL, NSF, Box 376.
57. Rostow to Rusk, 8 August 1963, USNA, RG 59, S/PC 1963-64, Box 256, USSR.
58. Talking Points for Secretary, n.d., USNA, RG 59, EUR/RPM: RPA 1957-66, Box 12, NAP.
59. On NATO's détente debates in the fall and winter of 1963, see Christian Nuenlist, 'Into the 1960s: NATO's Role in East–West Relations', in *Transforming NATO in the Cold War: Challenges beyond Deterrence in the 1960s*, eds Andreas Wenger et al. (London: Routledge, 2007), 67–88, 80ff.
60. AAPD 1963:2, 349. In 1963, Bonn had established trade missions with Poland, Romania, and Hungary, expecting a spill-over to the cultural and the political sphere. On Schröder's 'policy of movement', see Franz Eibl, *Politik der Bewegung: Gerhard Schröder als Aussenminister, 1961–66* (Munich: Oldenbourg, 2001), 256–78.
61. Rusk to US Embassies, 16 December 1963 RG 59, CF, Box 334, NATO Ministerial Meeting 12/63.
62. MemCon Zinchuk-Manning, 20 December 1963, USNA, RG 59, CDF 1963, Box 3696, DEF 4.
63. MemCon of NSC Meeting, 5 December 1963, LBJL, NSF, NSC Meetings Files, Box 1. See also Ball, OHI, LBJL, 17.

64. Morf, *Building Bridges*, 27f.; Rusk, *As I Saw It*, 340; Schwartz, *Johnson*, 22–5.
65. Bundy to Johnson, 3 December 1963, LBJL, NSF, Memos to the President, Box 1.
66. Ball, OHI, LBJL, 17.
67. PPC Paper, 'The US and Germany: A Policy of Movement', 3 April 1964, LBJL, NSF, Country Files, Germany, Box 183. For a detailed analysis, see Morf, *Building Bridges*, 49–55. See also Mitchell Lerner, 'Lyndon Johnson, Bridge Building, and the End of the Prague Spring', *Diplomatic History* 32, no.1 (2008): 77–103.
68. Rostow to Rusk, 'Arms Control and the Alliance: Or How to Persuade Allies to Make Peace', 6 April 1964, LBJL, NSF, Subject File, Box 23.
69. http://www.presidency.ucsb.edu/ws (accessed 21 June 2008). LBJ formalised the policy in early June, see FRUS 1964–8:17, 12.
70. Morf, *Bridge Building*, 59f.
71. Note by Johnson, 21 December 1963, LBJL, Statements of LBJ, Box 91.
72. Cohen, *Rusk*, 200f.
73. Rusk to Johnson, 8 April 1964, LBJL, NSF Subject File, Box 23. See also FRUS 1964–8:13, 35f.
74. FRUS 1964–8:11, 155.
75. Rusk to Schröder 13 January 1965, LBJL, NSF Subject File, Box 25. See Andrew Priest, 'From Hardware to Software: The End of the MLF and the Rise of the Nuclear Planning Group', in *Transforming NATO*, 148–61, 151; Thomas Gijswijt, 'Multilateral Force', in *Encyclopedia of the Cold War*, ed. Ruud van Dijk (New York: 2008), 601–4.
76. Rusk interview, quoted in Schertz, *Deutschlandpolitik*, 292.
77. FRUS 1964–8:13, 35.
78. Rusk OHI, LBJL, 11ff. See also Cohen, *Rusk*, 299.
79. Garret Martin, 'A Gaullist Grand Strategy?', in *International Perspectives on de Gaulles Foreign Policies, 1958–69*, eds Christian Nuenlist et al. (Lanham, MD: Rowman & Littlefield, 2009); Garret Martin, 'Untying the Gaullian Knot: France and the Struggle to Overcome the Cold War Order, 1963–68', PhD dissertation, LSE, 2006; Wenger, *Crisis*, 30–4; Erin R. Mahan, *Kennedy, de Gaulle, and Western Europe* (Houndmills: Palgrave Macmillan, 2002), 22–8, 143–162.
80. Rusk OHI, LBJL, 178.
81. Rusk to Kennedy, 23 June 1962, JFKL, POF, Box 88.
82. Schertz, *Deutschlandpolitik*, 157.
83. Rusk to Kennedy, 8 October 1962, JFKL, NSF, Box 71a.
84. George W. Ball, *The Past Has Another Pattern* (New York: Norton, 1982), 271f.; Rusk, *As I Saw It*, 268.
85. Quoted in Anna Locher, 'A Crisis Foretold', in *Transforming NATO*, 107–27, 111.
86. Dirk Buda, *Ostpolitik à la française* (Marburg: VAG, 1990), 78–81; Frédéric Bozo, *Deux stratégies pour l'Europe: de Gaulle, les Etats-Unis et l'alliance atlantique, 1958–69* (Paris: Plon, 1996), 144–8; Maurice Vaïsse, *La grandeur: Politique étrangère du général de Gaulle, 1958–69* (Paris: Fayard, 1998), 421–5.
87. Quoted in Morf, *Bridge Building*, 89. See also Wenger, *Crisis*, 34f.
88. FRUS 1964–8:13, 206f.; Finletter to Rusk, 25 May 1965, LBJL, NSF, Country File, Box 2; Klein to Bundy, 5 May 1965, ibid., Box 171. See also Schertz, *Deutschlandpolitik*, 313.
89. Fredrik Logevall, 'America Isolated: The Western Powers and the Escalation of the War', in *America, the Vietnam War, and the World: Comparative and International Perspectives*, eds Andreas W. Daum et al. (Cambridge: Cambridge University Press, 2003), 175–96.
90. Locher, *Crisis Foretold*, 117ff.
91. FRUS 1964–8:13, 209f.
92. Schertz, *Deutschlandpolitik*, 315. For Britain's prominent role in Western contingency planning, see also James Ellison, 'Defeating the General: Anglo-American Relations, Europe and the NATO Crisis of 1966', *Cold War History* 6, no. 1 (2006): 85–111.
93. Position Paper, 'France and NATO', 25 September 1965, LBJL, NSF Country File, Box 3.
94. Schoenbaum, *Waging Peace*, 421.
95. On 16 March, Komer recommended that Johnson followed a conciliatory, defensive stance rather than answering 'State's clarion call to propaganda battle'. FRUS 1964–8:13, 335–8. In 1966, Bator established himself as LBJ's 'man for Europe' – he had enormous influence on

Johnson's policy towards Europe. See Schertz, *Deutschlandpolitik*, 347–50; Wenger, *Crisis*, 35–9; and Schwartz, *Johnson*, 100–10.

96. Lawrence S. Kaplan, *NATO Divided, NATO United: The Evolution of an Alliance* (Westport, CT: Praeger, 2004), 32ff.

97. FRUS 1964–8:13, 409.

98. See Schwartz, *Johnson*, 143–59; Thomas Holderegger, *Die trilateralen Verhandlungen 1966/67: Der erste Schritt der Johnson-Administration zur Lösung der NATO-Krise* (Zurich: CSS, 2006).

99. FRUS 1964–8:17, 54f.

100. http://www.presidency.ucsb.edu/ws (accessed 21 June 2008). For the preparations for the speech, see Morf, *Bridge Building*, 161–72.

101. On the Harmel exercise, see – besides the studies by Haftendorn, Wenger and Schwartz mentioned in note 8 – Frédéric Bozo, 'Détente versus Alliance: France, the United States and the Politics of the Harmel Report 1964–8', *Contemporary European History* 7, no. 3 (1998): 343–60.

102. FRUS 1964–8:8, 618.

103. Ibid., 641ff.; Schwartz, *Johnson*, 213.

104. FRUS 1964–8:13, no. 304.

105. *Time*, 9 August 1982, http://www.time.com/time/magazine/article/0,9171,925631,00.html (accessed 21 June 2008).

John Foster Dulles: moralism and anti-communism

Dianne Kirby

Department of History, University of Ulster, Belfast, Northern Ireland, UK

With a grandfather and an uncle who had also been secretaries of state, the life of John Foster Dulles was marked by participation in key international developments from an early age. In 1919 he was at Versailles involved in economic and reparations negotiations. During the 1920s Dulles was part of the significant international expansion of American business and banking. In the 1930s he became involved with the ecumenical movement, Christian churches seeking unity, as it strove to halt the tides of war. During the Second World War, Dulles chaired the Federal Council of Churches' Commission on a Just and Durable Peace (CCJDP) intended to study the question of world order and to change the American public mind towards taking an active role in reforming international relations. Following the war, he consolidated his reputation as a 'Christian statesman' and strengthened his position in the Republican Party, especially as a 'bipartisan' internationalist acting as a foreign policy advisor to the Truman administration.

Perhaps the key lesson Dulles derived from his long association with United States' foreign policy was how his nation was strong and united when confronted by danger. Without a discernible threat, however, the United States was divided not simply over what its global role should be, but even whether or not it should have a global role.[1] Dulles had witnessed America's rejection of Wilsonian internationalism in the aftermath of the First World War. He saw that it was not Roosevelt's rhetoric or Nazi aggression that united the American people behind the Allied war effort, but Pearl Harbor. He was himself a participant in the public exaggeration of the Soviet threat required to ensure that the American people supported the Truman administration's global interventionism that it deemed essential for America's economic well-being.

Wilson, Roosevelt and Truman all called upon the righteous nation narrative to engender national unity in support of an interventionist foreign policy. This required the idealisation of America and the demonisation of the 'other', for which all three presidents drew on the notion of divine choseness that has informed American history, and indeed the very concept of America, from its colonial beginning.[2] Presidential rhetoric was infused with religious language that reinforced the image of a righteous, chosen nation with a God-given mission, intended to encourage as well as justify the assumption of world leadership.

Prior to the Second World War, Dulles had addressed international affairs in his speeches and writing in terms of national self-interest. His arguments drew on political, economic, social and security concerns.[3] They did not rely on moral persuasion and there was no indictment of an 'other' within a framework of mission, the key ingredients of his later position and when he was secretary of state in the 1950s.

During Dulles's first foray into the international arena at the end of the First World War, Dulles learned a valuable lesson about European unity. He observed how 'the Paris Peace Conference made a host of decisions, all of which in varying degrees, were designed to check Bolshevism'.[4] Shortly after becoming President Dwight D. Eisenhower's secretary of state in January 1953, Dulles explained to the Senate Foreign Relations Committee in April 1953 that a 'coalition is held together very largely by fear'.[5] By then Dulles fully appreciated the continuing strength of anti-communism as a powerful common denominator. Consequently, the religio-political stance for which Dulles is remembered, embodying the proclaimed logic of the Cold War, the containment and eradication of evil, reflected a calculated and pragmatic choice in the context of the challenges inherent to the job at home as well as abroad.

By the end of the 1940s Dulles's direct involvement with the churches and international Christianity had been effectively curtailed by his political career. Yet his religious moralism notably increased once he became secretary of state. Indeed, former allies in the religious field were uneasy with Dulles's 'religiosity' in office. Reinhold Niebuhr, America's pre-eminent religious intellectual and a fellow member of the Commission for a Just and Durable Peace, complained in the 1950s that 'Mr Dulles' moral universe makes everything quite clear, too clear … Self-righteousness is the inevitable fruit of simple moral judgements'.[6] Richard Immerman attributed Dulles's later loss of public support to his excessive moralism: 'In large part he owed his declining popularity to his public image, that of a Presbyterian moralist ever ready – and eager – to do battle with the devil.'[7] Yet, as Seth Jacobs has pointed out, in the beginning it was precisely this image 'that had made Dulles so widely respected and his appointment as secretary of state such a foregone conclusion'.[8]

It is important to realise that Dulles's attitudes and behaviour were far from unusual in post-war America.[9] Dulles became secretary of state with America in the throes of a religious revival encouraged by society's core institutions, from the presidency down.[10] Henry Luce, the influential publisher who coined the term 'American Century', promoted religious revival as essential to winning the Cold War.[11] Two of the era's most notorious figures, Senator Joseph McCarthy[12] and FBI director J. Edgar Hoover,[13] paraded as defenders of Christianity against communist atheism. This was the era when the words 'one nation under God' were added to the Pledge of Allegiance on 14 June 1954, Flag Day.[14] Also in 1954, Congress required all US coins and paper currency to bear the slogan 'In God We Trust', and two years later that became the official US motto.[15]

In addition to having practical application at home, the religious dimension was also helpful in consolidating the transatlantic alliance. A shared Christianity served as a reminder of the common cultural traits and values that united Europe and America. Equally important, America's European allies had already learned both how to respond to and how to manipulate the way in which the United States presented itself and projected its power.[16] Britain, for example, had a 'Religions Division' section of the Ministry of Information during the Second World War through which direct appeals were made to American public opinion.[17] After the war, a common cultural heritage and shared religion became an important means of assuaging the British public's suspicions about US intentions and values as America began to exercise its power around the world.[18] Noteworthy is the extent to which the Truman administration's provision of an ideological rationale based on Christianity to justify political actions in the international arena enabled European governments to offer calculated responses.

Recognising the importance of ideological solidarity to the United States, America's allies responded by presenting the basic division between their democracies and the totalitarian states as a conflict between religion and communism. In doing so they formulated the basis for a theory of totalitarianism that raised the question of the structural similarities between National Socialism and Stalinism which provided a useful taxonomy of repressive regimes that justified the post-war switch from one enemy to another.[19] In the process, the defence of Western civilisation and Christianity became anti-communism's central rhetorical device, consolidating the two fundamental contentions on which the policies of initially Truman and then Eisenhower rested: that communism was a supreme and unqualified evil and that its purpose was world domination. Anti-communism thus provided a powerful ideological basis of agreement between the governing conservative forces in the United States and their Social and Christian Democratic counterparts in Western Europe. The latter played a vital role in legitimising the Cold War, in enrolling labour movements into the anti-communist crusade and in bringing to fruition a form of social reformism that did not threaten the established order.

Dulles began his new role convinced that an embellished anti-communism and an exaggerated Soviet threat were pre-requisites to the task in hand. This included how to manage recalcitrant Republicans and non-compliant European statesmen, plus publics either side of the Atlantic that he feared might not otherwise live up to the demands of the sort of world order he envisaged. Dulles's wartime meetings with European Christian and secular leaders had acquainted him with the widespread conviction in Europe that the Second World War should be fought not only to defeat the Axis enemy, but also to achieve a new social and political order. Dulles, already worried that Stalin might not remain content with his allowed 'security zone',[20] was worried even more about the inspirational potential of communism. He fretted about the appeal of a creed that promised 'from each according to his ability, to each according to his need' in a world disillusioned with and critically questioning the system that had delivered slump, fascism and war.

More than Soviet aggression, Dulles feared the lack of an international ethos in the West could cause disunity, undermining the sort of politically structured societies he envisioned: 'Even if the Soviet threat were totally to disappear, would we be blind to the danger that the West may destroy itself?'[21] Dulles was convinced that a universal values-based creed was essential for world order. Soon after Eisenhower's first inauguration, Dulles spoke with the president about the need for a comprehensive education programme that would assure popular understanding 'of the "American mission" and its problems'.[22] Shortly afterwards, *Reader's Digest*, in language resonant with Dulles' own sentiments, reported that Eisenhower wanted to use his influence and his presidency to encourage 'a spiritual turning point in America, and thereby to recover the strengths, the values, and the conduct which a vital faith produces in a people'.[23] Ira Chernus has tellingly illustrated the extent to which Eisenhower understood the power of ideological language to advance pragmatic ends and to have pragmatic interests serve ideological commitments.[24] Joining the president and the secretary in recognising the value of a politico-religious entente was the West German Chancellor, Konrad Adenauer, whose Christian Democratic Union had been founded to combat nationalism, materialism and atheism. All three perceived in Christianity a crucial base for transatlantic relations and European union.

Few secretaries of state came to office having given the time, thought and commitment to America's relationship with Europe as had Dulles. He experienced Europe as a student, a diplomat, an international lawyer and a churchman. His main encounter with his European cousins derived from his vocation as a lawyer dealing with international finance and commerce. His involvement with international banks and corporations sensitised him to the importance of economic factors and conflicts between states that could lead to war. A constant, if not the dominant factor in his thinking, was recognition that the economic health and stability of Europe and the United States were interdependent. Whether as a representative of government, church or an American investment house, Dulles's lifelong interest in a peaceful, prosperous Europe and his support for European unity stemmed from the importance that he attributed to transatlantic commercial and financial ties for the well-being of American capitalism.

During the 1952 election campaign, Dulles was critical of Truman's foreign policy, promising a more dynamic approach, including an 'endeavour to bring about the liberation of the enslaved people'.[25] It was a means by which the Republicans could gain electoral advantage by charging that containment abandoned East Europeans to Soviet brutality. Dulles and Eisenhower stood on a platform that claimed containment was immoral and Truman was 'soft' on communism. They also promised a 'New Look', which subsequently became identified with 'massive retaliation', defined by Dulles as 'maximum deterrent at a bearable cost'.[26] Intended as a means of providing adequate defence and an active foreign policy more economically, it was dubbed 'more bang for the buck' by Eisenhower and conveyed the impression of an administration overly enamoured with nuclear weaponry. However, in office the actual policies pursued were markedly similar to Truman's approach to containment and liberation.[27] Dulles and Eisenhower assumed office in a year when concerns about a decline in American prestige became potentially dangerous owing to the death of Stalin, which raised European hopes for de-escalation of the Cold War, threatening to widen already existing 'cleavages in the Free World'.[28] The electoral success of Joe McCarthy's party heightened European anxiety about the direction of the US at a time when western political élites feared the removal of Stalin could compromise and weaken popular hostility toward the Soviet Union.

By the early 1950s, opposition to McCarthyism had become a way to vent resentment of American domination and traditional feelings of Europe's cultural superiority although without unsettling the basic links that bound the United States and Europe. Upon entering office, Eisenhower and Dulles immediately confronted a Europe-wide clemency campaign on behalf of Ethel and Julius Rosenberg. Found guilty of conspiracy to commit treason for allegedly conveying the secret of the atomic bomb to the Soviets during the war, they were condemned to the electric chair.[29] The clemency campaign became a major left-wing cause. However, it also managed to secure support across the political spectrum. Appeals for commutation of the death sentence came from leading West European church and statesmen, including the vehemently anti-communist Pope Pius XII.[30] The demonstrations for clemency that dominated the European media in the days leading up to the Rosenbergs' execution in early 1953 illustrated how the European Cold War consensus embraced both anti-communism and anti-McCarthyism. Portrayed by the left as victims of McCarthyism, their case became an outlet for expressing the anti-Americanism evoked in Europe by a combination of McCarthyite excesses, the Korean War and fear of a US precipitated nuclear confrontation.[31]

In policy discussions at home, Dulles revealed himself to be aware of and sensitive to emotive issues that would confirm the worst fears of those Europeans already worried about the new Republican administration. His concern, of course, was Europe becoming less adverse to the 'Soviet inspired' peace movement and more inclined toward neutrality or appeasement.[32] Although roundly repudiated by Western statesmen as a sinister ploy intended to weaken the free world, Dulles recognised the extent to which the peace movement struck a visceral chord in peoples still scarred by the horror of war. The record shows that Dulles was much exercised about the dilemmas inherent in the possession of nuclear weapons. Dulles long time association and involvement with the churches, where nuclear weapons and war were deeply debated topics, meant that he was well acquainted with the moral dimension as well as the strategic, political and military questions.

Knowing the moral repugnance nuclear weapons aroused, Dulles realised how: 'Propaganda picturing us as warmongers on account of our atomic capabilities has done incalculable harm.'[33] He considered that America's stated willingness to use nuclear weapons could be counter-productive: 'The Russians are smarter on this question because they never talk about using atomic weapons.'[34] Dulles worried that if the United States did not strike the right stance or put forward seemingly constructive proposals, then America's moral leadership could be compromised and even pass to the Soviets.[35]

The security policies Dulles advocated required allied cooperation and were a mix of flexibility and firmness. Acknowledging the potential for nuclear exchanges to destroy Western civilisation as well as the Soviet regime, Dulles counselled against aggressive policies that might lead to war. He recognised that American superiority and Soviet weaknesses might result in the disintegration of the Soviet bloc, but he also understood that American aggression would alienate allies.[36] Whilst Dulles wanted the Soviets to know that America would not tolerate military aggression, he preferred non-provocative actions that would not 'inevitably broaden … into total nuclear war'. Caution was necessary 'to assure the support of our allies against aggression and to avoid risks which do not promise commensurate strategic or political gains'.[37] In effect, 'massive retaliation' shifted to 'graduated deterrence', with Dulles acknowledging the importance of NATO's conventional strength even as he warned that a major attack would incur a nuclear response.[38]

Deeply worried about the potential of the 'Soviet peace offensive' to undermine the coherence of the Western alliance, Dulles also had to contend with unwelcome peace initiatives from Winston Churchill, re-elected as British Prime Minster in October 1951. Whilst some historians have commended Churchill's summit diplomacy as wise and far-sighted, others have dismissed it as hopelessly unrealistic.[39] Klaus Larres has persuasively presented Churchill's advocacy as an 'imaginative and perhaps even visionary policy through which he attempted to revive his country's declining fortunes and prevent or undo major catastrophes before the First World War, in the course of the Second World War and during the Cold War years'.[40] Churchill lacked the support of his cabinet colleagues and the trust of the Soviet leadership, and his advocacy of East–West peace negotiations brought him into conflict with Dulles. Churchill wanted a global détente that would provide the opportunity for Britain to reassert itself as an economic and military power. However, the long-term goal of the Eisenhower administration remained to reduce, if not rollback, the power of international communism and the Soviet system.

The importance to which Dulles attributed a strong Western alliance in this process is reflected by the time and effort Dulles devoted to European affairs, not least the arduous and frustrating struggle over a European Defence Community (EDC). The historical consensus now is that in his drive toward the fully integrated, united states of Europe that was his goal, Dulles was more flexible and creative than commentators realised at the time. Contemporary observations, however, were based on substantive foundations. Dulles's tactics included a coercive mixture of threats and calculatedly exaggerated predictions. The former included Dulles threatening both Paris and London with unilateral German rearmament and a United States–German alliance. The latter is best represented by his 'agonising reappraisal' speech, a calculated bluff that also illustrated the complementary roles played by president and secretary. As Eisenhower quietly worked toward a consensus, Dulles 'drew the public fire and presented the tough choices',[41] sure in the knowledge that in the final reckoning his European counterparts were as keen as he to halt Soviet influence. Certainly Dulles pandered to some of his allies' conceits,[42] a sound procedure when he well knew the extent to which European statesmen had the unenviable task of trying to maintain American support without losing that of their own electorates. Openly bowing to United States' dictates risked the label 'American puppet'. European statesmen were very well aware of the possible consequences inherent in the potential isolationism and fiscal conservatism of the new Republican administration that militated against high expenditure on defence and foreign aid. But they equally well understood their value to the United States in its rivalry with the Soviet Union.

EDC represented a supra-national federation that required a radical restructuring of defence policies and a considerable surrender of national sovereignty on the part of member states. With a rationale of providing security for as well as against West Germany, the scheme was inevitably controversial in Europe. Dulles had inherited EDC. It originally derived from the Pleven Plan, a French strategy that proposed German troops be integrated into a European command composed of hybrid units. Intended to form the hard core for a greater NATO that would include Italy, the Netherlands, Belgium and Luxembourg, as well as France and Germany, it was seen as a means to bring the French to accept German rearmament. It was also meant to secure German allegiance to the West and prevent future hostilities among the European powers. The question of German rearmament was inevitably contentious. Stalin was prepared to accept a unified Germany, but only if it was not in a military alliance. However, this would deprive the West of the German resources, troops and buffer zone considered key to EDC strategy.[43] Naturally, Stalin's proposal appealed to many Germans, albeit not the West German chancellor, Konrad Adenauer, whose long-term goal was sovereignty on terms of near equality with Britain and France.[44] Yet many Europeans, the French above all, remained uneasy at the prospect of a re-armed and rehabilitated Germany. The British, always suspicious of schemes for European unity, were determined not to compromise their sovereignty and her national defence system and resisted commitment, despite strong American pressure. Churchill, moreover, was far from convinced that a neutral Germany would necessarily move toward the Soviet side.

In August 1954 the French Parliament refused to ratify EDC. Having anticipated just such an outcome, the British Foreign Office had prepared an alternative solution, which they much preferred all along, the NATO-Western European Union (WEU) plan. Dulles moved quickly to support it. Dulles's understanding of the difficulties confronting his European counterparts meant that he was prepared to defer to and defend the British proposals, although Vice President Richard Nixon suggested resentment of US leadership would doom any alternative American proposal. Dulles's ready acceptance of and cooperation with the British plan contributed significantly to its subsequent success. Dulles's diplomacy to help secure what the Europeans called the 'Eden Treaty' involved give-and-take, carrot-and-stick, high level 'linkage' negotiations in which British interests in the Middle East and French concerns in Indochina became factors in securing America's goals in Europe.[45] The Federal Republic of Germany obtained its semi-sovereignty and membership of NATO in May 1955, achieving Adenauer's objective of integration with the West. Celebrated by historian Frederick W. Marks as Moscow's greatest Cold War diplomatic defeat, Robert Divine considered its pursuit as a missed opportunity for an earlier thaw and détente.[46] Whichever interpretation is accepted, Dulles's intricate exertions on behalf of EDC are the cornerstone for the revisionist literature moderating previous criticism of his statesmanship.

The perception of Dulles as a devious manipulator derives from the contrast between the ruthless pragmatism with which he pursued American interests to the moral guise in which he presented them. From the European perspective this was particularly the case with Dulles's anti-colonialism, which he seemed well able to suppress when EDC and then WEU were his priorities. Otherwise his rhetoric placed him in the traditional American mould of instinctively opposing colonialism. Privately, however, his views were far more ambiguous, or, as his European detractors would claim, hypocritical. During a wartime visit to England in 1942, Dulles revealed himself an adherent to the Wilsonian concept whereby conflicts among the great powers had to be eradicated but not the exploitative relationship between them and the developing world.[47] As secretary of state, Dulles pursued a course that required the cooperation of Western powers reluctant to relinquish their colonies. Dulles indicted colonialism at the same time as he supported France and Britain as key American allies.[48] A further consideration was the nationalist aspirations of the developing world, an important factor in US–Soviet rivalry for hearts and minds. Dulles sought an orderly decolonisation that would facilitate the spread of American influence and prevent Soviet penetration, a process deeply resented by major European allies when it seemed the US was exploiting colonial crises for its own benefit. Anthony Eden complained of the American determination to replace the French in Indochina and the British in Egypt: 'They want to run the world.'[49]

If Dulles did want the United States to run the world, it had to be without the taint of colonialism that would engender resistance at home and in the non-European world. But the United States needed the support of its European allies, particularly as a bridge into the developing world for American influence. Suez brought to the fore Dulles's worries about rapid and tardy decolonisation, the former might cause instability, the latter revolution. Concurrent events in Hungary, combined with elections at home, forced Dulles to take a principled stand against colonialism, which offended the British for whom Suez was a law and order issue.[50] But Suez significantly raised American prestige, throughout the Middle East especially. Notably, however, once the British announced their withdrawal, Dulles not only moved to restore Anglo-American relations quickly, he suggested that he wished the mission to remove Nasser had succeeded.[51]

Dulles's concern about the damage inflicted by America's image as a collaborator with Western colonialism had always to be balanced against America's reliance on its European allies to facilitate American expansion in the developing world and the containment of communism. Whether Dulles prioritised the former or the latter depended on Washington and the White House. Eisenhower revisionists have clearly demonstrated that it was the president who made the decisions.[52] Although no longer seen as the inflexible and dogmatic ideologue he appeared to many contemporaries, Dulles the man and his record as secretary of state remain contentious. Revisionist assessments portray Dulles as sophisticated, flexible, even a creative and imaginative statesman. But if his diplomacy now warrants commendation, the outcomes remain contested, as does his relationship with the president. Interpretations of the Dulles–Eisenhower relationship have evolved considerably from the common wisdom of the period and early studies that thought that the secretary's was the dominant voice in the policy-making process.[53] The historical consensus now agrees that Eisenhower was the decision-maker. For some historians this diminished Dulles, who emerged from Eisenhower revisionism as an unequal partner mainly responsible for implementing the president's policies.[54] Subsequent scholarship stressed shared views and values, aims and aspirations, presenting a close working relationship, an interdependent partnership based on mutual respect in which both shared responsibility for the direction of US foreign policy.[55]

In assessing Dulles's diplomacy it is worth considering an interpretation that claims to go beyond 'post-revisionism'. Peter G. Boyle presents Dulles as one of a number of presidential appointees that 'acted as a lightning rod to attract criticism and allow Eisenhower to appear to be the genial, unifying head of state …'. Sufficiently knowledgeable himself about foreign policy, the need was for someone with diplomatic expertise who could also 'deflect from Eisenhower some of the consequences of more difficult foreign policy decisions'.[56] The diaries and memoirs of Dulles's contemporaries suggest that, if indeed a deliberate Eisenhower ploy, it was effective. Certainly Khrushchev blamed Dulles for the hard line that the United States maintained toward the Soviet Union, especially after the death of Stalin.[57] Equally, Churchill blamed Dulles for frustrating his pursuit of dramatic high level negotiations aimed at some form of rapprochement with Soviet leaders: 'Only Dulles could be "clever enough to be stupid on a rather large scale".'[58]

An often-neglected third party in the Dulles/Eisenhower relationship was the secretary's brother, Allen Dulles. Allen Dulles was credited by Eisenhower 'for helping make him a major political figure' and appointed as director of the CIA.[59] His expertise in clandestine operations and his intimacy with the president and secretary of state adds a profound dimension to their foreign policy that is difficult to explore.[60] Covert activity offered significant advantages. In addition to plausible deniability, the lack at that time of congressional oversight, combined with easy access to generous funding, offered the president and his secretary seemingly attractive options that circumvented the usual diplomatic channels and constitutional constraints on presidential power. However, covert activities exacerbated Soviet mistrust and possibly encouraged adventurism amongst Western allies seeking to protect and promote their own national interests. It also compromised the idealism on which both president and secretary drew heavily to justify, legitimate and promote their foreign policy.

However nuanced Dulles's discussions with fellow statesmen, in the public eye he seemed 'to personify the Cold War as an unambiguous struggle between good and evil'.[61] Dulles behaved as though the Cold War was a morality play in which he was acting the part of an old style preacher. He insisted the Soviet Union was an evil and untrustworthy nation with which America and its allies should have no dealings. His insistence that the Soviets were unfit for the diplomatic niceties that convey legitimacy signalled to its leadership the irreconcilable nature of the conflict. Dulles's strident rhetoric exacerbated Soviet insecurities. Fear of Western subversion was inevitably heightened by an exceptionally moralistic secretary of state, aggressively committed to liberation in the 1952 elections, and whose brother, ominously, was subsequently appointed head of the CIA. Dulles inherited 'absolutist' anti-communism from Truman. Absolutist anti-communism, couched in extreme moralistic terms with strongly religious connotations, insisted that the Soviet Union was the incarnation and main source of evil. The exalted rhetoric precluded validation or explanation and repudiated accommodation, negotiation and compromise as evidence of weakness and corruption. Truman had invoked it to move America into permanent military, political and economic intervention on a world scale at tremendous cost. Confronted by the Republican Party's potential isolationism and fiscal conservatism, allied electorates increasingly resistant to US leadership, plus an unstable environment in which the UN was not yet effective and European unity remained elusive, Dulles had few alternatives. His subsequent adoption in public of a rigid absolutism revealed his realisation that America's most precious Cold War asset was the image of an aggressive, evil Soviet regime dedicated to world conquest – the godless Soviet bogey.

Truman had deliberately exaggerated the Soviet threat and fashioned a particular brand of anti-communism to ease America's transition to global engagement, interventionism and leadership. The conviction within the Truman administration among figures such as Dean Acheson and George Kennan was that absolutist anti-communism was a temporary device that America would shed as it matured into its world role. Dulles had little confidence that sufficient maturity had been achieved by the time that he and Eisenhower took over the reins of power. The Soviet threat, moreover, had proven crucial to effective management of the Western alliance; hence Dulles's ready rejection of Soviet overtures and Churchill's summitry. Dulles dismissed both by claiming the basic situation and danger remained unchanged.[62] Dulles was criticised at the time and since that his inflated rhetoric might have provoked the Soviet Union into a reckless response. However, Dulles was able in part to resort to such tactics precisely because he was confident that a Soviet attack on the West was highly improbable.[63]

Contemporary diplomatic historians no longer rate Dulles as among the worst five American secretaries of state.[64] Nonetheless, at the time of his death in 1959, relations with the Soviet Union were deteriorating after a decade in which he had supported and contributed to a foreign policy largely informed by a narrow and absolutist anti-communism. Accordingly, his own legacy was a significant contribution to the institutionalisation of the Cold War, with its attendant costs and consequences, not least a divided Europe.

Notes

1. Walter Russell Mead, *Special Providence: American Foreign Policy and How It Changed the World* (New York: Routledge, 2002).
2. This is a well-explored theme in American history books. See Conrad Cherry, ed., *God's New Israel: Religious Interpretations of American Destiny* (Chapel Hill: University of North Carolina Press, 1998).
3. R.W. Pruessen, *John Foster Dulles: The Road to Power* (New York: The Free Press, 1982), 186.
4. A.J. Mayer, *Politics and Diplomacy of Peacemaking, Containment and Counter-revolution at Versailles, 1918–1919* (New York: Alfred Knopf, 1967), 9.
5. US Congress, *Senate Foreign Relations Committee, Executive Sessions of the Senate Foreign Relations Committee*, vol. 5, 83rd Congress., 1st session, 1977, 315.
6. Reinhold Niebuhr, 'The Moral World of John Foster Dulles', *New Republic* (1 December 1958), 8.
7. Richard Immerman, ed., 'Introduction', in *John Foster Dulles and the Diplomacy of the Cold War* (Princeton, NJ: Princeton University Press, 1990), 3.
8. Seth Jacobs, *America's Miracle Man in Vietnam* (Durham, NC: Duke University Press, 2004), 275.
9. See, for example, the work of James Burnham, philosophy professor and CIA consultant, *The Struggle for the World* (1947), *The Coming Defeat of Communism* (1950) and *Containment or Liberation* (1953).
10. J.F. Dulles, 'Thoughts on Soviet Foreign Policy and What to Do About It', *Life* (3 June 1946), 20.
11. James Baughman, *Henry R. Luce and the Rise of the American News Media* (Boston, MA: Twayne Publishers, 1987).
12. D.T. Miller and M. Nowak, *The Fifties: The Way We Really Were* (New York: Doubleday, 1977), 38, 91.
13. Kenneth O'Reilly, *Hoover and the Un-Americans: The FBI, HUAC and the Red Menace* (Philadelphia, PA: Temple University Press, 1983).
14. M. Silk, *Spiritual Politics: Religion and America since World War II* (New York: Simon & Schuster, 1988), 96–7.
15. The proposal had originated some years previously in Roman Catholic circles. Silk, *Spiritual Politics*, 99.
16. Alessandro Brogi, '"Competing Missions": France, Italy, and the Rise of American Hegemony in the Mediterranean', *Diplomatic History* 30, no. 4 (September 2006): 741–70.

17. Dianne Kirby, 'The Church of England and Religions Division during the Second World War: Church-State relations and the Anglo-Soviet Alliance', *Journal of International Relations* 1, no. 1 (electronic) (May 2000).

18. Diane Kirby, 'Divinely Sanctioned: The Anglo-American Cold War Alliance and the Defence of Western Civilisation and Christianity, 1945–48', *The Journal of Contemporary History* 35, no. 3 (July 2000), 385–412.

19. Hitler's mobilisation of religion, as part of his 'crusade' against the Soviet Union, was disregarded. See S.M. Miner, *Stalin's Holy War: Religion, Nationalism, and Alliance Politics, 1941–1945* (Chapel Hill: University of North Carolina Press, 2003).

20. At the Potsdam conference, Secretary of State James Byrnes initially refused reparations, before concessions that historian Marc Trachtenberg has interpreted as a policy of 'amicable divorce' by which the Americans demonstrated their willingness to tolerate a Soviet 'security zone'. W.A. McDougall, *Promised Land, Crusader State* (Boston, MA: Houghton Mifflin, 1997), 158.

21. Foreign Relations of the United States (henceforth FRUS), 1952–1954, V, 461–468.

22. Ibid., 362.

23. Stanley High, 'What the President Wants', *Reader's Digest* 65 (April 1953), 2–4.

24. Ira Chernus, 'Operation Candor: Fear, Faith, and Flexibility', *Diplomatic History* 29, no. 5 (November 2005), 785–9.

25. *New York Times*, 5 October 1952.

26. Dulles's statement to the North Atlantic Cuncil, 23 April 1954, FRUS 1952–54, 5: 509–14.

27. Scott Lucas, *Freedom's War: The US Crusade against the Soviet Union, 1945–1956* (Manchester: Manchester University Press, 1998). For a contemporary comment on the distance between Dulles's rhetoric and policy, see Joseph C. Harsch, 'John Foster Dulles: A Very Complicated Man', *Harper's Magazine* 213 (September 1956), 27–34: 'He has appeared to be a crusading knight bearing the cross of righteousness on his shield, his sword upraised against the foe and his voice calling for the charge. But if your glance descends from this stirring picture, you notice that the charger he bestrides is ambling placidly in the opposite direction.'

28. E.M. O'Connor to G.A Morgan, 27 May 1953; 'US Prestige Abroad', Box 17, PSB 092, Eisenhower Library.

29. Ronald Radosh, *The Rosenberg File* (Austin, TX: Rinehart & Winston, 1983).

30. Dulles was the first secretary of state to have an official audience with the pope. Frederick W. Marks III, *Power and Peace: The Diplomacy of John Foster Dulles* (London: Praeger, 1995), 77.

31. D. Kirby, 'Ecclesiastical McCarthyism: Christianity and Cold War Culture', *Journal of Contemporary British History* 19, no. 2 (June 2005), 185–201.

32. Memorandum of Dulles–Strauss telephone conversation, 29 March 1954, FRUS 1952–54, 2: 1379–80.

33. Foreign Relations of the United States, 1952–54, vol. XV, 1485, cited in J.L. Gaddis, *Strategies of Containment: A Critical Appraisal of American National Security Policy During the Cold War* (New York: Oxford University Press, 2005), 172.

34. Memorandum of NSC meeting, 5 August 1954, FRUS 1952–54, 2: 706–7.

35. The influence of Christian thinking about nuclear war, including the abolition of nuclear weapons, can be discerned in Dulles's recorded conversations with the president, 'Meetings with the President, August–December, 1956 (2),' Eisenhower Library, and in 'Papers on Nuclear Weapons 1/56 (1),' Eisenhower Library.

36. Memorandum of NSC meeting, 21 December 1954, FRUS 1952–54, 2: 833–836.

37. 'Basic National Security Policy (Suggestions of the Secretary of State)', 15 November 1954, FRUS 1952–54, 2: 789–95.

38. Memorandum of US–UK conversation, 11 December 1956, FRUS 1955–57, 4: 125.

39. For a full historiographical discussion, see Klaus Larres, *Churchill's Cold War: The Politics of Personal Diplomacy* (New Haven, CT: Yale University Press, 2002).

40. Ibid., xx.

41. Brian R. Duchin, 'The "Agonising Reappraisal": Eisenhower, Dulles, and the European Defence Community', *Diplomatic History* 16, no. 2 (Spring 1992), 201–222.

42. Alessandro Brogi, '"Competing Missions": France, Italy, and the Rise of American Hegemony in the Mediterranean', *Diplomatic History* 30, no. 4 (September 2006), 741–70.

43. Rolf Steininger, 'John Foster Dulles, the European Defence Community, and the German Question', in *John Foster Dulles and the Diplomacy of the Cold War*, ed. Richard H. Immerman (Princeton, NJ: Princeton University Press, 1990), 80.

44. Hans-Jurgen Grabbe, 'Konrad Adenauer, John Foster Dulles, and West German-American Relations', in *John Foster Dulles and the Diplomacy of the Cold War*, ed. Richard H. Immerman (Princeton, NJ: Princeton University Press, 1990), 120. Grabbe argues that the skillful management of what was still a fragile, difficult relationship was one of Dulles's lasting achievements, p. 132.

45. Frederick W. Marks III, *Power and Peace*, 62–9.

46. Frederick W. Marks III, *Power and Peace*, 62; Robert A. Divine, 'John Foster Dulles: What You See is What You Get', *Diplomatic History* 15, no. 2 (Spring 1991), 277–86.

47. R.W. Pruessen, *John Foster Dulles*, 211.

48. Wm. Roger Louis, 'Dulles, Suez, and the British', in *John Foster Dulles and the Diplomacy of the Cold War*, ed. R. Immerman (Princeton, NJ: Princeton University Press, 1990), 135.

49. Evelyn Shuckburgh, *Descent to Suez: Diaries 1951–1956* (London: Weidenfeld and Nicolson, 1986), 187.

50. It was, of course, Dulles's withdrawal of the Anglo-American offer to fund building the Aswan Dam, following Nasser's recognition of China in May 1956 that prompted the crisis.

51. Lloyd to Eden, 18 November 1956; FO 371/118873, National Archives.

52. Fred I. Greenstein, *The Hidden-Hand Presidency: Eisenhower as Leader* (New York: Basic Books, 1982).

53. Townsend Hoopes, *The Devil and John Foster Dulles* (Boston, MA: Little Brown, 1973).

54. Stephen E. Ambrose, *Eisenhower, the President, 2* (New York: Simon and Schuster, 1984).

55. Chris Tudda, *The Truth is Our Weapon: The Rhetorical Diplomacy of Dwight D. Eisenhower and John Foster Dulles* (Baton Rouge: Louisiana State University Press, 2006).

56. Peter G. Boyle, *Eisenhower* (New Jersey: Pearson Education, 2005), 18 & 37.

57. Strobe Talbott, ed., *Khrushchev Remembers* (London: Andre Deutsch, 1971), 361.

58. Klaus Larres, *Churchill's Cold War: The Politics of Personal Diplomacy* (New Haven, CT: Yale University Press, 2002), 285.

59. James Srodes, *Allen Dulles: Master of Spies* (Washington, DC: Regnery Publishing, 1999), 432.

60. Blanche Weisen Cook, *The Declassified Eisenhower: A Divided Legacy* (New York: Doubleday, 1981).

61. Leo Ribuffo, 'Religion and American Foreign Policy', *National Interest* 52 (Spring 1998): 36–51.

62. Lloyd Gardner, 'Poisoned Apples: John Foster Dulles and the "Peace Offensive"', in *The Cold War after Stalin's Death*, ed. Klaus Larres and Kenneth Osgood (New York: Rowman & Littlefield, 2006).

63. Van Dusen, ed., *The Spiritual Legacy of John Foster Dulles* (Philadelphia, PA: Westminster Press), 118.

64. Robert A. Divine, 'John Foster Dulles: What You See is What You Get', 277.

President Harry Truman's Secretaries of State: Stettinius, Byrnes, Marshall and Acheson

Michael F. Hopkins

Department of History, University of Liverpool, UK

Following the end of the Second World War the United States found itself in a position of unprecedented peacetime involvement in global affairs – as the leading sponsor of new international economic machinery and the United Nations Organisation, with occupation forces in Germany and Japan and the need to frame post-war settlements in Europe and Asia. The Second World War had familiarised Americans with engagement in the world but institutionally the US was ill-prepared: the State Department, the federal agency best-suited to handling these tasks, had played a limited role in wartime diplomacy and enjoyed low public regard. America faced these challenges with a new, inexperienced President, Harry S. Truman. Unlike his predecessor, Franklin D. Roosevelt, he turned to his Secretary of State for guidance. Four men occupied the post during Truman's presidency: Edward S. Stettinius (November 1944–June 1945), James F. Byrnes (July 1945–January 1947), George C. Marshall (January 1947–January 1949) and Dean Acheson (January 1949–January 1953). If Truman's approach offered an opportunity for the secretary and his department, their effective impact was not automatic. Their performances would depend upon the interaction of their personalities and talents, relations with the president, their running of the department, their policy vision and handling of the key issues of the day.

Franklin D. Roosevelt and the making of American foreign policy

As president Franklin Roosevelt kept control of foreign policy in the White House, preferring to use trusted intermediaries like Harry Hopkins rather than the Secretary of State Cordell Hull. He adopted the same approach in foreign affairs that he deployed in domestic policy: he tried different, often inconsistent alternatives so long as he accomplished his goals. His charm and strong personality usually allowed him to overcome the misgivings of his colleagues and allies. Scholars debate the extent of his consistency. Roosevelt rarely committed his thoughts to paper. He let his advisers compete in arguing their cases. Nevertheless his was the last word, and to prevent him from changing a decision once it was reached, those who understood the presidential style developed a practice that guaranteed finality. Subordinates drew up a memorandum and Roosevelt initialled it 'FDR, OK'.

Roosevelt might have made the foreign policy decisions, but he eschewed the normal channels of communication. He established the White House Map Room, so named because it contained maps of the theatres of war, as his means of communication with diplomats and military commanders. As a result, the State Department was often uninformed about the latest initiatives. He adopted this practice because he disdained the department: he declared that he could not 'get a damned thing through the State Department'.[1] He failed, thereby, to provide presidential direction and policy goals for his diplomats.

Roosevelt chose Cordell Hull as Secretary of State because he needed someone with standing in the Democratic Party but who would bend easily to his wishes. Tennessee-born Hull was the quintessential Southern gentleman in speech and appearance. He was deeply religious, indeed rather rigid in morality, disliked socialising, preferring the company of his long-established friends, and rather provincial in outlook. Yet, he was a type of professional figure that appealed to many Americans – he was regularly declared the most popular member of the administration after the president.[2]

In developing and executing his foreign policy Roosevelt turned not to Hull but to Harry Hopkins. The president and Hopkins kept control of American foreign policy by working with various second level officials in the different federal agencies. In the State Department the Under Secretary, Sumner Welles, worked directly with the president until his dismissal in 1943. Welles and FDR shared a similar background: each was born into a wealthy family and was educated at Groton and Harvard. He and the president also shared a similar foreign policy outlook. In addition, Welles was much abler than Hull. He had an incisive, quick mind and the ability to get things done. Hull resented his treatment, which created a State Department divided between the Welles men, who looked to the Under Secretary, and the Hull men, who sought guidance from the chief.[3]

Edward R. Stettinius

Edward R. Stettinius was Secretary of State when Harry Truman became President in April 1945, having held the post since November 1944 when Hull had retired through ill-health. Like Hull he had to defer to presidential domination of foreign policy, but did so more willingly than Hull. Born in Chicago in 1900, he began work in the stock room of the Hyatt Roller Bearing Division of General Motors at 44 cents per hour in 1924 and rose to become the chairman of the board of US Steel in 1938 with an annual salary of $100,000. He sympathised with much of FDR's New Deal recovery, relief and reform programme. He and his fellow members of the Business Advisory Council, which included businessmen not unduly opposed to the New Deal, acted as advisers to Harry Hopkins while he was Secretary of Commerce (1938–1940). Hopkins recommended Stettinius to Roosevelt who appointed him head of the War Resources Board in 1939. Stettinius acted as Lend-Lease Administrator in 1942–1943 and then succeeded Welles as Under Secretary in September 1943. He impressed the White House with his genial demeanour, social skills, administrative ability and loyalty to the president. Although clearly not an intellectual, he was not the empty-headed manager of his critics. Charles Bohlen, appointed as State Department liaison between the Secretary and the White House in Stettinius's December 1944 reorganisation designed to improve the efficiency of the department, described him as decent and outgoing, not given to intrigue, and possessed of Boy Scout enthusiasm, but someone who made some awkward slips. His strengths lay in organisation and public relations and not in a grasp of the complexities of international affairs.[4]

When Truman assumed the presidency on 12 April he turned to James F. Byrnes, a man whose prominence in domestic affairs led to the epithet 'assistant president'. He sought Byrnes's help in arranging FDR's funeral. Unlike Roosevelt, Truman did not wish to be his own Secretary of State. The highly capable Byrnes seemed the obvious choice. But he did not want to replace Stettinius until he had completed his work on the creation of the United Nations. Stettinius's term was typical of FDR's approach to foreign policy, minimising the role of the State Department in major decisions. Yet Stettinius did have some achievements. He initiated the much-needed reorganisation of the department, improved liaison with other government agencies and began the process of improving its public standing. His most significant contribution came with the successful negotiation of the final stages in the foundation of the United Nations Charter at the San Francisco Conference of April–June 1945.[5] Once that was achieved, Truman appointed Byrnes as Secretary of State in July.

James F. Byrnes

Born into humble circumstances in Charleston, South Carolina in 1879 or 1881, Byrnes went on to enjoy an impressive career. He put himself through law school while working as a court stenographer; served as a Senator, 1931–1941; was an Associate Justice of the Supreme Court, 1941–1942; and was chosen by Roosevelt to co-ordinate the work of all the war agencies and federal departments, operating as a fixer, negotiator and conciliator on behalf of the president. As his biographer notes, 'Byrnes had always exuded confidence in his own abilities to solve any negotiable problem, including those of foreign diplomacy'.[6] A further ingredient in Truman's choice was Byrnes's association with Roosevelt's policies as the war was ending. He was one of Roosevelt's advisers at Yalta, keeping extensive shorthand notes that would prove useful to Truman as a guide to the Roosevelt–Stalin agreements. Byrnes became Roosevelt's 'Yalta salesman' to the Senate and the press. Unfortunately, he offered an incomplete and sanitised version of Yalta that elicited unrealistic expectations for US–Soviet cooperation.[7]

Byrnes's term started with much promise but deteriorated in the face of poor relations between him and the president. The secretive and freewheeling secretary did not feel he needed to refer all his decisions to the president. An early indication came when he ended Bohlen's role as liaison with the White House. Truman had not been as perceptive as Roosevelt about Byrnes's character. In a revealing exchange, Roosevelt accepted Stettinius's summing up of his reservations: 'Jimmy might question who was boss'.[8] Byrnes had a huge ego, though it was rooted in considerable skills as a political operator and efficient administrator. He possessed deep knowledge of Congress and the federal bureaucracy and knew how to achieve political deals. A journalistic portrait in 1940 observed: 'Byrnes, whom enemies call the slyest, and friends the ablest, member of the Senate, does not appear to have been born to wear the toga. A small, wiry, neatly made man, with an odd, sharply angular face from which his sharp eyes peer out with an expression of quizzical geniality, he has not a trace of the majestic.'[9] He believed he could apply the same techniques as Secretary of State. For Bohlen, one of the few members of the State Department to work closely with him, 'Byrnes's personal style was to operate as a loner, keeping matters restricted to a small circle of advisers ... Thus he failed to get the most out of the talent and expertise of the State Department', though he effectively used humour to ease tensions. He

> did a better job as Secretary of State than he was given credit for. He had to deal with possibly the most difficult period of any since World War II. He had to shift from a wartime alliance to a policy of facing up to the emerging Soviet menace'.[10]

Relations between the President and the Secretary of State were good at first because Truman esteemed Byrnes. But an early sign of future difficulties was Byrnes's feeling that he should have been chosen as FDR's vice-president in 1944 rather than Truman. Soon Byrnes was acting after limited, or no, consultation with the president.

Byrnes arrived at the State Department without much experience of foreign affairs. Truman described him as 'my able and conniving Secretary of State'.[11] Byrnes was always attentive to domestic considerations in shaping a foreign policy: as a Senator he was sensitive to the personal foibles and to the interests of his fellow Senators. He was, by his own admission, away from the department for 350 days out of his 562 in office.[12] He spent 62% of his time abroad. Hull had been abroad 22% of his time. The figures for Marshall and Acheson were 47% and 25%.[13] He therefore came to rely a good deal on Dean Acheson, whom he appointed as his Under Secretary.[14] Byrnes's relations with his colleagues in the State Department were, at a minimum, complicated. The British Ambassador, Lord Halifax, noted that 'Mr Byrnes is known to regard the State Department with a highly critical eye and to be irritated by the manner and outlook of the typical career man'. There is also the claim by the State Department official, Theodore Achilles, that Byrnes declared, 'Hell, I might tell the president sometime what happened . . . but I'm never going to tell those little bastards at the State Department anything about it'.[15]

In a memoir, published in 1947, Byrnes wrote that he recognised that it was important for US representatives abroad to understand policy. So he initiated a series of policy statements on individual countries that were sent to US missions around the world and to the Joint Chiefs of Staff. He also established area committees to 'review the policies set forth for each country . . . to make sure that our aims were consistent'. He chose to 'bring in fresh minds to review the statements with critical detachment'. The first of these committees examined Latin America and comprised Samuel F. Bemis of Yale University, Dana G. Munro of Princeton University and Dexter Perkins of the University of Rochester. Byrnes was convinced of the value of the resulting policy statements because they required a 'consistent program of action' and because they forced 'the responsible officers to look ahead, to plan for the crises of tomorrow.[16] He might have acknowledged that it was Hull in late 1944 who had commissioned a manual containing the essentials of US foreign policy on issues and on geographical areas, based on policies and directives of President and Secretary of State, so that all in the department would have the same understanding of policy. Versions appeared in January, April and September 1945.[17]

Byrnes recognised that structural and procedural changes would only be effective if the right personnel were in place. Acheson proved a particularly effective figure – in Byrnes's words, a man of 'unusual ability and energy'. He presided at staff meetings during the Secretary's frequent absences abroad, when the various office directors met; and he kept Byrnes informed of developments. Whilst he recognised the skills and commitment of State Department officials, Byrnes felt the department was 'inadequate for the tasks we must perform in the world'. He therefore continued the restructuring of the State Department's responsibilities and staff into the geographical 'divisions' and 'offices', begun by Stettinius. The Kee-Connally Act, signed into law on 13 August 1946, was the first legislation on the Foreign Service since the Rogers Act of 1924. It brought improved salaries but also placed 'more rigid requirements on training and promotion'.[18] Acheson, in his memoirs, however, commented unfavourably on Byrnes's organisational methods.[19]

Byrnes relished his role as Secretary of State: he was confident that he could preserve good relations between the United States and the Soviet Union, believing in his talents as a negotiator to overcome the obvious difficulties. He became the prototype of the globetrotting diplomat in search of solutions to challenging problems. *Time* magazine named him 'Man of the Year' for 1946. He made his debut at the Potsdam conference of July–August 1945. For a time he favoured atomic diplomacy – he advocated use of the bomb against Japan and spoke of American possession of the weapon as a means of pressurising the Soviets – but soon realised its limited efficacy. Instead, he reverted to deal-maker, believing that he could work with Moscow, that Stalin would negotiate like any other politician to achieve a deal on Germany and the regimes of Eastern Europe. The Soviets demanded that Germany pay $20 billion in reparations and that half of this sum should go to them. Byrnes negotiated an agreement that became known as the 'Byrnes Package Deal'. Each of the occupying powers would be permitted to collect reparations from their zones. In addition, the Soviet Union could take a further 10% of 'such industrial capital equipment as is unnecessary for the German peace economy' from the British and American zones. The Soviet Union was also given an additional 15% in return for food and other commodities from its zone. The Soviets agreed to Italy's admission to the United Nations and Britain and the United States accepted the Oder-Neisse German-Polish border, meaning German territories east of the Neisse River would come under Polish administration.[20]

At Potsdam the victorious powers agreed to establish a Council of Foreign Ministers which would hold periodic conferences to tackle problems of the post-war peace. The first CFM met in London in September–October 1945. It soon encountered difficulties. The Soviets insisted that they be involved in the administration of Japan and that Britain and the United States recognise the new, Soviet-installed regimes in Bulgaria and Romania. The Soviets also refused to allow France and China a role in making peace treaties. Britain and the United States wanted all five CFM members involved. The conference ended on 2 October after failing to reach agreement on these issues.[21] In his report, broadcast on CBS on 5 October, Byrnes noted the stalemate but he would not let this prevent him from pursuing a 'second and better chance to get on with the peace'.[22] The Secretary of State, however, still sought to find a way forward. He made a number of conciliatory moves. The United States recognised the provisional governments in Austria and Hungary in return for a Soviet promise that free elections be held. Byrnes then sent a special emissary – Mark Etheridge of the *Louisville Courier-Journal* – to Bulgaria and Romania. Finally, Byrnes drafted a cordial letter to Stalin from Truman, which stressed America's earnest wish for an agreement on the European peace treaties.

Byrnes then arranged another CFM meeting in Moscow in December. The British resented Byrnes's failure to consult them, feeling that he took them for granted, but reluctantly attended. A number of agreements were achieved. The Soviets accepted an American scheme for international control of atomic energy, but the plan would run into the sand by mid-1946. A deal was reached to broaden the political composition of the Bulgarian and Hungarian governments. This allowed Byrnes to claim the regimes deserved American diplomatic recognition. In order for plans to go ahead for a formal peace conference, he had to yield to the Soviet wish that only the Big Three should draft the treaties. Byrnes produced a typical compromise: the full CFM could 'review' the drafts and offer comment for 'consideration'. In addition, the Americans granted the Soviets a small role in the administration of the occupation in Japan.[23] Despite these agreements, Byrnes's manner was beginning to rankle Truman, who was growing in confidence as president. Byrnes seemed to feel he and not Truman was in control of US diplomacy. For example, the US Ambassador, Averell Harriman, claimed that he refused to telegraph Truman to bring him up to date with developments at Moscow, declaring that he could not trust leaks from the White House. Historian Robert Messer disputes this. Yet, Byrnes's release of the Moscow conference communiqué before consulting Truman demonstrated his attitude.[24]

Meanwhile, a growing number of Congressional leaders and administration officials were becoming concerned at Soviet behaviour. For them Byrnes's compromise settlements conceded too much to the Soviets. There was talk of him as an 'appeaser'. This anxiety about Soviet policy and Byrnes's response resulted in tense exchanges between President and Secretary of State. Truman objected to discovering what Byrnes was doing from the newspapers; accused him of 'losing his nerve' at Moscow and being too generous in the concessions he made. It seems clear that Truman was not happy with Byrnes's behaviour at Moscow but his later recollection in his memoirs exaggerated the extent of his disquiet. Moreover, the famous letter to Byrnes of 5 January 1946 saying he was tired of babying the Soviets was never sent; rather it was a summary of his feelings after seeing Byrnes. Yet, the fact that Truman took the trouble to compose such a letter indicates that the issue mattered to him. Moreover, he had asked Byrnes to see him immediately after his return from Moscow on 29 December and was mildly critical. It was the White House Chief of Staff, Admiral Leahy, who delivered the sharper comment. The meeting ended with Byrnes complaining about exhaustion and the need to prepare a radio speech. As David Robertson notes, Byrnes was quick tempered and would almost certainly have resigned had he faced the serious criticism in the letter. After all, he had offered to step down on a number of occasions during the war when he had felt insulted, only for FDR to refuse the requests. Truman was a 'more impulsive and decisive man than Roosevelt' and would 'have accepted Byrnes' resignation had his secretary angrily offered it'.[25]

Pressure to be tougher towards Moscow came not only from the president, Congress and the public. George F. Kennan, chargé d'affaires at the US Embassy, wrote the famous 'Long Telegram' of 22 February 1946 outlining Soviet expansionist tendencies. Byrnes began to adopt a firmer attitude to the Soviet Union. In a talk to the Overseas Press Club on 28 February he remarked, 'We will not and we cannot stand aloof if force or the threat of force is used contrary to the purposes and principles of the Charter'.[26] A crisis over Iran provided the first indication of this new approach.

During the war Britain and the Soviet Union had jointly occupied Iran to prevent its pro-Axis government from giving the Germans access to its oil. The Americans had also placed some troops in the country to facilitate the movement of Lend-Lease aid to the Soviets. At the London CFM it was agreed that the allied forces would leave Iran six months after the end of war with Japan. This meant that the deadline was 2 March 1946. At Moscow in December Byrnes warned the Soviets that if they did not offer promises about the withdrawal, then Iran would take the case to the UN. When no reassurances arrived, Iran presented the issue to the UN Security Council on 19 January. The Soviet response was to temporise: they denied the allegations and promised to negotiate. On 4 March, two days after the deadline had passed without any troop movements, Truman and Byrnes met. The next day a message was sent to Moscow claiming that the Soviet Union had broken its Tehran commitment to the territorial integrity of Iran.[27] That same day also brought reports of Soviet troop movements near Iran. On 17 March Kennan cabled from Moscow, warning that the Soviets were likely to try and intimidate the Iranians into appointing a pliant government.[28] On 25 March the Security Council met by which time moves towards a settlement were underway: that same day the Soviet press agency, Tass, announced that Soviet troops would leave within six weeks. In a move designed to heighten the drama of the issue, Byrnes then took over from Stettinius, the official US representative at the UN Security Council.[29] Byrnes, always inclined to be legalistic, asserted his commitment to upholding international law but he was almost certainly also influenced by Iran's position as the world's fourth largest producer of crude petroleum. Robertson describes the Iranian crisis as Byrnes's 'finest performance as a diplomat'.[30]

Byrnes made a further effort to negotiate with the Soviets in the spring and summer of 1946 at the Paris CFM which aimed to produce peace treaties. He tabled his proposal for a 25 year treaty between the four main powers that would demilitarise Germany. The Soviets at first agreed to consider the suggestion but insisted on reparations first. The result was that the offer went nowhere and persuaded Byrnes that he could no longer reach an agreement with the Soviets on Germany.[31] The Americans were now working increasingly closely with the British. In June they agreed to the economic merger of their occupation zones – the Bizone came into effect in January 1947. Then, in September 1946, Byrnes spoke in Stuttgart and committed the United States to rebuilding the western zones of Germany whether or not the Soviets agreed. He announced that 'the German people throughout Germany, under proper safeguards, should now be given the primary responsibility for the running of their own affairs … The United States favors the early establishment of a provisional Government for Germany'. He added, 'If complete unification cannot be secured, we shall do everything in our power to secure maximum possible unification'. Byrnes ended this major speech by implicitly warning the Soviet Union: 'We do not want Germany to become a satellite of any power. Therefore, as long as there is an occupation army in Germany, American armed forces will be part of that occupation'.[32]

September 1946 also saw another important indication of a tougher US policy to the Soviet Union: the Clifford-Elsey report, 'American Relations with the Soviet Union', of 24 September 1946.[33] It was a reaction to growing anxiety among various figures about Soviet behaviour. In July 1946 Truman asked his special counsel, Clark Clifford, to prepare a record of Soviet violations of international agreements. Clifford consulted his assistant George Elsey, who suggested that they should investigate the views of senior officials to discover whether there was a consensus about the Soviets. On 16 July Truman sanctioned such a report. Clifford and Elsey decided to consult Admiral Leahy, as a representative of the Joint Chiefs of Staff; James Byrnes and Dean Acheson from the State Department; the Secretary of War, Robert Patterson; Secretary of Defense James Forrestal; Attorney General Tom Clark; CIG Director Sydney Souers. They made special use of George Kennan's expertise; and also consulted Charles Bohlen. Byrnes reacted somewhat sharply to their enquiries, feeling the task should have been given to the State Department.[34]

If relations with the Soviet Union dominated Byrnes's term, there was another, slower-burning issue – communist advances in the Chinese civil war. Americans since the late nineteenth century had felt a particular attachment to the fate of China. During the Second World War American forces under General Stillwell had fought the Japanese, enjoying variable support from Chiang Kai-shek's nationalists and Mao Tse-tung's communists, who suspended their civil war. After defeat of the Japanese in 1945 the civil war resumed. Anxious to avoid another communist victory, in November 1945 Truman appointed General George C. Marshall, recently retired as Chief of Staff of the Army, to undertake a mission to assess the situation in China.[35] By December Marshall's draft plans for the mission were approved. Acheson was to be his 'rear echelon': he would co-ordinate contacts between Marshall and the president.[36] The report Marshall submitted in 1946 did not make agreeable reading for those in Congress and among the American population who favoured all-out support for Chiang. It suggested that there was little point in further US aid, for the nationalists were losing and were doing so because of poor performance. The so-called 'China lobby', which favoured support for Chiang soon grew critical of Truman and Acheson.[37]

By this time, Byrnes's days as Secretary of State were numbered. Truman accepted a letter of resignation Byrnes had written the previous April, when a misdiagnosis indicated he had a heart condition. Byrnes left office on 20 January 1947.

George C. Marshall

George Marshall served as Secretary of State until January 1949, a pivotal period in the development of US policy. The successor to Byrnes could hardly have been more different in character or in his impact on US policy. Marshall was born in Uniontown, Pennsylvania and served almost his entire adult life in the US armed services. He was Army Chief of Staff during the Second World War and attended key conferences at Casablanca, Quebec, Cairo, Tehran, Yalta and Potsdam. He retired in November 1945 only to be recalled to try to broker a settlement in the Chinese civil war but the task proved impossible. The respected journalist, James Reston, neatly captured Marshall's character and compared him with his predecessor. Marshall evinced 'moral grandeur' and was 'severe and aloof and courteous in manner, but with none of the Virginian's love of people and capacity for humor'. Byrnes, on the other hand, 'is a warm, happy man with a rare capacity for political manipulation and a wonderful stock of illustrative anecdotes'.[38] Marshall brought integrity, a non-partisan outlook and his wartime experience of global affairs and acquaintance with leading statesmen.

Above all, he held his post on the basis of the deeply rooted trust of the president. Truman 'thought General Marshall was ... the greatest man he ever knew'.[39] It was the foundation on which Marshall sought to build a more effective national policy. He saw his main task as identifying the central needs of the nation and determining the policies best suited to meet those needs. Although he served for only two years, his term saw significant departures in American policy.

In pursuit of these goals, Marshall set about improving the State Department as an organisation. Charles Bohlen noted how Marshall brought order after the previous inadequate secretaries. 'He gave a sense of purpose and direction. His personality infected the whole Foreign Service ... the department functioned with as much efficiency as I was to note in my nearly forty years in the Foreign Service'. 'There was a greater clarity in the operation of the State Department than I had ever seen before or have seen since'.[40] He established more effective channels of communication and achieved a clear line of command. 'Believing in staff work and deeply secure in himself, Marshall willingly placed responsibility for policy-making on subordinates from whom he invariably garnered loyalty and respect'.[41]

Marshall preferred difficulties to be settled before they reached him, for his under secretary to bring him more or less completed proposals. This meant that figures below the secretary could play an important role; and left him open to the charge that they held too great an influence. Indeed, Acheson, urged him to give more guidance, but the Secretary did not welcome this task. Marshall left matters in the hands of his successive deputies, Dean Acheson and Robert A. Lovett. Clark Clifford has captured Lovett's talents very effectively:

> I respected Acheson greatly ... but despite his great stature, he did not possess Lovett's ability
> – unsurpassed in my entire Washington experience – to get people to work together with a
> minimum of friction. Where Acheson was decisive and impatient, Lovett was thoughtful and
> conciliatory. In informal settings, he was witty and charming, with a fine sense of detachment
> and irony ... these charming qualities ... skilfully concealed an immensely tough interior'.[42]

Marshall also decided to duplicate in the State Department the War Department's Strategy and Policy section that addressed long-range planning. In May 1947 he established the Policy Planning Staff and appointed George F. Kennan as its first director.

Marshall soon appreciated the problems facing him when he attended the Moscow CFM of March–April 1947, which witnessed a serious deterioration in relations with the

Soviet Union. He left the meeting deeply dispirited, concluding that the Soviets did not want to reach agreements on pressing issues and on Germany especially.[43] Nearly simultaneous with this failure of diplomacy was the unprecedented peace time commitment of US financial and military assistance, which emerged from a crisis in the eastern Mediterranean. Since 1945 the British military had assisted the royalists in the Greek civil war, and had extended financial aid to Turkey. On 21 February the British said they could no longer afford to finance these commitments and that their forces would quit Greece by 1 April. Preoccupied with the Moscow CFM, Marshall gave responsibility for the issue to Acheson, who agreed with Truman that the Americans should replace the British commitment, lest Greece and Turkey fall under Soviet influence or control. Marshall accepted this as the right decision and then, together with Acheson, persuaded Congressional leaders that they should support a programme of aid. All the parties to this discussion agreed that the president should present the case to the American public. On 12 March Truman spoke to a joint session of Congress and enunciated what became known as the Truman Doctrine, offering help to those nations in danger of internal or external subjugation. He sought $400m of aid to Greece and Turkey. The speech, and the testimony of Marshall and Acheson, spoke in apocalyptic terms of a global threat. Although the Soviet Union was not mentioned in the speech, it was abundantly clear to all that it was the focus of the administration's anxieties. Congress accepted Truman's request and the president signed it into law on 22 May.[44] The administration's commitment to the aid package pointed to Marshall's readiness to cooperate with Britain – after all, as Army Chief of Staff he co-ordinated Anglo-American strategy during the Second World War.

Continued unease about Soviet intentions in Germany and the possible damage to Europe's economy led Marshall to say on 28 April: 'The patient is sinking while the doctors deliberate'. He asked Kennan and his PPS staff, even though not yet formally established, to investigate and suggest possible solutions. On 8 May Acheson spoke in Cleveland, Mississippi giving a clear sign of the administration's concern about Europe's economic ills. Internally this was followed on 22 May by a PPS paper recommending a major economic aid programme for Europe.

Then on 5 June Marshall spoke at Harvard University proposing a major scheme of American aid to Europe. Unlike the Truman Doctrine, this time the appeal was more humanitarian than geopolitical. 'Our policy is directed not against any country or doctrine but against hunger, poverty, desperation and chaos'. He urged the Europeans to draft a joint plan for recovery that the US could support. The Europeans quickly responded, formulating a detailed scheme by September, which was then subjected to Congressional scrutiny. Marshall had frequent meetings with politicians and was usually highly effective in persuading them. However, in seeking finance for the first 15 months, he suggested that Congress should either fund what was needed or not undertake the scheme at all. Despite some resentment at this, funds were allocated. The European Recovery Program (ERP), popularly known as the Marshall Plan, brought nearly $13 billion to help various West European countries between 1948 and 1952.[45] At the time this was regarded as absolutely vital to economic recovery. More recent writers have suggested its primary value lay in the impetus it provided for better economic reorganisation and for the psychological boost it offered to European economic confidence.[46]

As the first instalments of Marshall Aid were reaching Europe, there arose a crisis over Berlin in June 1948, when the Soviets imposed a blockade of the western sectors that would last until May 1949. Germany had been divided into four zones of occupation and its capital, Berlin, which was located within the Soviet zone, became a miniature version with four sectors. By 1948 the American, British and French sectors were increasingly regarded as a single entity. In June these three powers introduced a reformed currency into West Berlin. The Soviets saw this as a challenge to the economic security of their sector and so imposed a blockade on all movement by train, road and waterway into the city. Both President Truman and Marshall would not back down to this pressure. They decided on an airlift to provide supplies for the 2,500,000 people in West Berlin, while rejecting any idea of using force to reopen routes to the city. Both the British and French supported Truman and Marshall's general approach.

This crisis only confirmed the worst fears of many in Washington, Paris and London. The London CFM of December 1947 had broken up in acrimony, leading the Americans, British and French to meet to discuss possible joint responses.[47] The extension of communist control over the governments of East Europe, and the coup in Czechoslovakia in particular, caused a good deal of unease in Britain and the United States. Secret talks were held at the Pentagon in March 1948 on the possibility of some kind of treaty or guarantee for West European security. In July 1948 formal talks on a North Atlantic Pact began in Washington with six other powers – Britain, Canada, France, and Benelux. By December the negotiators had produced a draft treaty.[48]

While Marshall's term was dominated by European issues, the situation in China deteriorated. Because the bipartisan approach to foreign policy did not apply in Asia, the administration faced frequent condemnation. In 1947 and 1948 Marshall watched events but opposed Republican appeals for American intervention. Nevertheless, he had to make some concessions: the May 1948 Foreign Assistance Act allocated $338m for economic aid and $150m for military assistance to the nationalists. Despite the bitter nature of many criticisms of the administration's policy on China, Marshall encountered little personal criticism. It was only in 1949 that the collapse of the nationalists and the communist victory unleashed direct attacks on the Secretary of State, who was now Dean Acheson, for Marshall had been compelled to resign through ill-health.

By the close of his term Marshall could reflect on his twin achievements: the hugely successful aid programme and the emergence of the clear strategy that he sought. Given that the policy of containment, though coined by Kennan and advocated by Marshall, owed most to efforts of Dean Acheson, it was entirely appropriate that Acheson should be the new secretary whose central task would be the development of this strategy.

Dean Acheson

Dean G. Acheson was born in Middletown, Connecticut in April 1893, educated at Yale University and Harvard Law School, served as Under of the Treasury in 1933 and then as Assistant Secretary of State from 1941 to 1945. As Under Secretary of State he had made a major contribution to the Truman Doctrine and the Marshall Plan and the emerging policy of containment of the Soviet Union. After 18 months out of office but still involved in supporting government initiatives, he returned as Secretary of State in January 1949. A tall, dapper, self-confident man of considerable intelligence, Acheson possessed a talent for cutting to the heart of issues. He took pains to ensure that the State Department continued to operate as efficiently as it had done under Marshall. If he could not quite match Marshall's ordered administration, he gave a greater sense of policy direction to the department. He articulated an increasingly tough policy to the Soviet Union and, after October 1949, to Mao's China. Even more than Marshall, he favoured transatlantic co-operation to meet the growing challenges.

By the close of 1946 Acheson and President Truman had developed a relationship of considerable mutual respect. Acheson clearly preferred the direct and straightforward

Truman to what he saw as the imperious condescension of Roosevelt. President and Secretary had very different characters and backgrounds. One was the worldly-wise East Coast lawyer, the other the plain speaking product of Missouri machine politics. Yet they enjoyed excellent relations. Acheson 'respected Truman's political talents, his hard work, his decisiveness, and especially his willingness to take Acheson's advice'.[49] Truman appreciated Acheson's loyalty after the Democrats' Congressional defeats in 1946 and his mastery of his brief. Acheson was always careful to keep the president informed. As Truman said in his memoirs:

> He was meticulous in keeping me posted on every development … He had a deep understanding of the President's position in our constitutional scheme and realized to the fullest that, while I leaned on him for central advice, the policy had to be mine – it was.[50]

They held daily meetings or, if he was absent from Washington, the Secretary of State reported to the President each day. In addition, they enjoyed a shared vision for American policy. In consequence, as James Chace observed, 'No secretary of state in this century possessed the power Truman granted to Acheson.'[51] In this secure relationship with the president and solid institutional framework Acheson was able to perform his duties as secretary.

From the outset he sought to pursue Byrnes's and Marshall's bipartisan approach to the Soviet Union and European issues, not least because he had played an important role in cultivating this as Under Secretary. In his first task – the completion of the negotiations for North Atlantic Pact – he was especially attuned to this need. Acheson was surprised to discover how little had been done to inform the Senate. He met Senators Tom Connally (Democrat, Texas) and Arthur Vandenberg (Republican, Michigan), the incoming and outgoing chairmen of the Senate Foreign Relations Committee, who expressed concern at the apparently automatic nature of the obligation clause of the draft treaty. Connally was unhappy at the inclusion of 'military' action. Acheson, however, worked assiduously with the British Ambassador, Sir Oliver Franks, with whom he had established a relationship of extraordinary confidence, to produce a text for article 5 that met both the European need for a suitably strong commitment and the Senators' constitutional concern to preserve Congress's prerogative to declare war. By mid-March the remaining details had been settled. The North Atlantic Treaty was signed in Washington on 4 April and ratified in August. The Mutual Defense Assistance Program, a scheme designed to assist the North Atlantic Treaty powers in their defence measures, was signed into law by Truman on 6 October 1949.[52]

Acheson then oversaw moves to end the Berlin blockade. After Stalin raised the possibility of a solution when he spoke to an American journalist, talks were held between Jacob Malik, the Soviet UN Representative, and Philip Jessup, the American Deputy Representative. They revealed a Soviet readiness to terminate the blockade if another CFM was called before the Americans, British and French moved forward with their plans to create a West German state. After the North Atlantic Treaty signature, the three allies met to consider the situation and asked Jessup, Franks and Couve de Murville for France to draft a message to Moscow. By 5 May an agreement was reached – the blockade would be removed at midnight on 11 May and another meeting of the CFM would begin in Paris on 23 May. Despite his strong words about Soviet behaviour and his important role in the formation of NATO, Acheson had still not abandoned the hope of negotiating with the Soviets, especially on Germany. However, Soviet behaviour at the Paris CFM only convinced Acheson that an agreement on a unified Germany was not possible, and so he sanctioned the creation of the West German state.[53]

Success in the first half of the year gave way to difficulties in the final quarter of 1949: the discovery of a Soviet nuclear explosion in September and the communist victory in China in October led to a Republican onslaught against Acheson and Truman. The administration felt even more embattled as the charges of communist infiltration of US institutions by the House Un-American Activities Committee were joined by the Senator Joseph McCarthy's accusation that there were communists in the State Department. Such an atmosphere almost certainly contributed to Acheson's increasingly tough attitude to the Soviet Union. Already persuaded of the need to be firm, he also clearly wanted to demonstrate to the public that he was not going to be 'soft on communists'. In a press conference and then in a speech in February 1950 Acheson articulated his notions of how to use American power in the face of Soviet communism. He spoke of the necessity for total diplomacy involving all the agencies of government in order to develop 'situations of strength', since the Soviets only understood power. He commissioned a report, NSC 68, which proposed substantial increases in defence expenditure.[54]

The most serious crisis of his term came when the Soviet-backed North Koreans attacked American-supported South Korea on 25 June 1950. He quickly took a leading role, advising the president to send military assistance to the South. Acheson and Truman were convinced that the invasion was Soviet-inspired and required a firm response. The Secretary gave the president his legal opinion that he had the authority to send forces without having to secure Congressional sanction, something that would prove a handicap when military operations went badly later in the year, for members of Congress could criticise the conduct of war without being accused of opposing something they had voted for.[55]

Like Truman and the UN commander, General Douglas MacArthur, Acheson was buoyed by the dramatic success of the UN operation at Inchon in September and the subsequent rout of the North Koreans – all were dismissive of the risks of Chinese intervention. When the Chinese did intervene in November the UN forces, which were overwhelmingly American, seemed in danger of catastrophic defeat. Although he kept his head in the face of widespread consternation in Washington, he was not immune from panic and did resort to some bluster. Nevertheless, he realised that MacArthur's suggestion that attacks be launched against the Chinese mainland was unwise. Instead, he counselled against expanding the war. Thereby, the Americans conducted the first limited war of the Cold War era. Thanks to the leadership of General Matthew B. Ridgway, who replaced MacArthur in April 1951, the front stabilised and remained in stalemate for the next two years.[56] Both the Korean War and communist triumph in China hurt Acheson's standing. His Asian policy was markedly less popular than his European initiatives. Yet it did have one success – the signature of the Japanese Peace Treaty in September 1951. Indeed, his televised performance as chairman of the conference made him a celebrity for a while. It was a brief bright spot in the final rather beleaguered phase of his secretaryship.

Conclusion

American foreign policy under Harry S. Truman was as much the policy of the president as had been the case under Roosevelt. It genuinely expressed his foreign policy outlook. Nevertheless, it did not spring directly from the president. He understood that he needed to utilise the best talents of the nation and in a co-ordinated way. From the outset he recognised the value of using the Secretary of State and his officials. But their advice had to be on the basis of proper consultation with the president. Byrnes's failure to honour this precept resulted in the steady decline in his effectiveness and then his departure. Byrnes,

Marshall and Acheson each contributed to the content and tone of US policy. Byrnes articulated the initial worries and tough words and policies towards the Soviet Union over the Near East and Germany. He was an adept negotiator who overcame some difficult issues (reparations, East European regimes) but failed over Germany and atomic energy and encountered problems with Iran and Turkey. Above all, his relations with the president were poor; as, indeed, were his relations with the State Department. He adopted a tougher attitude in 1946 but never succeeded in converting it into a coherent strategy. He was seen as the arch-dealmaker when deals were no longer popular.

Marshall enjoyed extremely good relations with the president and with officials in the State Department. He tried and failed to reach agreements with the Soviets. His judgment that the task was proving impossible due to the obduracy of Moscow was immediately accepted by Truman because of the enormous respect he felt for him. Marshall oversaw and lent authority to the significant policy initiatives of the Truman Doctrine and the Marshall Plan and approved the opening of talks on a North Atlantic Treaty. However, American foreign policy under Truman owed most to one individual, Acheson, who had played a vital role in all the key developments – the Truman Doctrine, the Marshall Plan, the North Atlantic Treaty and the Korean War.

Acheson's opportunity to exercise influence in developing American policy arose because of his position of trust with Truman but also because his department was given the chance to have a significant input into policy-making. Acheson's role was not like one of the advisers of FDR. His impact arose partly from personal relations with the president but also from the chief executive's readiness to leave most matters of foreign relations to the Department of State. This would not have worked had the department not delivered. It underwent a number of reforms and changes that turned it into a much more effective instrument for assessing international affairs and proposing workable policies. Again, Acheson was at the centre of developments. In successive posts before 1949 he helped to implement reforms. Then as Secretary of State he instituted changes designed to improve the efficacy of the department. Acheson was also a major source of new ideas. Above all, he offered the robust, carefully reasoned policy of containment of Soviet communism. Most contemporaries were impressed with this resolute strategy. Distance from the events allows us to see that the philosophy of 'situations of strength' was prone to harden divisions and limit the opportunities for a lessening of tensions, though accusations that Acheson's policies needlessly militarised East–West confrontation under-estimate Soviet ambitions and the pressure to make a strong American response. He epitomised the spirit of American co-operation with Europe that, despite vicissitudes, continues to this day. Perhaps no other Secretary of State in the twentieth century had such an influence on the ideas, institutions and policies of the United States in international affairs.

Notes

1. Martin Weil, *A Pretty Good Club* (New York: Norton, 1978), 105.
2. William D. Leahy, *I Was There* (New York: Harper, 1950); George M. Elsey, *An Unplanned Life* (Columbia: University of Missouri Press, 2005), 18–47; Richard L. Walker, *E. R. Stettinius, Jr* (New York: Cooper Square Publishers, 1965), 12–14; Irwin F. Gellman, *Secret Affairs: FDR, Cordell Hull, and Sumner Welles* (New York: Enigma Books, 2002), 1–19, 20–30.Warren Kimball, *The Juggler: Franklin Roosevelt as Wartime Statesman* (Princeton, NJ: Princeton University Press, 1994).
3. Robert E. Sherwood, *Roosevelt and Hopkins* (New York: Harper, 1948); Dean Acheson, *Present at the Creation* (New York: Norton, 1969), 12.

4. Walker, *Stettinius*, 1–26; Randall Bennett Woods, *A Changing of the Guard: Anglo-American Relations, 1941–1946* (Chapel Hill: University of North Carolina Press, 1990), 154–5, 210; Charles Bohlen, *Witness to History 1929–1969* (New York: W. W. Norton & Co. 1973), 166.
5. On reorganisation, see *Department of State Bulletin* X, no. 238 (15 January 1944), 43–67 and vol. XI, No 286A Supplement, 17 December 1944, 777–814; on the UN, see Stephen C. Schlesinger, *Act of Creation: The Founding of the United Nations* (Boulder, CO: Westview Press, 2003). Walker, *Stettinius*, 60–83. Stettinius served as the first US Representative to the UN, December 1945–June 1945; he died in 1949.
6. David Robertson, *Sly and Able: A Political Biography of James F. Byrnes* (New York: Norton, 1994), 446.
7. Robert L. Messer, *The End of an Alliance: James F. Byrnes, Roosevelt, and the Origins of the Cold War* (Chapel Hill: University of North Carolina Press, 1982), 31–70.
8. Thomas M. Campbell and George C. Herring, eds, *Diaries of E.R. Stettinius, Jr, 1943–1946* (New York: New Viewpoints, 1975), 184.
9. Joseph Alsop and Robert Kintner, 'Sly and Able', *Saturday Evening Post*, 20 July 1940; Robertson, *Sly and Able*, 447.
10. Bohlen, *Witness to History*, 256–7.
11. Robertson, *Sly and Able*, 443, citing Robert H. Ferrell, ed., *Off the Record: The Private Papers of Harry S. Truman* (New York: Harper & Row, 1980), 49.
12. James F. Byrnes, *Speaking Frankly* (New York: Harper, 1947), 245. He later published *All in One Lifetime* (New York: Harper).
13. Barry Rubin, *Secrets of State* (New York: Oxford University Press, 1985); Henry Wriston, 'The Secretary of State Abroad', *Foreign Affairs* (July 1956), 523.
14. Robertson, *Sly and Able*, 443.
15. Robertson, *Sly and Able*, 446; Messer, *End of Alliance*, 126. Achilles made the claim in his oral history interview for the Dulles Oral History Project but omitted it in his Truman Library Oral History.
16. Byrnes, *Speaking Frankly*, 246.
17. Clemson University, Special Collections, Walter Brown Papers, Box 7, Folder 15, Foreign Policy Manual, September 1945.
18. Byrnes, *Speaking Frankly*, 246–7; Robertson, *Sly and Able*, 443; Clemson University, Special Collections, James F. Byrnes Papers, State Department, Box 11, folder 18, News Clippings, 1945–1946, Frank Gervasi, 'New Statesman – New World', *Collier's*, 20 October 1945, 14–15, 80–82 describes Byrnes's working practices.
19. Acheson, *Present at the Creation*, 163.
20. *FRUS: The Conference of Berlin, 1945* 2 vols; the protocol encompassing the main conference agreements is in vol II, 1478–98 (quotation at 1486).
21. *FRUS 1945 II*, 99–559.
22. James F. Byrnes, 'Report on First Session of the Council of Foreign Ministers', 5 October 1945, in *Department of State Bulletin* XIII, no. 328 (7 October 1945), 507–12.
23. *FRUS 1945 II*, 560–826.
24. W. Averell Harriman and Elie Abel, *Special Envoy to Churchill and Stalin 1941–1946* (London: Hutchinson; 1976), 524. Messer, *End of Alliance*, 259 n32 claims that Byrnes communicated regularly with Washington, citing *FRUS 1945 II*, 609–10, 760, 815–24.
25. Robertson, *Sly and Able*, 454–7.The text of the letter was first published in William Hillman, *Mr President* (New York: Farrar, Straus and Young, 1952), 21–3.
26. George F. Kennan, *Memoirs, 1925–1950* (New York, 1967), 549–51 contains the text of the Long Telegram. James Byrnes, '. . . we have pinned our hopes to the banner of the United Nations', 28 February 1946, in *Department of State Bulletin* XIV, no. 349 (10 March 1946), 355–8 (quotation at 358).
27. *FRUS 1946 VII*, 340.
28. *FRUS 1946 VII*, 362–4.
29. Robert J. Donovan, *Conflict and Crisis: The Presidency of Harry S. Truman, 1945–1949* (New York: W. W. Norton, 1977), 194–5.
30. Robertson, *Sly and Able*, 462–3.
31. *FRUS 1946 III* (CFM) and *IV* (Peace Conference).
32. The text of the speech is in *Department of State Bulletin* XV, no. 376 (15 September 1946), 496–501.

33. Arthur Krock, *Memoirs: Sixty Years on the Firing Line* (New York: Funk & Wagnalls, 1968), 421–82.
34. Clark Clifford with Richard Holbrooke, *Counsel to the President: A Memoir* (New York: Anchor Books, 1991), 110–12; Elsey, *An Unplanned Life*, 138–44.
35. Byrnes, *Speaking Frankly*, 226.
36. Dean Acheson, *Sketches from Life* (London: Hamish Hamilton, 1961), 144–5.
37. For full details of Marshall's efforts, see State Department, *United States Relations with China with Special Reference to the Period 1944–1949* [The China White Paper] (Washington, DC: USGPO, 1949).
38. Clemson University, Special Collections, James F. Byrnes Papers, State Department, Box 20, Folder 3, United Nations News Clippings 1947–1953, James Reston, 'Marshall Held Aloof at Conference in Moscow', *New York Times*, 30 April 1947.
39. Harry S. Truman Library, Oral History Interview with Charles Murphy, Special Counsel to the President, 27. Acheson shared Truman's opinion, saying that he admired Marshall more than any other living person; Douglas Brinkley, *Dean Acheson: The Cold War Years* (New Haven, CT: Yale University Press, 1992), 7.
40. Bohlen, *Witness to History*, 259.
41. Wilson D. Miscamble, *George F. Kennan and the Making of American Foreign Policy, 1947–1950* (Princeton, NJ: Princeton University Press, 1992), 5.
42. Clark Clifford, *Counsel to President*, 16.
43. *FRUS 1947 II*, 139–576.
44. *FRUS 1947 V*, 32–45; US Senate, Foreign Relations Committee, Historical Series, *Legislative Origins of the Truman Doctrine (March–April 1947)* (New York: Garland Publishing, 1979). See also Joseph M. Jones, *The Fifteen Weeks (February 21–June 5, 1947)* (New York: Viking, 1955), a vivid, indeed heroic, account by a former State Department official that influenced many later studies, which contains the texts of key speeches by Truman, Acheson and Marshall.
45. *FRUS 1947 III*, 197–484; *FRUS 1948 III*, 352–400; Marshall's 28 April speech is in *Department of State Bulletin* XVI, no. 410 (11 May 1947), 919–24.
46. Harry B. Price, *The Marshall Plan and Its Meaning* (Ithaca, NY: Cornell University Press, 1955) is an early study that stresses ERP's vital role. Alan S. Milward, *The Reconstruction of Western Europe 1945–51* (London: Methuen, 1984) questioned such claims. Greg Behrman, *The Most Noble Adventure* (New York: Free Press, 2007) is the most recent study; it is positive about the benefits but more reserved in its claims.
47. *FRUS 1947 II*, 728–72 (CFM meetings), 811–30 (post-CFM talks).
48. US Senate, Foreign Relations Committee, Historical Series, *The Vandenberg Resolution and the North Atlantic Treaty (May, June 1948; February, March, April, June 1949)* (New York: Garland Publishing, 1979); *FRUS 1948 III*, 333–43 (draft treaty).
49. Walter LaFeber, *The American Age: US Foreign Policy at Home and Abroad, 1750 to the Present*, 2nd edn (New York: Norton, 1994), 468.
50. Harry S. Truman, *Memoirs II: Years of Trial and Hope* (New York: New English Library edn, 1965), 487.
51. James Chace, *Acheson: The Secretary of State who Created the American World* (New York: Simon & Schuster, 1998), 441.
52. For details of these negotiations see Michael F. Hopkins, *Oliver Franks and the Truman Administration, 1948–1952* (London: Frank Cass, 2003), 108–14, and Sir Nicholas Henderson, *The Birth of NATO* (London: Weidenfeld & Nicholson, 1982). On military assistance, see Chester P. Pach, *Arming the Free World* (Chapel Hill: University of North Carolina Press, 1991).
53. Acheson, *Present at the Creation*, 267–88; *FRUS 1949 III*, 709–16.
54. *Department of State Bulletin* XXII, no. 555 (20 February 1950), 272–74; *Department of State Bulletin* XXII, no. 559 (20 March 1950), 427–9; *FRUS 1950 I*, 246–85.
55. On Acheson's legal argument, see *Department of State Bulletin* XXIII, no. 57 (31 July 1950), 173–8.
56. *FRUS 1950 VII* and *FRUS 1951 VII Part 1* provide details on Korean policy.

Index